£8.50

COMBAT
KILL

As part of our ongoing market research, we are always pleased to receive comments about our books, suggestions for new titles, or requests for catalogues. Please write to: The Editorial Director, Patrick Stephens Limited, Sparkford, near Yeovil, Somerset BA22 7JJ.

COMBAT KILL

The drama of aerial warfare in World War 2
and the controversy surrounding victories

HUGH MORGAN &
JÜRGEN SEIBEL

Patrick Stephens Limited

© Hugh Morgan and Jürgen Seibel 1997

First published in 1997

British Library Cataloguing-in-Publication Data
A catalogue record for this book is available
from the British Library

ISBN 1 85260 536 7

Library of Congress catalog card no. 97-72303

Patrick Stephens Limited is an imprint of
Haynes Publishing, Sparkford, Nr Yeovil,
Somerset BA22 7JJ.

Tel: 01963 440635 Fax: 01963 440001
Int. tel: +44 1963 440635 Fax: +44 1963 440001

E-mail: sales@haynes-manuals.co.uk
Web site: http://www.haynes.com

Haynes North America, Inc.
861 Lawrence Drive, Newbury Park,
California 91320 USA

Designed & typeset by
G&M, Raunds, Northamptonshire
Printed in Hong Kong

Further information on the front cover illustrations:

These three views are taken from good quality gun
camera footage showing the final moments leading to
the destruction of a Bf 109. From the Battle of Britain
onwards gun camera film became an increasingly
significant feature in the assessment of combat claims
made by Royal Air Force fighter pilots. Unfortunately,
such film was not always of this quality and was often
inadequately stored in battlefield conditions so that
little of value survives today.

Contents

Acknowledgements   7
Introduction   9

Chapter One   Royal Air Force   19
Chapter Two   Soviet Air Force   50
Chapter Three   United States Army Air Force   74
                 3-view colour drawings   97–104
Chapter Four   Italy   107
Chapter Five   Finnish Air Force   140
Chapter Six   The Luftwaffe   164

                 Bibliography   194
                 Index   197

Colour Plates

1/72 scale 3-view colour drawings of aircraft of the Fighter Aces, by John Weal.

Page 97 – Supermarine Spitfire VB (LO-Y/BM113) of No. 602 'City of Glasgow' Squadron, RAF, flown by Flt Sgt Len Thorne, Kenley, April 1942.

Page 98 – Hawker Tempest V Series I (R-B/JN751) flown by Wg Cdr R. P. Beamont, Wing Leader, Newchurch Tempest Wing, Newchurch, June 1944.

Page 99 – Lavochkin La-7 (White 23) flown by Major V. Orekhov, CO of 1 Sqn, 32 Giap, 3 Giad, 1 Giak, VVS (Soviet Air Force), Latvia, September 1944.

Page 100 – Republic P-47D-5 Thunderbolt (YJ-K/serial unknown) of 351 Fighter Squadron, 353 Fighter Group, USAF, flown by Ltn Robert C. Strobell, Raydon, June 1944.

Page 101 – Fokker D.XXI (Blue 7/FR-110) of 3/LLv 24, Ilmavoitot (Finnish Air Force), flown by Ltn V. Pyotsiä, Tammikuu, early 1940.

Page 102 – Curtiss Hawk 75A (Yellow 0/CUw-560) of 1st Flight, LeLv 32, Ilmavoitot (Finnish Air Force), flown by 2nd Ltn K. Karhila, Suulajärvi, May 1942.

Page 103 – Messerschmitt Bf 109G-10/AS (Black 7/Werk-Nr. 491353) flown by Cap. Ugo Drago, CO of 4ª Sq., II° Gr.C., ANR (Italian Republican Air Force), Aviano, February 1945.

Page 104 – Messerschmitt Bf 109F-4 trop (White 2) of II./JG 27, German Luftwaffe, flown by Oberfeldwebel Emil Clade, Quotaifiya/Egypt, August 1942.

Acknowledgements

The research for this book has spanned several countries, and considerable support has been freely and generously given by historians, archivists and former wartime fighter pilots. Quite properly, we should make mention of all those whose assistance, advice, leg-work, material and expertise was instrumental in guiding and informing the published findings. Perhaps the most appropriate way of doing this is to acknowledge those who have contributed on a country-by-country basis.

For the chapter on the Soviet Air Force, information provided by historians Andrei Alexandrov in St Petersburg and Sergey Kul'baka of Minsk, together with the photographic assistance of Gunnedy Petrov, has been critical. Nigel Eastaway of the Russian Aviation Research Trust also supplied many photos and other reference material – like Bill Gunston and Alex Boyd, he also read drafts of the chapter, making pertinent and expert comments which we hope have been taken on board. Thanks also go to Professor John Erickson for earlier advice on appropriate material for the chapter. Finally, Malcolm Passingham and Peter Kostelnik were instrumental in facilitating significant translation of the Russian language into English.

The chapter on the Luftwaffe's fighter operations has benefited greatly from Jürgen Seibel's interviews with *Experten* Emil Clade, and also with wartime German aviator Martin Hoffmann, who supplied extensive information on pilot training. Our thanks also go to Günther Rall and Alfred Ambs for written contributions. Inevitably, much of the primary research for this chapter took place at the Bundesarchiv Koblenz and the Bundesmilitärarchiv in Freiburg. Therefore, appreciation for help is extended to Frau Hoffmann in Koblenz and to Frau Scholl, Frau Waibel and Herr Moritz in Freiburg. Thanks are also due to Thomas Hampel and Beate Weiss. Finally, Dr David Baker generously read the draft chapter and provided informed comment.

The compilation of the Finnish chapter benefited from photographic material provided by Hannu Valtonen, Director of the Finnish Air Force Museum at Tikkakoski, and Liisa Knudsen, Archivist at the Defence Training Development Centre, Photographic section, in Helsinki. Special notes of appreciation go to Kari Stenman, who not only proof-read the draft chapter but also put the authors in touch with one of Finland's greatest fighter pilots, Kyostia Karhila. Capt Karhila's anecdotes of combat were highly important, and gratefully received. Thanks also go to Carl-Fredrik Geust and again to Nigel Eastaway.

The Italian chapter has benefited tremendously from the input of several people. Personnel recollections were provided by Gen (ret) Giuseppe Biron and Maresciallo (ret) Aldo Barbaglio, whilst Gen (ret) Marcheze of the Associazione Arma Aeronautica in Treviso also gave excellent advice. Historians Nino Arena, Umberto Bonvicini and Giovanni Massimello have been very helpful, and a special thank you to Ferdinando D'Amico for both the provision of material and primary research towards the section on awards and decorations. Ferdinando also read the draft chapter providing expert analysis and comment. Final thanks for the help provided by relations and friends, including Christiane and Adriana!

The chapter on the USAAF has benefited from much help derived from official archival sources. Thanks are due to Dr Daniel Haulman, Essie Roberts, Lt Johnna A. Perdue and Mickey Russell, all of HQ AFHRA, Maxwell AFB, Alabama; David Giordano National Archives, Maryland; and D. Menard, USAF Museum Wright-Patterson AFB, Dayton, Ohio. It is, however, the personal recollections which bring the chapter to life, and for sharing these with us we would like to thank Fred Lefebre and Robert Strobell – after completing his combat tour on P-47s, the latter became one of only a very select group of Allied pilots to fly captured Me 262s in May/June 1945, prior to ferrying them to the USA. Appreciation is also due to Hugh V. Morgan (no relation!) and Roger Freeman.

The RAF chapter derived much from the personal recollections of Len Thorne, whilst contributions made by Roland 'Bee' Beamont and Eric Carter were also gratefully received. Eric was one of the RAF pilots assigned to 151 Wing when it was sent to the USSR in 1941 to teach Soviet pilots to fly the Hurricane. Further assistance in telling the tale of the wing in combat was derived from Peter Fearn, Managing Director of the present day Broquet International, author (and former Hurricane and Typhoon pilot) John Golley and researcher Mark Sheppard, who has meticulously researched 151 Wing.

Finally, thanks are also due to Michael B. Connolly, Paul Sergeant at the Imperial War Museum, Dave Hatherell of the Aviation Bookshop in London, Barry Ketley of Hikoki Publications, Nick Beale, John Weal for the profiles, Tony Holmes, who brought the authors and publisher together and Alison Roelich, Peter Nicholson and Darryl Reach at PSL.

Hugh Morgan and Jürgen Seibel

Introduction

This book is about the experiences of fighter pilots involved in the Second World War hailing from six air forces, comprising three from the Axis powers and three from the Allies. It is an account which weaves narrative around the recollections of those fighter pilots who experienced for themselves the intensity of aerial combat and, through their success, submitted claims for the destruction, or damage, of opposing aircraft. Sometimes these aerial victories were solely earned, whilst on other occasions two or more fighter pilots may have put a claim in for a share of the kill.

Structure of each Chapter

The main structure of the book is based around 'snapshots' relating to the experiences of fighter pilots flying as members of air forces from Britain, Germany, Finland, Russia, USA and Italy. For each air force, the training of a nations' fighter pilots is explored, combat tactics described and the process of claim submission and verification identified. Reference is also made to the psychological impact of combat upon fighter pilots, and the recognition and responses to it made by the air forces in question. Finally, brief profiles of fighter pilots are given for each air force, plus details of the major awards and decorations made by each country to these men.

Notwithstanding the above comments, within the broad parameters given, each chapter has individual emphasis. This has much to do with the authors' own preferences for concentrating upon elements which have personal appeal, without, it is hoped, repeating previous literature on the subject. For example, rather than intensively focus upon the potential minefield of combat claim submission and accreditation by the USAAF (which has been so ably described by other researchers), this chapter spends time exploring training, followed by contemporary accounts detailing combat stress, which encourages comparisons to be made between three different theatres of operation. By way of contrast, the Italian chapter tries to focus a greater degree of emphasis on the often confused claim process employed by the Regia Aeronautica and, later, the Aeronautica Nazionale Repubblicana.

Qualifications and Terminology

The operational focus of the text in this book is on daylight operations flown by pilots in single-engined fighters. For nightfighter pilots, a very different tactical scenario unfolded where combat was rarely visual until, perhaps, the last moment, as electronic aids played a major role in helping them pinpoint their target. The emotive terms 'ace' and 'kill' have often clouded the issue when it has come to evaluating combat victories. The latter is difficult to define, for 'kill' may mean the downing of an aircraft without necessarily implying with any degree of certainty that the machine was indeed damaged beyond repair (and therefore unable to fly again in combat), nor that its pilot was killed as a result of the action. In any air war, overclaiming by aggressive and optimistic fighter pilots was rife, and in many cases there was no definitive proof that the enemy aircraft had in fact been destroyed. Rather than using the word 'kill', perhaps the all-embracing terms 'aerial' or 'combat' 'victory' should be used. This signifies that an aircraft was claimed as destroyed, regardless of whether or not definitive proof of its destruction existed.

The same basic criterion applies to the term 'ace', for it was not consistently used by the air arms involved in the Second World War. Individual air forces would have their own process of awarding claims, the accumulation of which led to the term 'ace' being bestowed upon a successful pilot. Comparisons between air arms founded upon the scores of their most successful pilots is a nebulous argument due the variety of factors involved in the theatre of war in which the victories were achieved. Inevitably, there were differences in the operational fronts, the conditions under which air forces operated, the style of mission flown (defensive or offensive), the performance of the fighter used, and the quality of the enemy (both in respect to their natural flying ability and the aircraft they employed). Training, tactics and opportunity also played critical roles in determining the survivability and success of a fighter pilot.

Despite these widely-varying criterion, both wartime and postwar lists were produced detailing high-scoring pilots. The leading aces of many of the nations involved in the air war are as follows, and they appear in no particular order: Stanislav Skalski (Poland), who attained 18 combat victories with the RAF, having earlier achieved at least 4 in the Polish Air Force; Svein Heglund (Norway), who claimed at least 14 personal aerial victories with the RAF's 331 and 85 Squadrons; Marcel Albert (France) flew with three air forces – the French, the RAF and finally over the Eastern Front in the Soviet Air Force's

Normandie Neimann regiment – whilst in the process of scoring 23 victories; Karel Kuttelwascher (Czechoslovakia) gained 18 during his time with the French air force, and then the RAF; John Frost (South Africa) got 16 whilst flying exclusively with the South African Air Force; Colin Gray (New Zealand) achieved 27 with the RAF; Ivan du Monceau de Bergendael (Belgian) flew with 609 and 530 Squadrons, RAF, to gain eight combat victories; Wang Kuang-Fu (China) obtained seven with the USAAF's Chinese-American Composite Wing; and Congressional Medal of Honor winners Joseph Foss with 26 victories and David McCampbell with 33 personal claims became the highest scoring fighter pilots of the US Marine Corps and Navy respectively.

For the Axis powers, Constantine Cantacuzene (Romania) claimed 60 victories; Hiroyoshi Nishizawa (Japan) is credited with around 87 claims for combat victories whilst flying with the Navy, and Satoshi Anabuki (Japan) 51 for the Army; whilst Stojan Stojanov (Bulgaria) was credited with 15 combat victories.

Measuring the Qualities of a Fighter Pilot

It would be unfair to measure the capability of the fighter pilot purely on the number of combat victories he obtained. From literature – especially the published recollections of those fighter pilots who flew during the Second World War – it can be suggested that the qualities of an outstanding fighter pilot were not only his ability to shoot down large numbers of enemy aircraft (and thus demonstrate that he was a great aerial shot), but also his effectiveness as a leader of other pilots. The latter meant looking out for the 'weakest links' in the operational 'chain' and nurturing them to improve their fighting skills. This was usually achieved through communication with his men, instructing them to perform as a team, rather than as individuals, through the employment of effective tactics.

Nevertheless, there are outstanding examples of fighter pilots with vast numbers of aerial victories who never attained senior rank within a squadron. Examples include Air Master Sergeant Oiva Tuominen, who became the first Finnish fighter pilot to receive his country's top military award, the Mannerheim Cross, and the RAF's James 'Ginger' Lacey, who gained 23 of his eventual 28 combat victories whilst still a sergeant pilot.

Critical characteristics in the make-up of the successful combat fighter pilot were identified during the war. Surviving wartime studies delineate these characteristics, which were derived directly from observation of fighter pilots undergoing combat flying. For example, it is clear that the quality of flying training in terms of preparing a pilot for combat flying played a significant role. In later years, combat flying in various conflicts has presented us with the opportunities to identify, and evaluate, the key features of the combat fighter pilot. One succinct appraisal of the essential characteristics came recently from Vietnam-era U.S. Navy fighter pilot, Rear Admiral (Ret) Paul T. Gillcrist, in his foreword to the autobiography of Finland's foremost fighter pilot, Illu Juutilainen. The former cautioned that it was unlikely that any single pilot would ever fit all the characteristics he identified, which are:

1) Attack. The advantage will always lie with the one making the attack.
2) Superb situational awareness.
3) Incredibly good eyesight combined with a good lookout doctrine.
4) A natural shot with outstanding ability to estimate deflection.
5) A sound knowledge of the strengths and weaknesses of both his aeroplane and the enemy's. A capacity to capitalize on these.
6) A natural and gifted pilot.
7) A willingness to fly the fighter to the ragged edge of its capabilities, and to sustain the combat at the edge of the envelope.
8) High physical endurance under very harsh operating conditions.
9) Supremely confident in his own abilities.
10) Coolness under fire.

The Changing Face of Aerial Combat

Compared to the Great War, there were fundamental, but significant, differences in aerial combat when exploring the specific characteristics of the Second World War. The former conflict was largely shaped by infantry and artillery, but in the second, aerial power was to play the key role. In the First World War, engagements often took place between individual machines, or between small flights of aircraft – even by 1918 combat between vast numbers of aircraft from either side was uncommon. In the Second World War, larger formations of aircraft often became embroiled in combat, with fighting taking place both at higher altitude and at greater speeds. Pilots of the later conflict were also equipped with parachutes, which gave them a higher chance of surviving from an engagement in which their aircraft had been damaged. By comparison, their predecessors in the First World War were forced into trying to land their machines, or perish in the attempt, due to the unwillingness of senior commanders to issue parachutes to the frontline.

The Second World War heralded two further distinct developments in the history of aerial war – the control of aircraft from the ground and the advent of the early warning system. Radio and radar created both the opportunity for aircraft to be controlled from the ground and enabled advance (and accurate) warnings to be given of incoming attacks by enemy aircraft. In July 1935, the then Air Member for Research and Development on the Air Council, AM Sir Hugh Dowding, presented a report to the British Air Defence Research Committee strongly advocating the practical implementation of 'radio direction finding'. For the first time, radar became a critical factor in the defence of Britain, and during the summer of 1940 it provided information on the height, range and composition of belligerent formations, thus allowing the RAF to be more efficient in exploiting the opportunities it presented for interception. Radio, radar and fighter controllers were not common to all theatres of combat, however, this technology having little part to play in operations conducted by the Luftwaffe over the Eastern Front, for example.

Gun Camera

The origins of the use of the gun camera as a tool for claim verification in aerial warfare can be traced back to the First World War. The gun camera was used by the Royal Flying Corps as an aid to gunnery training, for it was constructed so as to physically represent a Vickers or Lewis machine-gun, which would be fitted in both single- and twin-engined aircraft. Its use enabled the operator to engage in gunnery practice without risking damage to the target, and was particularly useful in simulated dogfights. The gun camera also allowed the aim of the operator to be evaluated once the film had been developed,.

The RAF continued to use the gun camera as a training aid throughout the interwar period, fitting them to fighter aircraft like the Bristol Bulldog and Hawker Hart. However, it was not until the Second World War that the function of the gun camera altered significantly from its use as a simple training tool to its employment as a method of verifying the effectiveness of fighter armament, and thus by consequence providing a method of independently evaluating combat claims made by pilots.

In the process of claim verification, victory submissions were generally considered to be more accurate when supported by gun camera footage. However, the employment of gun cameras has led to infrequent accusations that scores were boosted between wingmen, who would co-operate to duplicate each others' claims when in fact it was the same single aircraft that had been shot down. Nonetheless, gun camera was often used to provide evidence to support claims for victories where no other evidence existed. The RAF began installing G.22 gun cameras in their fighter aircraft from early 1940, this equipment utilizing 16-mm black and white film. Later in the war the RAF also used 35-mm film, which enabled a superior quality of image to be obtained. The USAAF made use of both colour and black and white 35-mm film, as well as 16-mm stock, in their fighter aircraft – the colour images of aerial combat over Guadalcanal and the Marianas remain as vivid today upon viewing as they did when first seen over 50 years ago. In the USSR, gun cameras were used by some units, but the earliest employment of good quality colour film can be traced only as far back as 1946. In Finland, gun cameras were not widely available, whilst only limited (if any) use was made by the Italians. The Luftwaffe situation is quite similar, although some footage exists using BSK 18 cameras fitted with 16-mm over the Eastern Front.

Surviving gun camera footage from any air force is now extremely rare, primarily due to two factors. Firstly, the film was never intended for archival treatment, rather it was intended to be used as a source of intelligence – i.e. to verify damage to enemy aircraft and other targets, and in many cases was almost immediately discarded after review. And secondly, many units operating 'in the field' either failed to receive the proper film, or when they did receive stock, did not have the appropriate equipment to process, develop and store it.

Psychological Stress

Combat stress, or combat fatigue, seems to have been acknowledged by each of the six air forces examined within this volume, but the emphasis placed on the observation and treatment of it appears to have differed considerably. For example, the USAAF actively pursued the recognition and treatment of those fighter pilots affected by combat fatigue, whereas until the final year of the war that the Luftwaffe – whose pilots had no defined length of operational tour – provided rest and recuperation centres, where tired pilots were quickly posted to re-charge their psychological batteries. By contrast, the RAF focused their attention to identifying early on in the aircrew selection process those who it believed would be 'temperamentally unsuitable' for combat flying.

An important point to mention in this introduction is that some aircrew seemed to 'get by' without showing obvious signs of undue stress, but then in postwar years suffered the reccurrence of memories of the terrible conflicts in which they had fought. For some, nervous debilitation and breakdowns occurred in the immediate postwar years, whilst for others, recurring nightmares still continue some 50+ years after the traumatic events took place. Combat stress took many forms, and the residual effects have not been adequately identified in postwar years.

INTRODUCING THE AIR FORCES

The Luftwaffe

At the beginning of 1934 the Rhineland programme of German Air Force expansion commenced. This programme was to realize an increase in production of over 4,000 military aircraft for the newly-instigated Reichsluftwaffe by mid-1935. This figure included 245 fighters, a total further increased following Gen Milch's revised expansion plan of January 1935. On 14 March that same year, the Luftwaffe began a large recruiting campaign based on the nostalgic appeal of the famous German pilots of the First World War, which also saw squadrons and groups re-christened. For example, 132 Fighter Squadron became *Jagdgeschwader Richthofen Nr 2* (*Richthofen* Fighter Group No 2), whilst an adjunct of JG 2 became known as *Geschwader Immelmann*. In October 1935, Milch introduced Lieferplan (production plan) No 1, increasing the number of fighters by April 1936 to 970.

Production plan No. 4 became highly significant in this series, for in addition to the requirement for a total of 18,000 military aircraft by May 1938, new types such as the Bf 109 were specified for the first time. Whilst British political disinterest was attempting to stifle F/L Frank Whittle's attempts to develop a functional jet engine, by 1937 the German Air Ministry had set up Project X – the secret rocket research programme placed under the leadership of Dr Alexander Lippisch. Also at around this time Hans Pabst von Ohain conducted his first successful runs of his turbojet engine at the University of Göttingen. Possibly the finest radial-engined fighter of the war in the shape of the Focke-Wulf Fw 190 made its first flight at Bremen on 1 June 1939. The third great German fighter, in addition to the piston-engined Bf 109 and Fw 190, was the turbojet-powered Me 262, which did not make its (belated) first flight until well into 1942.

In terms of tactical preparation for the Second World War, the Luftwaffe held a big advantage over its adversaries by having honed its combat tactics in the Spanish Civil War. Germany's involvement in this conflict stemmed directly from a request for military assistance made by Spanish Nationalist Capt Francisco Arranz to Hitler on 25 July 1936, the Sonderstab W plan seeing military support to Spain within a matter of weeks – the Luftwaffe was heavily involved in supporting Franco until March 1939. At the beginning of its Spanish 'sojourn', it appeared that German pilots had forgotten the lessons of air combat in the First World War, choosing instead to rely on the training its pilots had received from the Italian Air Force, where aerobatics and tight formation flying had been the name of the game.

The pilots of the 'voluntary' Condor Legion had commenced the conflict in Heinkel He 51 and Arado Ar 68 biplanes on ground support operations, and they quickly appreciated that close formation flying placed them at a disadvantage to the American Curtiss Hawk biplane and Soviet I-16 monoplane – known to the Germans as the Rata. The introduction of the Bf 109 (which First World War ace Ernst Udet had earlier claimed would 'never make a fighter') changed the shape of aerial conflict in Spain, and provided the foundation for the Luftwaffe fighter tactics that were eventually used in Poland, the low countries and France.

The Red Air Force

In Spain, the primary function of the pilots of the Red Air Force was to provide support for the ground forces. The Russians were perceived by the Condor Legion pilots to be tactically naive, maintaining small but tight and defensive formations. Inadequate combat training was masked by initial successes over the German biplane fighters, but following the Luftwaffe's introduction of the Bf 109B, the Russians found themselves out-paced and out-fought by their German opponents. In the hands of an expert pilot, the Polikarpov I-16 (the first monoplane fighter with a retractable undercarriage and enclosed cockpit) was a fair match for the Bf 109, but the biplane I-15 was hopelessly outclassed. The latter had been introduced to Spain in September 1936, followed just a month later by the far superior I-16. Within weeks Russian pilots discovered an inherent vulnerability in tight formation flying, which not only inhibited their opportunities for manoeuvring, but also reduced the effectiveness of the cover they could offer each other in combat.

Russian fighter pilots were also involved in combat with the Japanese prior to the outbreak of the European phase of the Second World War. Here, they seemed to fare slightly better than in Spain. Their Japanese opponents had practised air raid alerts for many years in anticipation of a Sino-Japanese War, which eventually commenced in 1937. Four Soviet I-15 fighter and two SB-2 bomber squadrons formed as part of the second Volunteer Air Group were duly sent to defend Soviet bases in China at Lanchow, Nanking, Hankow and Chunking.

NII-VVS test pilots, including Stepan Suprun, who had already been awarded the Order of the Red Star, were amongst those sent, and another, Grigori Kravchenko, was put in command of the 22nd Fighter Regiment, based at Khalkin Gol. This unit went on to claim 32 Japanese aircraft destroyed for the loss of only one pilot. Kravchenko later achieved high distinction, and rank, whilst in combat with firstly the Finns and then the Luftwaffe, before being killed on the Volkhov Front in 1943.

In the late 1930s, the Soviet Air Force, suffering enormously from Stalin's purges of senior military figures, including highly experienced and knowledgeable air force leaders, was ill-prepared, despite potentially over-whelming numerical superiority, to wage war with Finland, and later Germany.

Finnish Air Force

The roots of the Finnish Air Force (FAF) stretch back to 1918, and over the following 20 years, despite very limited resources in terms of Finnish equipment and personnel, the FAF was acutely conscious of their vulnerability to invasion from the threatening expansionist policies of the USSR. By the mid-1930s, defence strategy had gained increased importance, and the FAF actively pursued a policy of combat training for its fighter pilots. Highly effective gunnery training, allied with the development of a strong – almost unshakeable – sense of squadron camaraderie, were targeted high within the air force's list of objectives. The extraordinary 'kill/loss' ratio achieved against Soviet aircraft during the Winter and Continuation Wars of 1939–40 and 1941–44 respectively are testimony not only to the courage of the FAF fighter pilots, but also to their skill, which had been developed through the implementation of a highly effective combat flying training programme. Whilst the Winter War lasted just five months between November 1939 and March 1940, the Finns decided in 1941 to align themselves with Germany primarily as a defensive measure in light of the continuing avaricious intent of the Soviet Union.

The Regia Aeronautica

Benito Mussolini instructed the Regia Aeronautica to attack Ethiopia on 3 October 1935 in support of ground forces driving into the African country. Included were eight fighter squadrons, three of which were equipped with Fiat CR.20 biplanes. Being a great advocate of the employment of biplane fighters in modern warfare, Italy had ordered the new Fiat CR.42 Falco as late as 1938, despite the development at the same time by the company of the new monoplane G.50. On 10 August 1940, the Macchi C.202 Folgore made its first flight, powered by a Daimler-Benz DB 601A liquid-cooled engine – it went on to become arguably the most successful Italian fighter of the war. On 10 June 1940, Benito Mussolini declared war on Britain, Holland, Belgium and Luxembourg. At the time of the declaration the Regia Aeronautica boasted a fighter force totalling some 594 aircraft.

During the First World War, all Italy had learned of the exploits of its highest scoring pilots, who were feted as heroes. Subsequent conflicts in Ethiopia and Spain produced a new generation of men who attained scores that afforded them 'ace' status, but by then the Regia Aeronautica (the Italian Royal Air Force) had developed a policy of avoiding focusing attention on specific pilots. Rather, they sought to promote the concept that fighter combat victories resulted from the efforts of several aircraft working together as a team, as opposed to individual flying skill.

Combat flying training was focused upon aerobatics and formation flying, with comparatively little attention being paid to gunnery training. By 1943 the situation had changed dramatically, as many Italian fighter pilots re-mustered into the Mussolini-inspired Aeronautica Nazionale Repubblicana (ANR), whilst others left to fight on the side of the Allies. ANR pilots began to receive individual recognition for their exploits, and the Luftwaffe provided support and guidance – albeit rather limited – in combat training and, more importantly, in the provision of Bf 109s.

Royal Air Force

Unlike the Luftwaffe, the RAF had no pre-war proving ground, even though operations in the middle-east in the late 1920s and early 1930s had sown the seed of strategic bombing. Like the Luftwaffe, the RAF had also forgotten the lessons learned from the First World War, although the latter did not have the alibi that it needed to reconstitute a complete air force from scratch. The RAF's lack of preparedness stemmed from political indifference, which brought with it an almost blasé regard for events happening in Europe. The political isolation was reflected in the organization of the Royal Air Force, which for the early part of the 1930s adopted a somewhat carefree existence.

Britain had been completely unsuccessful in their attempts to ban military aircraft at the multi-nation talks held in Geneva in 1934, and seemed unaware of the rapid build-up of national air forces by other nations. Limited political recognition of the re-armament of other European countries came with the implementation of the five-year expansion programmes starting in the aftermath of the Geneva conference. The government announced that the RAF was to receive under Scheme A an additional 41 squadrons, and that the training of aircrew was to increasingly become a priority over the subsequent five years.

Scheme C was introduced in May 1935 in direct response to bragging from senior Nazi officers that the Luftwaffe had already achieved an air force just as capable as the RAF. A further 35 fighter squadrons were planned by 31 March 1939, whilst the subsequent Scheme F of February 1936 instructed further expansion – however, for fighter squadrons there was to be no increase in either the number of units or aircraft produced. Later expansion plans were not approved until Scheme M in 1938, which called for a force of 638 fighters. Fighter Command was formed in July 1936, with the first AOC in C appointed being AM Sir Hugh Dowding. In October 1935 the British Joint Planning Committee (including G/C Arthur T. Harris) filed a secret report which concluded that war with Germany was inevitable, and therefore went on to propose strategies for the defence of the low countries and France. In the meantime, the ponderous move towards expansion coincided with Air Ministry specifications for aircraft with higher-performance, allowing the Royal Air Force to rather belatedly prepare for conflict.

On the outbreak of the Second World War, Fighter Command had only 35 squadrons, including 22 equipped with the latest fighters,

the Hawker Hurricane (600 of which were ordered by the RAF in June 1936) and the Supermarine Spitfire. Biplane fighters were still making their service debut with the RAF as late as 1937, with the last in this obsolete breed, the Gloster Gladiator, going on to serve with distinction with the RAF in Norway, Malta, Greece and North Africa, whilst lend-lease types were employed effectively by the Finns during the Winter War against Russia. The RAF began the war with combat flying training techniques which were rather more akin to the wing-tip to wing-tip formation flying of the Italians, rather than the combat techniques so ably learned and taught by the likes of Mannock and McCudden during the First World War.

The United States Army Air Corps

In June 1932 the United States Army Air Corps (USAAC) could boast just four fighter squadrons, despite the introduction of a five-year expansion plan in the late 1920s. It was not until 1937 that the USA gradually woke up to the increasing military preparedness of many European countries, President Roosevelt requesting that Congress approve an increase in Army Air Corps strength from 1,352 to 2,320 by 1940.

In January 1938, Maj Gen Frank Andrews and Maj James H. Doolittle of the USAAC reported to an aviation conference that the US lagged behind the standards in military aviation being established in several European countries. They suggested a complete reorganisation of the USAAC and a recruitment drive. Following the death of Maj Gen Oscar Westover on 21 September 1938, Maj Gen H. H. 'Hap' Arnold was appointed Chief of the USAAC. He was to play a critical role in developing the air force, especially in the establishment of a training curriculum and the creation of operational resources during the early war years. Roosevelt continued to badger Congress over the country's lack of military preparedness for war, and persuaded them to agree to produce a further 3,251 aircraft by June 1941. On the outbreak of the war in Europe on 3 September 1939, the USAAC still lagged far behind the Luftwaffe, having only 800 frontline aircraft and 26,000 personnel compared with 4,320 aircraft and 390,000 personnel for the German force. The situation had not significantly changed by the time the Japanese attack on Pearl Harbor on 7 December 1941 propelled the USA into war.

In June 1937 the USAAC had ordered the prototype Lockheed XP-38, which had been to fulfil the demanding X-608 specification for a long-range interceptor. Entering service as the P-38 Lightning, Lockheed eventually built over 11,000 aircraft – one of which became the first USAAF fighter to shoot down a German aircraft. Flying for the first time in 1937 was the prototype Bell Airacobra, an aircraft that was later to achieve greater success in the hands of Soviet pilots – who received some 4,773 examples – than with the Western Allies. In October 1938 the Curtiss P-40 made its first flight, and in April 1939 524 of the type were ordered by the USAAC (although only 199 had been delivered by 1940). By the end of the war, just under 14,000 P-40s had been built.

The Raymond Rice/Edgar Schmued designed North American NA-73 made its first flight on 26 October 1940, the Allison-engined fighter having been built to a specification drawn up by the British Purchasing Commission. Later dubbed the Mustang by the RAF, and eventually powered by the Rolls-Royce Merlin engine, this machine became arguably the most effective Allied piston-engined fighter of the war. The third great USAAF fighter, Republic's awesome XP-47B, was the last to take to the skies, the Pratt & Whitney-powered design completing its first flight on 6 May 1941. It was followed by some 15,683 Thunderbolts constructed for war service.

Although the USA did not enter the war until 7 December 1941, many American nationals voluntarily served with the RAF prior to this date. For example, on 17 August 1940, Hurricane pilot P/O William Fiske of 601 Squadron became the first American to lose his life on active service with the RAF. He had been part of the first contingent of seven US nationals that had volunteered to fight with the RAF upon the outbreak of war in Europe – only one survived the war. Some American nationals achieved notable scores whilst flying with the British in 1940/41.

In April 1941 President Roosevelt announced the formation of the American Volunteer Group (AVG), which was to be commanded by Maj Gen Claire Lee Chennault. The AVG were equipped with 100 ex-RAF P-40B Tomahawks, and supported Chiang Kai-shek's forces in China against the an overwhelming Japanese force. The AVG undertook its first operations some 13 days after the Japanese attack on Pearl Harbor.

The ten highest scoring fighter pilots within the air forces covered in this volume

Soviet Air Force

Name	Fronts	Victories	Top Awards
Kozhedub I. N.	St. F	62	HSU x 3
	Belor. F		
Pokryshkin A. I.	Kavk. F	59	HSU x 3
	Ukr. F		
Gulayev N. D.	Voron. F	57+4(sh)	HSU x 2
	Ukr. F		
Rechkalov G. A.	Kavk. F	56+5(sh)	HSU x 2
	Ukr. F.		
Yevstigneyev K. A.	Ukr. F	53+3(sh)	HSU x 2
Vorozheikin A. V.	Ukr. F	52	HSU x 2
	Prib. F		
Glinka D. B.	Kavk. F	50	HSU x 2
Skomorokhov N. M.	Ukr. F	46+8(sh)	HSU x 2
Koldunov A. I.	Ukr. F	46	HSU x 2
Popkov V. I.	Yuzhn. F	41	HSU x 2
	Ukr. F		

Key

HSU	Hero of the Soviet Union
St. F	Steppe Front
Belor. F	Belorussian Front
KavK. F	North Caucasion Front
Ukr. F	Ukranian Front
Voron. F	Voronezh Front
Prib. F	Baltic Front
Yuzhn. F	Southern Front

Finnish Air Force

Name	Fronts	Victories	Top Awards
Juutilainen E. I.	W. War	94 (1/6)	2nd Class
	C. War		MHC x 2
Wind H. H.	C. War	75	2nd Class
			MHC x 2
Luukkanen E. A.	W. War	56	2nd Class
	C. War		MHC
Lehtovaara U. S.	W. War	44 (1/2)	MHC
	C. War		
Tuominen O. E. K.	W. War	44	
	C. War		
Puhakka R. O. P.	W. War	42	MHC
	C. War		
Puro O. K.	C. War	36	
Katajainen N. E.	C. War	35 (1/2)	MHC
Nissinen L. V.	W. War	32 (1/3)	2nd Class
	C. War		MHC
Karhila K. K. E.	C. War	32 (1/4)	

Key

MHC	Mannerheim Cross
W. War	Finno-Russian Winter War 1939–40
C. War	Continuation War 1941–41

Luftwaffe

Name	Fronts	Victories	Top Awards
Hartmann E.	EF	352	KCOSD
Barkhorn G.	Br, EF, WF	301	KCOS
Rall G.	WF, Br, Rou, EF, WF	275	KCOS
Kittel O.	WF, EF	267	KCOS
Nowotny W.	EF	258	KCOSD
Batz W.	EF, Hun	237	KCOS
Rudorffer E.	WF, Br, Tun, EF, WF	222	KCOS
Bär H.	Br, EF, Sc, Tun, Med, Malt, WF	220	KCOS
Graf H.	WF, Med, EF	212	KCOSD
Weissenberger T.	Nor, EF, WF	208	KCO

Key

KCO	Knight's Cross with Oakleaves
KCOS	Knight's Cross with Oakleaves and Swords
KCOSD	Knight's Cross with Oakleaves, Swords and Diamonds
EF	Eastern Front
Br	Battle of Britain
WF	Western Front
Hun	Hungary
Rou	Roumania
Sc	Sicily
Med	Mediterranean
Malt	Malta
Nor	Norway

Royal Air Force

Name	Fronts	Victories	Top Awards
Pattle M. T. St J.	N.Afr, Gr	50(2)†	DFC*
Johnson J. E.	WF	34(7)	DSO**, DFC**
Beurling G. F	WF, Mal	31(7)	DS0, DFC, DFM*
Vale W.	N.Afr, Gr, ME	30(3)	DFC*
Lacey J. H.	WF, Br, Ind, Bma	28	DFM**
Malan A. G.	WF, Br	27(7)	DSO*, DFC*
Caldwell C. R.	ME, Pac	27(3)	DSO, DFC*
Gray C. F.	WF, Br, N.Afr, Mal	27(2)	DSO, DFC**
Stanford-Tuck R. R.	WF, Br	27(2)	DSO, DFC**
Finucane B. E. F.	Br, WF	26(6)	DSO, DFC**

Key

DSO	Distinguished Service Order
DFC	Distinguished Flying Cross
DFM	Distinguished Flying Medal
*	Bar to DSO, DFC or DFM
WF	Western Front
N.Afr	North Africa
Gr	Greece
Malt	Malta
Med	Mediterranean
Br	Battle of Britain
Ind	India
Bma	Burma
ME	Middle East
Pac	Pacific

† The 50+ score achieved by Pattle is not confirmed due to incomplete claim records for April 1941 following the German invasion of Greece.

United States Army Air Corps/Force

Name	Fronts	Victories	Top Awards
Bong R. I.	SW Pac	40	CMH
McGuire Jnr T. B.	SW Pac	38	CMH
Gabreski F. S.	ETO	28	
Johnson R. S.	ETO	28	
MacDonald C. H.	SW Pac	27	
Preddy G. E.	ETO	26.83	
Meyer J. C.	ETO	24	
Whetmore R. S.	ETO	22.60	
Schilling D. C.	ETO	22.50	
Johnson G. R.	SW Pac	22	
Kearby N. E.	SW Pac	22	CMH

Key

CMH	Congressional Medal of Honor
SW Pac	South-West Pacifc
ETO	European Theatre of Operations

Regia Aeronautica and Aeronautica Nazionale Repubblicana

Name	Score	Air Force
Martinoli T.	22	RA
Ferruli L.	21	RA
Lucchini F.	21	RA
Bordoni Bisleri F.	19	RA
Gorrini L.	19	15 in RA, 4 in ANR
Visintini M.	16	RA
Drago U.	15	4 in RA, 11 in ANR
Bellagambi M.	14	3 in RA, 11 in ANR
Baron L.	12	RA
Giannella L.	12	RA

Key

RA	Regia Aeronautica
ANR	Aeronautica Nazionale Repubblicana

Chapter One

Royal Air Force

There was no emphasis on proving 'victories' or 'confirmations'. This all came about much later in postwar years when historians became excited about the media scenes over 'scores'. It just did not matter at the time. What mattered was to attack the enemy, and mostly you never saw the final result when the aircraft went down into cloud. You then stated what you had done, and only occasionally a 'confirmation' would come back when wreckage had been found on the ground (none over the sea of course). The log book might receive an entry '109/190 (or whatever) destroyed/probably dest/or damaged'. If you knew that it had gone positively, you would just put 'at' and the location. The other 'confirmation' could be if one of your formation saw your target go in, but this seldom happened in 1940 when everyone was busy looking after their own tail!

W/C Roland Beamont

At the start of the Second World War, the RAF had under 160 squadrons and only 5,700 aircraft, most of which were unsuitable for front-line operation. The series of pre-war RAF Expansion Programmes had failed to deliver the volume of training aircraft and airfields required to produce a sufficient number of pilots to meet envisaged operational needs. During the Blitzkrieg in France and the defence of Britain, the need for

trained, and most of all combat experienced, pilots reached a premium. The problem was also compounded by the inclement British climate which, combined with the constant vulnerability of training flights and airfields to enemy attack, greatly impeded the pilot training programme.

Training
The key to the training of vast numbers of aircrew for the RAF came from the unofficial alliances that had been forged during the 1930s between Britain and other countries within the Empire. For example, the roots of the scheme in Southern Rhodesia (now Zimbabwe) can be traced back as far as 1934, whilst during the First World War, both Canadians and Americans had trained RFC and RAF pilots in Canada and Texas. During the Second World War RAF pilots were trained in countries as culturally diverse as Australia, India, New Zealand, Egypt, the West Indies, Canada, South Africa and Southern Rhodesia. Additionally, in early 1941 Britain entered into a clandestine deal with the Roosevelt administration in the US that saw thousands of RAF cadet pilots sent across the Atlantic to be trained in America by the USAAF, Navy and civilian instructors.

By 1941, the long haul to becoming a pilot commenced when the volunteer enlisted for service at a recruiting centre close to his home, where he was classified as an Aircrafthand/Pilot with the rank of Aircrafthand 2nd Class in the Royal Air Force Volunteer Reserve (RAFVR). In many cases this was followed by a period of deferred service, during which he would continue with his civilian employment, or studies, anxiously awaiting the call to report to the RAF. The long-anticipated letter from the air force would eventually arrive instructing him to report to the Air Crew Reception Centre (ACRC), bringing with him as few possessions as possible.

At the ACRC he would line up with hundreds of other hopefuls, and after form filling, be marched away to quarters. During the next two to three weeks at the ACRC there would be a maths exam, lectures, parades, guard and fatigue duties, and the issue of yet more equipment. Roll call on the final morning would lead to the identity of the Initial Training Wing (ITW) that the aspirant pilot would be posted to. He would quickly find that ITW was essentially a funnel through which potential cadet aircrew were filtered, before being selected to move onto a flying 'grading' course located at an Elementary Flying Training School (EFTS) somewhere in the UK.

Dual sorties in a DH.82A Tiger Moth, or a Miles Magister, were likely to be the future fighter pilot's first introduction to flying, and he would need to 'go solo' after around 12 hours of such dual instruction if he was to stand any chance of being selected for pilot training, rather than other aircraft duties. 'Grading' had been introduced in late 1941, and was to become a pivotal factor in the early selection of men for pilot training. The reasoning behind the introduction of this system was logical enough, for in the early stages of the Empire Air Training Scheme, great financial and human resources were wasted in sending young men across the seas to train, only for many to be returned early when it became apparent that they had little aptitude for flying. By 'weeding out' those with little ability for becoming pilots in the UK, considerable wastage was minimized.

'Grading' successfully achieved, the potential fighter pilot would be reclassified as a Leading Aircraftman and re-mustered u/t (under training) Pilot. Posted to an Aircrew Despatch Centre (ACDC), he would be held here until receiving orders to proceed to his designated flying training base. For some, the destination would not be known until the point of departure from the UK, and even then, many were sent to a place they had never heard of before! For a puzzled few, the destination did not become apparent until they had arrived in the 'foreign' country.

For example, prior to America's entry into the war, several hundred RAF cadets were already training to become pilots in the 'States. During the summer and autumn of 1941, the cadet pilot wore his dress uniform on the ship over to Canada and at the Personnel Despatch Centre (PDC) in Toronto (and later to 31 PDC, Moncton). Just prior to crossing the border into the USA, he would change from his service uniform into the Burton's grey suit which had been issued to him by the RAF in England. From then on – and only until the Japanese attack on Pearl Harbor – civilian clothes be worn outside camp by RAF cadets, so as not to infringe or embarrass America's strict laws on neutrality.

The pilot would be posted to one of the several schools operated by the USAAC as part of the Arnold Scheme, or alternatively, to one of six (and, briefly, seven) civilian-operated flying training schools called, unsurprisingly, British Flying Training Schools (BFTS). Unlike those on the Arnold Scheme, RAF cadet pilots at the BFTS's, received all-through training on the one base – i.e. from Primary or Elementary stage on

Right *Graphic posters with explicit messages acted as visual prompts for fighter pilots, and were on display at many squadron dispersal points. Two examples are:*

'Temper Dash with discretion', which was an attempt to encourage a calm approach, as well as promoting the value of teamwork when making an attack. (via RAF Museum AD1305)

'Will Your Guns Fire?' makes a clear pictorial reference to the dangers of failing to check the temperatures and pneumatic pressure of the radiators prior to making an attack. The Spitfire's machine guns were heated by ducts running directly from the radiator in an effort to avoid the guns freezing at altitude. The optimum operational temperatures were between 80 to 90°C, whilst pneumatic pressure needed to be at 280 to 300lbs per square inch. Failing to examine radiator temperature and pressure could lead to the inability to fire at the critical moment, with the implication then being that the Spitfire is vulnerable to, and defenceless against, attack. (via RAF Museum AD1303)

TEMPER DASH with DISCRETION

Don't let your eagerness spoil a combined attack and incidentally make you a 'sitter' for the enemy.

THIS or THIS!

WILL YOUR GUNS FIRE?

THESE WILL

THESE WON'T

PT-17 Stearman, through Basic on Vultee BT-13 Valiants, to Advanced on AT-6 Texans, before gaining 'wings'. The Basic stage was phased out of RAF pilot training in America in 1942.

Those pilots who had come from universities were more likely to be commissioned on the completion of their training than cadets from other backgrounds. The cadet pilot could expect to receive a total of between 150 to 220 hours flying training in the US prior to gaining his wings. The considerable difference in hours was dependent on the time that the pupil entered the training syllabus, as the longer the war lasted, so the duration of the training programme increased. This was principally caused by the increasing congestion back in the UK at the Personnel Reception Centres (PRCs), which had been sparked by the massive influx of qualified pilots returning from abroad.

Once back in Britain, the future fighter pilot could expect a period of advanced flying and then operational, training. In 1942, the pilot would fly around 20 hours on Master Is and IIs at an Advanced Flying Unit (AFU), before moving to an Operational Training Unit (OTU) and completing some 50 hours on the Hurricane. He would then be deemed fit for posting to an operational squadron. So, the typical training for an inexperienced fighter pilot posted to a Typhoon squadron early in 1943, for example, would have seen him complete somewhere in the region of 270 flying hours prior to arriving in Fighter Command's frontline.

Tactics

The myriad lessons of fighter combat technique which had been learned in the harsh proving ground of the First World War seemed to have been lost by the time the RAF came to evolve tactics suitable for the Second World War. In the earlier conflict, combat flying had been shaped by great aces like Hawker, Ball, Mannock and McCudden, but their experiences had slipped into long-term memory during the bleak inter-war years, only to be rekindled some 20 or so years later after initial mistakes had been recognized. During the postwar years RAF fighter combat tactics were founded on wing-tip to wing-tip formation flying – like the German pilots who had trained in Italy.

Gunnery training was given a low priority, although pre-war RAF fighter pilots had, at least, the somewhat intangible benefit of the once a year summer gunnery camps. By the outbreak of the Second World War, RAF fighter pilots was less prepared tactically than their counterparts in the Luftwaffe. Out of necessity the former were to learn quickly. During the Battle of Britain, comparatively junior officer pilots of Fighter Command such as 'Gerry' Edge and John Dundas soon made their marks as brilliant tacticians, influencing the development of combat fighting amongst their colleagues. They were essentially the Hawkers and McCuddens of the new era.

At the age of 30, South African-born Adolf 'Sailor' Malan was considered an 'old man' during the Battle, but his outstanding performance as both a fighter pilot and leader led to the development of his ten 'commandments' for air fighting, which were subsequently to be displayed throughout Fighter Command stations during the course of the war.

Official recognition of the need to standardize the most efficient and effective forms of attack led to the production of authoritative guides. In 1940, Fighter Command published, and then updated, a document which sought to standardize the potential attack strategies which could be employed to attack incoming Luftwaffe aircraft during the Battle of Britain. The updated version of the Fighter Command Attack Document had six forms of attack:

No 1: An attack from Dead Astern and from Above Cloud
No 2: From Directly Below
No 3: (From Dead Astern) a) Approach Pursuit, b) Approach Turning, From Above Cloud.
No 4: (From Directly Below) Two Types of Approach
No 5: (From Dead Astern) Two Types of Approach
No 6: (From Dead Astern) Two Types of Attack.

As with the Luftwaffe, and indeed any of the other air forces covered in this volume, experienced, individual, pilots would employ tactics justified by their personal experience of combat. These were tactics which they intrinsically believed would work for them. Fighter leaders could also have a significant influence over the characteristics of a combat.

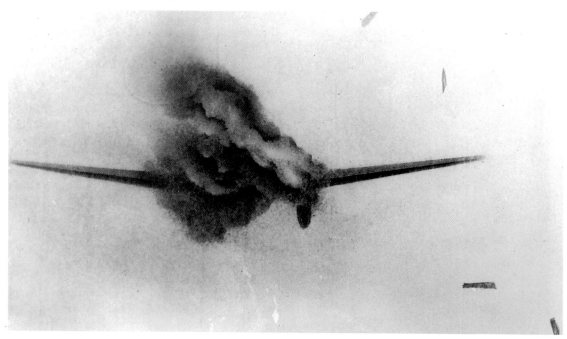

This gun camera shot captures the moment of destruction of a German aircraft by outstanding fighter pilot, and tactician, S/L Adolf 'Sailor' Malan. A native of South Africa, Malan was almost 30 years old by the time of the evacuation of Dunkirk, and had gained his nickname after having served for several years in the South African Merchant Navy. In 1936 he joined the RAF, and had risen to the rank of flight lieutenant by the start of the war. Malan was awarded an early DFC following his successes during Dunkirk with the Spitfire I, and this was followed in August 1940 with command of 74 Squadron, with whom he had served for the past four years. On more than one occasion over the next two years Malan was listed as Fighter Command's top scorer, and by the end of the war he had been decorated with the DSO and Bar, DFC and Bar, Belgian Croix de Guerre, and the Czech War Cross. In the early postwar years Malan returned to civilian life, where he eventually became a farmer in South Africa and was involved in human rights issues, leading protests against the withdrawal of voting rights for the black Cape community by the Nationalist government. During his final visit to the UK in 1959, 'Sailor' Malan flew in a Victor from RAF Cottesmore which, at that time, was commanded by G/C (later AVM) 'Johnnie' Johnson, another truly outstanding RAF fighter pilot. G/C Malan died following a long struggle with Parkinson's disease in 1963 at the age of just 52. (via IWM C1704)

Len Thorne, a Spitfire pilot with 602 Squadron, talks briefly of his impressions of flying into combat with two of the RAF's greatest fighter pilots, Al Deere and Paddy Finucane, during 1941–42:

My first CO in 602 was S/L Meagher, but he only remained for three or four weeks before Al Deere took over, who was with us from mid-1941 until being posted away in January 1942. I was very much a 'sprog' fighter pilot when I flew with Al Deere. He was a good leader in that whilst he would carry out his duties, he would also use his 'savvy' so that he did not lead the squadron into a situation where it was very likely to run into severe trouble. Just suppose we are flying at 13,000ft and there was a layer of cloud at 12,000ft. We were

sitting ducks – black flecks against white clouds, vulnerable to high flying enemy aircraft. In those circumstances, Al would either have gone up or down, or back – he would not have taken us on. Al was always sympathetic to us, but he was always in the thick of it – there were very few shows from which he did not come back with a few bullet holes in his aircraft.

'We had advance warning that Paddy Finucane was to take over from Al Deere in January 1942. At the time it was rumoured that Paddy came back from operations making claims to have shot down German fighters which nobody else had witnessed. This sort of throwaway remark made us a little cautious of Paddy, but I had the opportunity myself to view at close quarters his skills as a combat fighter pilot. I was, by then, fairly experienced, and towards the end I flew as number two to Paddy on a number of occasions. He had a very different approach to AI, although I have to say that flying as number two to Paddy could become a little hairy. However, on these occasions when Paddy made a claim, I was able to verify it with absolute certainty. As far as I can tell from the operations I flew with Paddy, he was a most wonderful and natural shot.

Filing Claims – Initial Criteria

During the Battles for France and then Britain in 1940, the Air Ministry recognized that there were large discrepancies between those aircraft claimed destroyed, and those destroyed supported by irrefutable evidence. Up to midnight on 13 August 1940, the criteria upon which claims could be submitted were as follows:

For a confirmed loss
a) the enemy aircraft had to be seen on the ground or in the sea by a member of a crew or formation, or confirmed as destroyed from other sources – e.g. ships at sea, coastguards, the Observer Corps and police.
b) the enemy aircraft had to be seen to descend with flames issuing. It was not sufficient if only smoke was seen.
c) the enemy aircraft must be seen to break up in the air.

For an unconfirmed loss
The enemy aircraft had to be seen to break off the combat in circumstances which led our pilot, or crew, to believe that it would be a loss

Therefore the two main categories were 'Destroyed Confirmed' and 'Destroyed Unconfirmed', and the onus of deciding into which category a particular claim fell lay with Fighter Command Headquarters.

In July 1940, the existing categorization was found to be suspect – not the least because the volume of combats, and claims arising from them, required considerable intelligence work to be undertaken to provide evidence to support or dismiss the claim. At the time, it was believed that the squadron Intelligence Officer was already overworked. There were, however, mixed feelings in the Air Ministry. Opposed to the alteration of existing claim criteria was AVM

Keith Park at 11 Group, who was keen to ensure that the category of unconfirmed loss should continue to be applied. He was anxious to avoid the situation whereby RAF pilots would follow their opponents down so as to mark the precise point where their foe hit the ground, and so provide evidence to gain a confirmed kill yet, almost inevitably, expose themselves to attack from above in the process.

Even so, serious questions had been raised by the sheer scale of claims when compared to admitted German losses, and those which could be ascertained by intelligence operations. In the week commencing 8 August 1940, the RAF claimed 279 Luftwaffe aircraft destroyed, yet unequivocal evidence was provided to support the claims of only 91 confirmed losses – the Germans admitted 98.

Just a week later, ACM Dowding himself wrote to the Secretary of State for Air, Sir Archibald Sinclair, asking that such large claims, which were running into three figures, should be taken as only 'an approximation of the actual numbers'. Dowding explained that detailed enquiry into claims was not possible due to pressure of time, and that pilots themselves had only an approximate idea of what subsequently happened to the enemy aircraft they attacked. He went on to say that the best control over unsubstantiated claims being made lay in the way in which a pilot's unofficial score was kept by a squadron, and that 'line-shooting' would soon lead to exposure from his colleagues, who had flown on the same sortie.

Towards the end of the Battle of Britain, Dowding wrote to the Vice-Chief of the Air Staff, Sir Richard Pierce, conveying his personal opinion that RAF claims were probably 25 per cent higher than actual losses suffered by the Germans. But the reality was that the overclaiming was certainly not a characteristic solely specific to the RAF, for the same was true in every operational air arm of the Allied and Axis powers. The RAF, however, actively sought to do something about the perceived issue. So, from midnight on 13 August 1940, the following revised categories were introduced:

Category I – Destroyed: to cover all cases in which the enemy aircraft was positively reported to have seen to hit the ground or sea, to break up in the air, or to descend in flames, whether or not confirmation by a second source was available (this term also covered cases in which the enemy aircraft was forced to descend and was captured).

Category II – Probably destroyed: to be applied to those cases in which the enemy aircraft was seen to break off combat in circumstances which led to the conclusion that it must be a loss.

Category III – Damaged: to be applied to those cases in which the enemy aircraft was obviously considerably damaged when under attack, such as undercarriage dropped or aircraft parts shot away.

By the end of May 1941, the Air Ministry had obtained a copy of the official regulations governing the criteria by which fighter pilots of the Luftwaffe, and associated air arms in Germany, submitted, and were accredited with, claims. The detailed document, the Luftwaffen Verordnungsblatt of 28 April 1941, was 'acquired' by the US Military Attache in Berlin, and passed via intelligence sources to the Air Ministry. The thoroughness of the claim submission criteria, and of the process of claim evaluation – dependent upon the availability of evidence – was at the least, the first real indication to the RAF that Luftwaffe pilots engaged in a stringent process of claim evaluation. It appeared that the Luftwaffe, like the RAF, were keen to minimize the effects of overclaiming – a charge that was laid against the Luftwaffe in postwar years.

A significant difference though was that RAF fighter pilots, unlike their counterparts in the Luftwaffe (and to a lesser extent in the USAAF), did not receive decorations based solely upon the achievement of a set number of combat victories. Indeed, reward targets appear not to have been such a motivational factor for RAF fighter pilots. Confirmations were usually not actively sought by pilots, nor indeed received. Indeed, there was no formal mechanism established by the Air Ministry until late in the war (covering 2nd TAF's operations in north-western Europe) for the issuing of formal confirmation of claims.

Roland Beamont, who flew operationally during the 1939-44 period, made the following point on victory accreditation within the RAF: '"Confirmations" seldom reached the squadrons, and were not thought about. There was also the

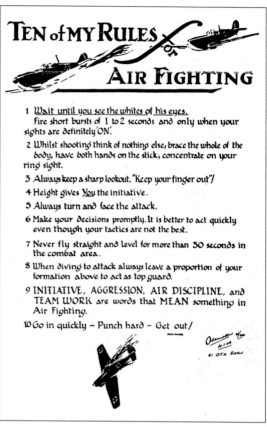

Displayed extensively throughout the squadrons of Fighter Command, 'Sailor' Malan's 'Ten of My Rules for Air Fighting' became the definitive aide-memoir for fighter pilots. This particular poster was signed by Malan when he was wing commander at Biggin Hill in January 1943, and was displayed at 61 OTU Heston.

element that it was improper and "not done" to appear to be trying to build up a "score".'

The Process

Fighter pilots would, with the aid of the squadron Intelligence Officer (IO), complete a combat report which would be passed for collation with other individual reports on Form 'F' – the Fighter Command Combat Report – by the group IO. Form 'F' was essentially a summary of the combat, and represented a collation of all RAF participants' reports, being a factual description of the action, not ascribing victories. Form 'F' would then be passed to group and then HQ Fighter Command, for judgement. Form 'F' would be also be used to record the combat report, together with any report of occurrences leading to personal injuries.

For example, Form 'F' was retrospectively completed for a combat action which took place over Dunkirk on 26 May 1940 by 605 Squadron pilot, P/O Ian J. Muirhead. Muirhead's typed account on Form 'F' gave striking evidence of this harrowing period in history. His Hurricane was hit possibly by Royal Navy guns and, having made his way north along the coast, Muirhead was forced to bale out of his stricken aircraft. Whilst hanging in his parachute he was by shot at by Belgian soldiers and civilians, and again after he had hit the ground. With two other aircrew, Muirhead made his way to the port at Ostend and boarded a small vessel, the *Aboukir*.

The ship had over 200 people on board – mostly refugees with many women and children, as well as several RAF and Army personnel. As the boat tried to make its way across the channel, it was strafed by the Luftwaffe, and Muirhead and his colleagues manned the *Aboukir*'s Lewis gun. An enemy motorboat then torpedoed it, and the passengers were forced into the water. The former then proceeded to cruise around at will shooting the swimming survivors, in particular those on the life raft. Only 32 of the 230 passengers and crew survived – Muirhead's

narrow escape from death was short lived and he was killed in action just four months later.

The squadron and group IOs clearly had a significant role to play in the process of claim submission. Involved in sweeps during 1941-42, Len Thorne describes the involvement of the IO directly on return from a sortie:

The normal procedure upon landing was to report to your ground crew at the side of the aircraft, then you would join the rest of the pilots who had landed in the dispersal hut where the IO was always waiting for us. He would go around the squadron and ask if anybody had got anything to claim. The IO would go to each of you, one by one, writing down the basic details of your claim. It would be difficult today to claim that this was a searching examination simply because the IO would not have had the time, nor the conditions, to be more thorough. Basic interrogation was always a bit light-hearted. You would find that half a dozen blokes would all be saying what had happened to them – whether they had been shot at, or had themselves shot at somebody. So the IO had a bit of a battle to get it right as you were in a high state of excitement and very relieved to be back at base.

The Hawker Hurricane was a mainstay of Fighter Command during the first three years of the war, being used in several differing roles as fighter, fighter-bomber, nightfighter, and as a ground attack aircraft. In the North African campaign the Hurricane was often employed in a ground attack role. This photograph, taken in colour, provides an excellent illustration of a Desert Air Force aircraft on a ground attack sortie. (via IWM TR 1012)

A 19 Squadron Spitfire I has its eight .303-in Colt Browning Mk II machine guns cleaned, rearmed with 300 rounds per weapons and its compressed air checked between sorties in September 1940. During the Battle of Britain many Spitfires were fitted with de Wilde tracer rounds, whilst a small number of late-production Mk Is were equipped with two 20-mm Hispano cannon that could fire 60 rounds per gun. (via IWM CH 1367)

Understandably perhaps, claims made during the early cross-channel sweeps significantly exceeded subsequent confirmation rates. Roland Beamont also recalled the role of the squadron IO:

Throughout the period 1939-44, *(in the autumn of 1944 W/C Beamont was shot down and taken prisoner)*, the procedure followed was for the fighter pilot to report the details of the action to the Station Intelligence Officer immediately after landing. He gave a verbal description and filed in a standard 'Combat Report' form. The pilot was discouraged from making extravagant claims, and the IO could, and often did, put his interpretation and emphasis into the final report to group HQ. The procedure involving the IO remained constant throughout the war.

Certainly the RAF IO's interpretation had a major effect on all our claims, but I can't emphasize too strongly that 'claims, victories and confirmations' were no big deal for us. You made your report and that was it. Feedback on 'confirmations' seldom reached the squadrons, but you knew if

1) Your e/a had crashed on land in the UK and could be found

2) If your No 2 saw it happen on land or sea

3) If HQ fed back evidence from your combat film.

After the early aerial combats of the Second World War had taken place, RAF IO's quickly became skilled in recognizing that whilst the immediate story of the combat was of course critical in determining what level of success, or failure, had been achieved, the fuller, and possibly more accurate, picture only came after the initial excitement had disappeared, to be replaced by more objectivity as the pilot's story slowly assumed greater validity.

But as Len Thorne retrospectively, and somewhat ruefully, observed:

I had a credited score of two destroyed, four probable and three damaged. If you had asked me at the time I would have said, 'Yes, I was absolutely sure that I shot them all down'. But today, I wonder if I really did. I was never in the position where you crept up quietly behind another aircraft and pressed the button and it blew up and disappeared in a flash of flame. It was usually a case of the aircraft going out of control, rolling over and going into a steep dive, streaming smoke – of course you could never be sure with the Bf 109s, as they would stream white vapour (due to the engine's water-injection system), which you always assumed was smoke. You didn't always see the result of a combat, as it was always so quick, but often one of the other chaps would see what happened to the aircraft.

Gun Camera

It is not precisely clear when the gun camera first came to be used by the RAF as a method of verifying the effectiveness of combat claims, although it had been used in a training capacity by the RFC back in 1917. At this time the gun

---

FIGURE 1 – Illustration of Report from February 1945

No 4 FILM PRODUCTION UNIT RAF

TYPHOON AUTOMATIC CINE CAMERA RECONNAISSANCE REPORT

THE FOLLOWING REPORT IS TO BE COMPLETED BY THE CAMERA OPERATOR FOR *EACH* CINE CAMERA CARRIED AND FORWARDED IN THE TIN WITH THE EXPOSED FILM

1	DATE	*20 JAN*
2	TIME	*1145*
3	TARGET	*RAILWAY TRAIN*
4	SQDN	*486*
5		*W/C BROOKER*
6	CAMERA OPERATOR	*DITTO*
7	WHETHER MEMBER OF THE CREW OR SUPERNUMERARY PILOT	
8	TYPE OF A/C	*TEMPEST*
9	A/C LETTER NUMBER	*B*

Type of film stock used	*SPECIAL NIGHT FILM*
Footage used over target	*90 FEET*
Aperture Set	*f 4.5*
Height of a/c during filming	*5,000 – 0 feet*
Light conditions	*GOOD*
Speed of A/C	*400*
No of frames per second	*56*
Type of attack	*GROUND ATTACK*

CAMERA LOADED BY
FITTED BY   *J. M. McCormack*
INSPECTED BY

Details of any failures

FURTHER POINTS OF INTEREST

1st SHOT	TEMPEST TURNING ABOVE CLOUD
2nd SHOT	ATTACK ON LOCOMOTIVE PULLING PASSENGER TRAIN
3rd SHOT	2nd ATTACK ON LOCOMOTIVE (FIRING)
4th SHOT	LONG SHOT OF 4 TEMPESTS ATTACKING TRAIN FROM ABOUT 2000ft

PHOTOGRAPHER:
When aircraft took off weather conditions were very bad indeed. Could you please rush this through as quickly as possible as the film was exposed by the Wing Commander i/c flying – the interest of whom I am anxious to cultivate as he can help our work no end.

J. M. McCormack,
Cpl

camera was more correctly referred to as a 'camera gun' – i.e. the photo lens of the camera replacing the machine gun. By contrast, the first film records of gun camera (i.e. photographs taken at the moment of a machine gun firing in order to capture the effect of ammunition expended) held today in the Imperial War Museum, London, indicate that some aircraft were equipped with G.22 (and later the G.42B)

camera supplied with 16-mm film as early as February 1940.

Gun cameras were fitted into the starboard wing root of the Spitfire IA, and on 22 February 1940, 602 Squadron pilots P/O Proudman and S/L A.D. Farquhar each claimed a share in the destruction of a Heinkel He 111P over St Abb's Head, which was captured by gun camera film. Fortunately for S/L Farquhar, his abortive

---

FIGURE 2 – Example of Claim Submission and Verification: 134 Squadron in Russia September/October 1941

Author's Notes:

The procedure followed after landing from a sortie:

1. interview by Squadron IO
2. completion of written Combat Report by pilot. No gun-camera used by 151 Wing in Russia
3. composite Combat Report produced by IO, consisting of a précis of all pilot's submitted Combat Report
4. Submission of all reports to 151 Wing IO for verification of claim. Instruction issued to squadron, determining acceptance or decline of claim

For example:
Action of 6 October 1941

14 Ju 88A-5s of 1./KG 30 attacked the Russian/RAF aerodrome at Vayenga in late afternoon. The Ju 88s, which were black with yellow-bordered black crosses, were due to be escorted by 6 Bf 109s of 1./JG77, which were late and missed connecting with the bombers by the time that they had reached the target. On arrival, the Ju 88s bombed the airfield, but found that most of the Hurricanes were already in the air on patrol. The Hurricanes got in amongst the Ju 88s and three of the bombers were claimed as destroyed, three as probable, and five as damaged. Duplicate claims were made on all Ju 88s which were hit, as there were so many combats in a period of 15 minutes' continuous fighting that a single Ju 88 could have been hit by any number of RAF pilots, and claimed as damaged, probable or destroyed dependent upon the point of time that the attack was made during the period of combat.

Combat Report submitted by F/O A. J. McGregor,

who was leading Yellow Section, A Flight of 81 Squadron claimed a probable.

The composite Combat Report (Form 'F') submitted by the IO said:

"Yellow Leader, F/O McGregor, opened fire at about 400 yards and saw hits register on a Ju 88 and smoke pour from its port engine. The E.A. opened up return fire, and our pilot broke away and repeated attacks with 3 more bursts of about 1 second each. Hits were seen to register on both engines, E.A. rapidly lost height and when last seen port engine was on fire. This is claimed as probably destroyed . . . Sight setting in all our aircraft were 60/250 yards. Return fire from E.A. was inaccurate and only 1 M.G. bullet in our aircraft is reported."

Slight modifications appeared to the RAF claims over the next few days. For example, on 9 October 151's IO wrote an addendum to the composite Combat Report, which was sent to Maj Gen A. A. Kuznetsov, the Commander of the Northern Fleet Air Force saying, 'Sgt/Pilot Kirvan's claim (Kirvan was another pilot with 134 Squadron) of one Ju 88 Probably/Destroyed has been disallowed, as further information received later does not give sufficient grounds for this claim'.

Available Luftwaffe loss records for the same action tell a rather different story of the total action, with two Ju 88s (Wk-Nrs 626 and 4155), piloted by Lt Hermann Serves and Uffz Robert Habermann respectively, failing to return to base and being reported as missing. The damaged Wk-Nr 292 managed to return to base at Petsamo where it made a belly landing – one of crewman, Uffz Walter Sellege, was injured.

attempt to land beside the downed Heinkel to arrest the crew before they could torch the aircraft was not captured on film, as his aircraft turned over upon landing on boggy ground and he had to be rescued by his German 'prisoners'!

Supermarine had also looked into the possibility of a wing-mounted gun camera which would also be synchronized with the Spitfire's eight .303-in Colt Browning machine guns. Eventually, the G.45 gun camera evolved for fitment to the Spitfire, and such was the quality of the footage shot by the equipment that it remained in regular use until the mid-1950s.

Standard commercially-produced 16-mm film was used by the RAF in gun cameras until it was replaced by 35-mm stock, which equipped gun cameras installed in Hawker's Typhoon and Tempest following the Normandy invasion. The use of 35-mm film gave a far superior definition to the quality of photographs, replacing the somewhat 'grainy' stills that can today be observed from gun camera footage.

Although the introduction of the gun camera improved the pilot's 'fall of shot', it never became the definitive answer to the verification of combat claims. For example, it could not cope with several pilots firing at the same target at the same time, as the camera was unable to differentiate between the shots fired from the various attacking aircraft. Len Thorne continues with his description of the process of claim submission by considering the impact of the gun camera:

The debriefing from the IO was only your preliminary report because the next thing to turn up

Undoubtedly staged for the camera, RAF Desert Air Force pilots are shown enjoying a beer on the makeshift bar, which is clearly the bullet-riddled tail section of a Bf 110. Although the primary task of the fighter squadrons throughout the campaign in North Africa was to act in support of ground forces, units also effectively blunted attacks from Axis bombers, and their escorts. (via IWM CM 2868)

was the ground crew member who had taken the camera out of the wing of your aircraft if you had made a claim. They knew whether you had fired of course, depending on whether the patches over the guns remained intact or not. Your cine film would go to the photographic section to be developed. The serious debriefing took place in the Intelligence section, where the cine film was shown to the CO, to you, and to any other pilots who had claimed to had been involved in the combat. Part of the evaluation was to work out exactly what your cone of fire was. If you got an enemy aircraft in the field of vision of the camera, the photographic section could say fairly definitely how many hits you had scored. They produced quite reasonable pictures. You did get cases when a pilot had claimed to have made a kill, but when the film was shown there was no enemy aircraft in sight. There were other occasions when the view was very fleeting, yet the pilot had still claimed to have hit the enemy aircraft. You wanted to have shot down an enemy aircraft, but there must have been many cases when the claims were greatly exaggerated.

Roland Beamont made the following point on gun cameras:

Gun camera was not reliable for many reasons – bad light, sun glare and camera failure. Right up to 1944, we had trouble with camera reliability, and even with the new Tempests the gun camera would bring back clear film of 1G ground attacks, but nothing in air to air combat when pulling more G. This was most frustrating, as I found with a Bf 109G-6 over Rouen on D-Day +2, and again with a Fw 190 over the Reichwald forest in October that year.

Measuring Stress within Fighter Pilots

It was recognized during the years following the First World War that many fighter pilots within the RFC/RAF suffered from the residual effects of combat stress which affected them long after the conflict had ended. Capt Roy Brown achieved lasting fame as the pilot who shot down Count Manfred von Richtofen on 21 April 1918. The Canadian-born Brown of 209 Squadron (RAF), was retrospectively interviewed in the late 1920s about his destruction of von Richtofen as part of the Air Historical Branch's effort to help clarify the circumstances surrounding the 'Red Baron's' death.

Brown co-operated fully, giving support to the operational combat reports from 1918 that stated that he had been the pilot that shot down von Richtofen. However, during the interview with the Canadian pilot, it was also discovered that he had suffered severely with 'bad nerves' – an indication of the psychological stress that fighter pilots operated under during that conflict. Some ten years after the end of the war, Brown, who had obviously been a fine combat pilot, was unable even to drive a car due to his nervous condition.

During the Second World War, the RAF paid greater attention to the condition of psychological stress amongst combat crew. Nevertheless, it was a gradual, and somewhat slow, process of increasing awareness and recognition. Indeed, until early 1942 the psychological impact of stress amongst flying personnel failed to be explored in any depth. The main function of research into psychological disorder that was then developed by the RAF Medical Branch was to introduce psychometric testing at an early stage in the aircrew selection process. Their aim was to 'weed out' those who were believed to be pre-disposed to psychiatric disturbance which might manifest under highly stressful circumstances. The Medical Branch coined the term 'temperamental unsuitability' to such applicants.

However, during the early postwar years, the validity of these tests as predictors of future psychiatric disturbance was called into question. The focus, therefore, was not so much upon the treatment of those who had developed symptoms of combat stress as a result of operational flying, but rather pre-empting a situation occurring through the removal of psychologically-vulnerable people from flying early in the aircrew selection process.

Nevertheless, the stresses and strains of combat flying amongst the operational fighter pilots of RAF Fighter Command did receive some limited acknowledgement, even if sufferers were not especially targeted for observation and treatment – after all, these were young men facing great, almost overwhelming, responsibility for not only their own lives, but for the lives and freedom of others.

During the early part of the war, it appears that individual RAF fighter pilots were largely left to

Although the censor deleted the unit number in this photograph, taken on 9 June 1941 in the Western Desert, it is highly likely that the outfit is 1 Squadron, South African Air Force. Its pilots and ground crew are seen celebrating reaching a 'ton' of enemy aircraft destroyed. Their 'scoreboard' is an Italian CR.42 biplane. (via IWM E.3414)

develop their own strategies for coping with the stress of continual combat flying. The individual awareness of the squadron commanding officer, and of the station Medical Officer (MO), to the effects of combat stress appears also to have been significant. J. H. 'Ginger' Lacey is quoted as saying:

Towards the end of the Battle (of Britain) I had taken just about as much as I could bear. My nerves were in ribbons and I was scared stiff that one day I would pull out and avoid combat. That frightened me more than the Germans, and I pleaded with my CO for a rest. He was sympathetic, but quite adamant that until he got replacements I would have to carry on. I am glad now that he was unable to let me go. If I had been allowed to leave the squadron feeling as I did, I am sure that I would never have flown again.

Some 20 months after Lacey's experience, Len Thorne was referred for medical treatment by his CO:

Most of us were stressed. I suffered a facial pain, something like sinusitis, which was enough to be worrying and was sent to the Royal West Sussex hospital at Chichester for X-rays and other types of examination. At the end of these tests, the doctor told me 'there really isn't anything there. I don't want you to take this the wrong way, but you are a fighter pilot and it is almost certainly that what you are experiencing is a form of nerves. I'm not saying that you are a nervy type, but its practically certain that your combat flying is the cause of the pain that you are feeling in your face'.

By 1942, in the drive to get increased knowledge of combat stress amongst fighter pilots, MOs were prepared to place themselves at risk – a few also held pilots' licences and, at times, sought to experience the same combat conditions as their subjects as a basis for measuring the effect of combat upon the psychological state of RAF fighter pilots. This attempt to empathize with the operational fighter pilot may, however, have also reflected a MO's desire to grasp the opportunity to take the fight to the enemy themselves. Inevitably, this could have tragic results, as Len Thorne recalls:

In the spring of 1942, 43-year-old G/C Hugh Corner AFC, a doctor at RAE Farnborough, was undertaking research into stress among operational fighter pilots. I suppose it would now be called battle fatigue, or something similar. He was also a qualified pilot, and in order to get first-hand experience of the sort of stresses the fighter pilots were suffering, he visited various squadrons and flew with them. On this particular day – 25 April 1942 – he appeared at Kenley fairly early in the morning and asked if he could join us in a show. It so happened that we were doing an air-sea rescue cover in which it was hoped to pick up some people who had been shot down near the French coast. This was a flight which lasted only three-quarters of an hour. There was no activity at all, we did not see any Germans, nor did we expect to. When we landed back at base, G/Capt Corner complained bitterly that we had taken him on a long show that did not prove anything and failed to help in his research. He asked to stay with the squadron for the

rest of the day, and to be included to fly on anything more interesting that might come up. He, of course, addressed his remarks to the squadron commander, Paddy Finucane. Paddy agreed 'if anything comes up sir, you can come along and I'll put you to fly as No 2 to Len Thorne, who is very experienced – you will be all right with him.'

At briefing we were told that the show would be a bomber escort to Lille – a deep penetration, and one that we were always a bit scared about. We went on the show and G/C Corner flew as my No 2. In my log book I made the following entry:

'I was Red three behind Paddy, with G/C Corner as my No 2. The section carried out attacks on a pair of enemy aircraft, then on four, and lastly on a single aircraft, at which I got a long burst. I ran almost out of ammunition and, as we approached the French coast, the G/C and myself were attacked by two 190s. Despite repeated calls to break, the G/C failed to turn with me and was badly hit, going down with smoke coming from the Spitfire. He pulled out and headed for home. The smoke stopped in mid-Channel, but at that point the 190s attacked again and I saw tracer going over and under both my wings. I pulled round and discovered two 190s shooting at him. I gave them

The Curtiss P-40B Tomahawk IIA and B was used extensively by the RAF, being used in the North African campaign at various stages by 113, 206, 250 and 260 Squadrons. It was replaced by the P-40E/F Kittyhawk I/II/III, which had a larger chin radiator and was equipped with six .50-cal machine guns (three in each wing), unlike the Tomahawk which had just four such weapons. Kittyhawks were used extensively in the Western Desert by 260 Squadron, which became the only RAF squadron to fly all first three marks of Kittyhawk in North Africa. (via IWM CM 2730)

the slip and went after Red 4 (G/C Corner), in time to see him go into the sea. His parachute did not properly open and he appeared to be dead. I returned to Lympne. Sgt Paul Green also missing.'

Today, my recollection of the event is that at the point when G/C Corner was hit the first time, Paddy who was flying as Red 1, saw it happen. Paddy called out 'Come on chaps, gather round, we can get this Spitfire home'. So in fact three of us were flying close when the 190s dived through us and hit him for the second time. G/C Corner was seen to be in the sea, floating in his Mae West, but his dinghy didn't open, and it was fairly obvious, indeed almost certain, that he was dead. I don't think he was ever picked up, having sank before the air sea rescue people could get to him. He was obviously an extremely good doctor, being very

dedicated to his task, but he should never have gone on that dangerous show. As a result there was a Court of Enquiry at which I, amongst others, was interviewed. Although no blame was attached to us over the loss of G/C Corner, I believed that he should never have been there in the first place. The result of the Court of Enquiry was that in future, senior officers, from group or Fighter Command, were banned from taking part as supernumeraries on squadron operations unless they were experienced on fighter operations.

Public Relations and Fighter Command – Getting Accounts of Action to the Public

During the First World War, the propaganda value attached to the raising of public morale through the combat exploits of air aces was a

28 January 1942 – W/C Bob Stanford-Tuck, DSO, DFC and Bar, was forced to crash-land his Spitfire VB in France after being hit by ground fire during a low-level sortie. A German photographer captured Tuck's aircraft on camera, and this is one of several photographs to survive. Twenty-nine aerial victories are recorded forward of the cockpit. (via BAK 598)

potent political tool, and one which served to unite the public behind the war effort. The successes of the air aces were easy for the public to identify with, for success could be measured in simple terms – i.e. by the number of enemy aircraft destroyed in a combat or by one pilot. Those pilots who were successful in this process – even though they were in the minority of the total number of pilots flying – were seen not only as individuals to be revered, but also representative of the efforts of the air operations as a whole from the political perspective. Their exploits helped galvanize public opinion behind the air arm.

During the first war, it was not until 1916 that the Germans, French and British began to recognize the political value of the publicizing of air aces. In Britain, Albert Ball received a high public profile and much adulation from an adoring public, whilst in France his contemporary was Georges Guynemer. On the German side, Count Manfred von Richtofen, Oswald Boelke and a handful of other pilots were portrayed to the public as national heroes whose personalities were far less important than their success in shooting down vast quantities of enemy aircraft.

It has been generally accepted that for Britain, the exploits of the 'aces' was a post-1945 phenomena, a concept that did not become an issue until historians began to seek evidence for the combat claims that were made, and to determine veracity of individual scores. Yet, casual browsing of contemporary national and local newspapers during the years of the Second World War will produce many examples of

cont. p.38

FIGURE 3 – Example of Combat Form and Pilot's Logbook Tally of Squadron Scores – 81 Squadron In Russia September/October 1941

On 24 October 1941, Chief of the Air Staff Charles Portal wrote to Prime Minister Winston Churchill. He was responding to Churchill's criticism that he had not been kept up to date with the developments of the small force of two RAF Hurricane squadrons that comprised 151 Wing in Russia. Portal reminded Churchill that 81 and 134 squadrons had been sent to protect the Russian port of Murmansk so that British light naval forces could use the port, despite German attempts to capture it.

By the time of Portal's reply to Churchill, it had become apparent that the aim of securing the 'Gateway to Russia' had not been successful in allowing British forces to use the port, and suggestions were made to transfer 151 Wing from Murmansk to the Russian left flank. However, it was found to be politically inexpedient to honour an earlier promise made by the RAF to leave the Hurricanes of 151 Wing to the Soviet Air Force, despite Stalin's refusal to permit any publicity to the gesture. The fighters therefore remained in Russia, and were the first of 2,952 examples of the Hawker fighter to be flown by the Soviet Air Force.

During the short period that 151 Wing was in the USSR it achieved notable success, for not only did it train Soviet pilots (including leading fighter pilot and Hero of the Soviet Union Boris Safonov) to fly the Hurricane, but it also escorted Russian bombers on operations over the Finnish border. The wing had 16 enemy aircraft confirmed as destroyed for the loss of only one RAF pilot. 134 Squadron's primary role was to train Soviet pilots, but they did achieve some success in combat, whilst 81 Squadron's main task was to escort Russian bombers, and therefore its pilots had more opportunities for tangling with the enemy.

Original material from two of 81 Squadron's stalwart pilots is reproduced here:

i) Scorecard Table from F/O Ray Holmes' Logbook
Ray Holmes' table lists the successes achieved by 151 Wing during the month of October 1941, shortly before they were posted home to the UK. Notable names on this list include P/O Walker, S/L Rook and F/Sgt Haw, all of whom gained 'ace' status. James Walker subsequently became a wing commander with at least nine personal and one shared destroyed before his death in April 1944. 'Wag' Haw was to become a squadron leader and 'Mickey' Rook a wing commander. The compiler of the logbook scorecard, Ray Holmes, had earlier found his place in history by shooting down the first enemy aircraft to be destroyed on a bombing raid over London during the Battle of Britain.

ii) Combat Report
Charlton 'Wag' Haw submitted this report claiming

the destruction of a Bf 109E on the afternoon of 12 September 1941. Haw was one of four 151 Wing pilots to be awarded the Order of Lenin, the others being W/C Ramsbottom-Isherwood, S/L Rook, and S/L Miller. An interesting feature of the RAF successes in Russia was that each combat kill was rewarded by the Russians with a bounty. W/C Ramsbottom-Isherwood refrained from sharing this bounty amongst his pilots, and felt that the safest option was to donate it to the RAF Benevolent Fund. It is believed that this financial reward is the only example of RAF pilots being paid a bounty for their combat success in the Second World War. Other examples of bounties being paid to fighter pilots were to be found in the Italian Regia Aeronautica and Aeronautica Nazionale Repubblicana and, of course, the Soviet Air Forces itself. (via Mark Sheppard)

YEAR 1941 MONTH / DATE		AIRCRAFT Type	No.	PILOT, OR 1ST PILOT	2ND PILOT, PUPIL OR PASSENGER	DUTY (INCLUDING RESULTS AND REMARKS)
—	—	—	—	—	—	TOTALS BROUGHT FORWARD
		SCORE BOARD FOR WING. (One Month's Flying Only).				
SQDN.	RK.	NAME.	✠	PROBABLE.	DAMAGED.	
81.	P/O	BUSH.	1.		1.	He.109. "110.
	F/Sgt	HAW.	3.			He.109. (Order of Red Banner)
	P/O	WALKER.	1.		1.	Me.109. Ju.88.
	Sgt	WAUD.	2.			He.109. He.126.
	S/L	ROOK.				
	Sgt	ANSON	1.			He.109 (81 Sq. also given
	Sgt	SIMS.				Me.110. which
	S/L	ROOK.	1.			no one claimed
134.	P/O	FURNEAUX				Ju.88.
81.	P/O	EDMISTON	1.	1.		Me.109.
	Sgt	REED	1.			Me.109.
	P/O	HOLMES	1.			Me.109.
	F/L	ROOK	1.			Me.109.
	F/O	McGREGOR		1.		Ju.88.
	P/O	RAMSAY		1.		Ju.88.
	Sgt	BISHOP			1.	Ju.88.
134.	P/O	CAMERON		1.	1.	Ju.88's.
	Sgt	GOULD			1.	Ju.88.
	F/O	ELKINGTON				Ju.88.
	F/Sgt	BARNES.	1.			Our Casualties.
		TOTAL.	15.	4.	5.	Sgt. Smith killed. F/Lt. Berg injured. TOTALS CARRIED FORWARD

GRAND TOTAL [Cols (1) to (10)]

Contains: { 11. Me.109's. 2. Ju.88's. 1. He.126. }

SECRET. FORM "F."

PERSONAL **COMBAT REPORT.**

Sector Serial No. _____ (A) Not given

Serial No. of Order detailing Flight or Squadron to Patrol _____ (B)

Date _____ (C) 12.9.41

Flight, Squadron _____ (D) Flight: A Sqdn.: 81

Number of Enemy Aircraft _____ (E) ONE

Type of Enemy Aircraft _____ (F) Me 109 E

Time Attack was delivered _____ (G) 1526 hrs

Place Attack was delivered _____ (H) Over enemy lines W. of MURMANSK

Height of Enemy _____ (J) 4,000 ft.

Enemy Casualties _____ (K) ONE Me 109 E.

Our Casualties _____ Aircraft _____ (L)

_____ Personnel _____ (M)

GENERAL REPORT _____ (R)

At 15.25 hrs on 12.9.41 whilst leading a patrol of five Hurricanes over the enemy lines I intercepted five Me 109 Es orbiting at 4000. My range was 3.500 ft. The E/A were approaching from ahead and slightly to the left, and as I turned towards them, they turned slowly to their right. I attacked the leader as he turned and gave him a 15 secs. burst from the full beam position. The E/A rolled onto its back, and as I was diving burst into their right, a similar one them, they turned into evasive action, but Red 2 confirms that it passed him in a 40° dive at 500 ft, smoke and flame still pouring from it.

Signature C Haw F/Sgt.

O.C. Section RED
Flight A Flight.
Squadron   Squadron No. 81

references – particularly of photographs – to 'ace' pilots of the period being awarded decorations (occasionally these individuals were named). National and local newspapers were desperately keen to receive newsworthy accounts of the exploits of their 'boys' of Fighter Command, as indeed were press from Allies overseas whose nationals were flying with the RAF.

So how was this achieved ? There was a close, if not always comfortable, relationship between the media and each group within Fighter Command, plus the Air Ministry. From the commencement of the war, a Public Relations Officer (PRO) was attached to each group. The function of the PRO was to gather news by working as closely as possible with Intelligence. PROs would however, seek to bypass Intelligence by interviewing fighter pilots directly, and then reporting back in the often colourful language used by the pilots themselves.

The PRO's aim was to obtain maximum publicity value from the exploits of the RAF fighter pilots, and they would often escort accredited pressmen – war correspondents, artists, photographers, newsreel and radio personnel of the British and Allied media – around operational airfields. The publicity value to be gained was reflected in recruiting figures, and in the status afforded the RAF fighter pilot by the nation as a whole.

The process of official approval of news items entailed the individual report being telephoned to the PR office at Command HQ, which was the 'newsroom' for the whole of Fighter Command's activities. Accounts from each group were collated, sub-edited, and a composite account produced reflecting the wider perspective of Fighter Command operations. The composite report was then telephoned to the Air Ministry for evaluation and approval, before being passed to the Ministry of Information for dissemination to the newspapers and BBC radio.

So, the Air Ministry was ultimately responsible for passing information about claims made by RAF pilots and anti-aircraft guncrews onto the press, and thus to the general public. Following initial verification of combat claims, involving only limited checking by Fighter Command's intelligence section due to the pressure they were under, the Air Ministry News Service figure was then passed to the BBC and the press, who often published it just hours after the relevant combat had finished. Understandably, more accurate figures pertaining to the RAF's own casualties were simultaneously released. It is not surprising, therefore, that the public accepted the German loss figures as categorical evidence of the success of RAF fighter pilots in action.

Whilst the official line of the Air Ministry was not to formally publish confirmation of claims to the public, it is clear that at the very least (principally through the efforts of Fighter Command PROs) the British public knew who their 'aces' were, and their impact upon the morale of the nation was not far removed from the public consciousness of the government. For example, by the end of March 1940, F/O Edgar 'Cobber' Kain, a Hurricane pilot of New Zealand extraction fighting with 73 Squadron in France, had became the first RAF 'ace' of the war. Despite official policy that the names of successful pilots should only be published if they were being awarded with a decoration, Cain's status afforded him high public profile.

After the first 18 months of war, PROs were permitted to mention by name the leader of 'notable' operational sorties made by Fighter Command pilots. As the conflict developed from the defence of France and the low countries to the RAF moving onto the offensive over the continent and in other theatres throughout the world, so more PROs were recruited.

This change in policy was first shown during the early fighter sweeps over the Channel in 1941, when the PRO at Fighter Command HQ would be given warning when a fighter sweep was to occur. Another PRO at group would be permitted to be present in the Operations Room to firstly observe the sweep being plotted on the ops table, and then monitor the combat reports from all squadrons engaging the enemy as they would be called in.

Right *The basic flying training of RAF pilots during the Second World War took place on several continents. In the USA alone, around 14,000 RAF pilots graduated with their wings to return home to the UK, and then on to operational training units. This unique, original, hand-written summary made by the RAF Delegation in Washington D.C., summarizes the statistics arising from the Arnold Scheme, in which young RAF cadet pilots were trained at US Army Air Force flying training schools.* (via PRO Air 45/11 196663)

Training Statistics "Arnold" Schools - U.S.A.

A. Effective Throughput.

Course.	Finally Graduated	Eliminated	Killed	Original ⊗ Effective Intake.	Remarks
42/A	240	254	9	533	⊗ Including
„ B	300	236	7	543	Transfers IN
„ C	356	248	5	609	but ignoring
„ D	342	296	6	644	Holdovers
„ E	344	354	3	734	except on dual
„ F	364	369	12	745	Course.
„ G	346	335	18	729	
„ H	415	338	5	758	
„ I	294	220	4	518	
„ J	281	209	3	493	
„ K	308	184	4	499	
43/A	338	185	2	525	46 Holdovers
43/B	342	158 38ˣ	3	541	8.6%
43/c	10	4ˣ		14	14 to 43/c
Total	4370	3392 42	81	7885	

Further Analyses - % at B   By Stages at C1   By Stages at D
Commissions at E   „ % at C2
Instructors at F

ˣ To Canada to finish training - after hospital

B. Graduations.

Course.	Percentage of Original Effective Intake.	Number.
42/A.	49.1 %	240
„ B.	55 (54)	300
„ C.	56.3	356
„ D.	52.5 (52.5)	342
„ E.	49.5	344
„ F.	47.9	364
„ G.	50.1	346
„ H.	52.8	415
„ I.	55.8	294
„ J.	55.1	281
„ K.	58.4	308
43/A	63.8	338
43/B	63.2	342
43/c		10
		4370

Summary

		%
Graduated	4370	55.4
Eliminated	3392	43.
Killed	8 × 2	1.
To Canada after hospital to complete Training	42	0.6
	7885	100.00 %

It was accepted practice for highly-successful RAF fighter pilots to be posted on a liaison trip overseas between operational tours. The opportunity was taken to 'spread the word' to the USAAF by the RAF during the months following Pearl Harbor. 'Sailor' Malan, Johnny Kent, Harry Broadhurst, Al Deere, R. Stanford-Tuck and the Texan-born Lance Wade were amongst those who made the trip to the 'States. Another top-scoring pilot from 1940 was H. A. V. 'Harry' Hogan (CO of 501 Squadron during the Battle of Britain), who was posted to the USA in June 1941, and later became Director of Flying (RAF) in America. Hogan was the lead RAF officer responsible for the establishment of the USAAC/F operated Arnold Scheme, the civilian British Flying Training School Programme, the

US Navy-based Towers scheme, and the Pan American Airways programme for observers. Hogan was keen that RAF fighter pilots on liaison and lecture duties in the USA should, wherever possible, visit the stations at which his RAF cadet pilots were training. This sequence of photographs, taken by RAF cadet pilot Alexander at No 4 BFTS in early 1942, captures the low flying demonstration in an AT-6A given by W/C Teddy Donaldson, a successful fighter pilot who was himself later to be decorated with the AFC for his instructional duties in addition to the earlier award of the DSO. The photographer successfully graduated as a pilot, but was killed in action later in the war. (via Mike Alexander)

On busy squadrons, a PRO would be allowed to be present during the pre-sortie briefing and at the de-briefing following the mission. He would then telephone his 'story' to his colleague at group HQ, who would, in turn, collate this information with the overall 'picture' gleaned from the Operations room, prior to passing the report onto Fighter Command HQ, from where the composite picture was developed. When the 'story' was not felt important enough to warrant national media coverage, the PRO would prepare the article for circulation and publication in the local press in the pilot's home area – this also applied to overseas nationals flying for RAF Fighter Command.

From the fighter pilot's standpoint, interesting interpretations of their actions during the Battle of Britain often appeared in the press, as Roland Beamont recalled:

'Vastly exaggerated claims reached the eager media in 1940. The pilot said what he thought he had done. The IO said in his report that the pilot had done it – and the Press said "50 more victories today!"'

Decorations and Awards

The Victoria Cross (VC) is the premier recognition of military valour for a member of the British Armed Forces, and it was awarded to 32 RAF airmen during the Second World War. Of this figure, just one was a fighter pilot – James Brindley 'Nick' Nicolson. Interestingly, the VC was awarded to Nicolson not for achieving a high number of aerial victories, but for a single act of outstanding bravery during the Battle of Britain – in only his first combat sortie. Nicolson survived this action to fight again, only to lose his life just a few days before the end of the war in Europe.

The VC was awarded very rarely, with the most commonly recognized decorations granted to RAF flying personnel during the Second World War being the Distinguished Service Order (DSO), the Distinguished Flying Cross (DFC), the Distinguished Flying Medal (DFM), the Air Force Cross (AFC), and the Air Force Medal (AFM). The latter four medals were all instituted on the occasion of the King's Birthday during the final year of the First World War, and were first notified for awarding to individual flying personnel in *The London Gazette* of 3 June 1918.

DSO

The DSO was the oldest of the decorations awarded to RAF pilots, having been instituted in 1886. Its aim was to provide a merit award for 'junior officers'. The criteria applied during the Second World War meant that the DSO could be granted for '. . . distinguished service under fire or under conditions equivalent to service in actual combat with the enemy'.

During the Second World War the DSO was awarded to 870 RAF officers, with 62 going on to receive a first bar, 8 a second bar, and 2 a third bar – bomber pilots/leaders are also included in this figure.

DFC

The DFC was established as a specific decoration for officers and warrant officers, and the criteria governing the award during the Second World War followed the instruction of 23 March 1932, which stated that the DFC was to be granted '. . . only for exceptional valour, courage or devotion to duty whilst flying on active operations against the enemy'.

Therefore, during the war the DFC was awarded not only for exceptional individual acts of bravery and flying skill, but also for the satisfactory completion of a tour of operations. On 11 March 1941, the DFC was extended to include the aircrew of the Fleet Air Arm. Inevitably perhaps, the DFC was granted with a far greater degree of frequency than the DSO, DFM, AFC and AFM.

In total, the DFC was awarded on 20,354 occasions to RAF aircrew, with a first bar to the medal being received by 1,550 pilots and 42 aircrew – it is not known how many of these awards were made to members of Fighter Command. Honorary awards of the DFC were also made on 964 occasion (including first and second bars) to aircrew from other countries, including King Albert of Belgium, who was flown on many occasions over enemy lines on reconnaissance missions in RAF aircraft.

DFM

The DFM was a decoration specifically designed to be awarded to non-commissioned officers

(NCOs), and during the Second World War some 6,637 RAF aircrew received the award (including a small number retrospectively in 1946-47 for actions during the recent conflict). Some 165 aircrew from countries other than Commonwealth also received the award. On 60 occasions the DFM was awarded as a first bar, but just one individual was awarded a second bar – Spitfire pilot Donald Kingaby of 92 Squadron. His citation read:

KINGABY, DONALD ERNEST, DFM and Bar.
745707.
Flight Sergeant. R.A.F.V.R. No 92 Sqn. L.G.
11th November, 1941.

This airman leads his section, and occasionally his flight, with great skill and courage. He has participated in 36 operational sorties during which he has destroyed 17, probably destroyed 6, and damaged a further 7 enemy aircraft. Flight Sergeant Kingaby has at all times displayed the greatest determination and sound judgement, combined with a high standard of operational efficiency.

AFM and AFC

Both the AFM and AFC were awarded for '. . . acts of valour, courage or devotion to duty performed whilst flying, though not in active operations, against the enemy'. The AFM was a decoration granted to NCOs and 'men', and the AFC its equivalent for officers and warrant officers.

The latter was awarded to 2,001 RAF aircrew, with a further 58 honorary awards being made to aircrew of other air forces. Some 26 bars to the AFM were also presented and, on one occasion, a second bar – to W/C H. J. Wilson on 8/6/44. By contrast, the AFM was awarded just 259 times during the Second World War, including on two occasions to Army Air Corps personnel.

Pilot Profiles

Gladiator Pilot – 'Pat' Pattle

Born in South Africa in 1914, Marmaduke T. St J. Pattle was almost certainly the highest-scoring RAF pilot of the Second World War. The fact that some doubt exists is simply because accurate, official, records are not held for the period in which many of his aerial victories were made – during the traumatic days leading up to the

evacuation of Greece in the spring of 1941.

Pattle originally joined the SAAF as a cadet, but transferred to the RAF before obtaining his pilots' wings in 1937. Posted to 80 Squadron, which was equipped with Gladiators, Pattle became a flight commander in 1939, by which time the unit had been posted to Egypt. He was to remain with 80 Squadron through to March 1941, achieving remarkable success against the Italian Air Force with the Gladiator I/II over Libya and Greece. Pattle scored 14 confirmed victories with the Gladiator, was forced to bale out of a stricken Gloster fighter aircraft on one occasion and awarded the DFC in February 1941 for his exploits.

The unit re-equipped with Hurricane Is during early March 1941, and Pattle continued to score freely as well as being promoted to the position of OC of 33 Squadron. By 20 April his score had unofficially reached 50, which can never be confirmed simply because no official verification of aerial victories was given by the RAF during this fraught period in Greece following the German invasion. It was on his third operation of the day on this date that S/L 'Pat' Pattle lost his life when he was shot down by two Bf 110s of II./ZG 26 over Piraeus Harbour.

Spitfire Pilot – Paddy Finucane

The enigma that was Brendan E. F. (Paddy) Finucane began his working life as a trainee accountant firstly in Dublin and then London. He had earlier been a successful rugby player at school, and he moved with his family from Dublin to Richmond in 1936. Interestingly, although Finucane's father was a Republican, and had earlier been actively involved in the conflict with Britain, Paddy Finucane and his two brothers all came to join the British Armed services – his younger brother Raymond also flew Spitfires for Fighter Command during the Second World War.

Paddy Finucane joined the RAF In August 1938, undertaking Elementary Flying Training at No 6 EFTS at Sywell, followed by Service Flying Training on Hawker Harts at Montrose. It was whilst at No 8 SFTS that he was graded 'below average' by the CFI and nearly dropped from the course. Almost as a last-ditch effort, the RAF transferred Finucane to continue his training with another flight, this time flying the

MEMORABILIA OF A 602 SQUADRON FIGHTER PILOT, IN 1942. All Credit: H. L. Thorne.

Left *A youthful Len Thorne is seen in the cockpit of his Spitfire in late 1941, 602 Squadron then still under the command of S/L Al Deere, who was replaced by Paddy Finucane in January 1942.*

Below *A cursory note, scribbled on a scrap of paper and pushed under a billet door late at night, may have been the first indication to an RAF fighter pilot that he was to be on Dawn Readiness for an operational sortie. This note shows that F/Sgt Len Thorne was to be on Dawn Readiness, transport to collect them from Sergeants' Mess arriving at 05.10. Interestingly, in the group of Sgt pilots who were to fly with F/Sgt Thorne were Bill Loud and 'Jock' Sanderson, who were both to subsequently achieve significant scores.*

Bottom *A page from Len Thorne's logbook covering the period 13 to 30 April 1942. The frequency, and intensity, of missions for a Spitfire pilot at this stage in the war is graphically illustrated.*

REMARKS

Dawn Readiness tomorrow.
F/Sgt Thorne — Leader.
Meyers.
Strudwick.
Loud.
Sanderson.
Any
transport from
1 B FLT Sgt of 602
Sgt to Mess
5-10 A.M.

LOG-BOOK · TIME IN AIR · ARRIVAL · DEPARTURE

YEAR 1942		AIRCRAFT		PILOT, OR 1ST PILOT	2ND PILOT, PUPIL OR PASSENGER	DUTY (INCLUDING RESULTS AND REMARKS)	SINGLE-ENGINE AIRCRAFT				MULTI-ENGINE AIRCRAFT					PASS-ENGER	INSTR./CLOUD FLYING (Incl. in cols. (1) to (10))	
							DAY		NIGHT		DAY			NIGHT				
MONTH	DATE	Type	No.				DUAL (1)	PILOT (2)	DUAL (3)	PILOT (4)	DUAL (5)	1ST PILOT (6)	2ND PILOT (7)	DUAL (8)	1ST PILOT (9)	2ND PILOT (10)	(11)	(12)	(13)
						— TOTALS BROUGHT FORWARD	55·25	306·15	3·30	8·25							3·30	9·35	7·4
APRIL	13	SPITFIRE	BM-187	SELF	—	LOCAL FLYING.		1·05											
"	14	SPITFIRE	BM-113	"	—	FIGHTER SWEEP (FECAMPS 17,000)		1·45											
"	14	SPITFIRE	BM-113	"	—	FIGHTER SWEEP		1·30											
"	15	SPITFIRE	BM-113	"	—	FIGHTER SWEEP		1·30											
"	16	SPITFIRE	BM-113	"		FIGHTER SWEEP		1·10											
"	17	SPITFIRE	BM-113	"		BOMBER ESCORT.		1·30											
"	17	MAGISTER	R-1915	"	L.A.C. CROOKS	TO MARTLESHAM.		1·00											
"	17	MAGISTER	R-1915	"	"	RETURN TO KENLEY.		·45											
"	25	SPITFIRE	BM-113	"		AIR SEA RESCUE		1·35											
"	25	SPITFIRE	BM-113	"		BOMBER ESCORT (LANDED AT LYMPE)		1·40											
"	25	SPITFIRE	BM-113	"		TO KENLEY		·20											
"	26	SPITFIRE	BM-113	"		BOMBER COVER ESCORT		1·35											
"	27	SPITFIRE	BM-148	"		RODEO 111. TO ST. OMER.		1·20											
"	27	SPITFIRE	BM-141	"		ESCORTED BOMBERS.		1·50											
"	29	SPITFIRE	BM-142	"		RAMROD 30 TO ST.OMER.		1·25											
"	29	SPITFIRE	BM-142	"		ESCORT COVER.		1·20											
"	30	SPITFIRE	BM-142	"		TARGET SUPPORT TO LE HAVRE.		1·30											
"	30	SPITFIRE	BM-142	"		RODEO OVER GRIS-NEZ.		1·25											
					GRAND TOTAL [Cols. (1) to (10)] 397 Hrs. 40 Mins.	TOTALS CARRIED FORWARD	55·25	330·20	3·30	8·25							3·30	9·35	7—

National and local newspapers were keen to capture 'scoops' with operational fighter pilots. The Evening Standard *printed these two photographs of F/Sgt Len Thorne giving a lecture to Air Training Corp cadets on Morse Code and engine handling.*

Hawker Fury. Finucane quickly gained confidence, and was awarded his wings with the assessment of 'average'. To his disappointment, Finucane was posted to Henlow to the pilotless Queen Bee target aircraft flight, and was with this unit when war was declared on Germany.

It was not until 27 June 1940, that Finucane finally got his wish for a posting to a fighter squadron when he was transferred to 7 OTU at Hawarden, which was one of three units set up to make good the losses inflicted on the RAF's flying personnel in May and June during the Battle for France. Here, Finucane converted onto Spitfires and completed just over 22 hours of flying time before being posted to 65 Squadron on 13 July 1940.

Assigned to 'B' Flight, the Irishman scored his first combat victory – a Bf 109E – on 12 August, together with a probable and a damaged. Whilst with 65 Squadron, Finucane was to gain five confirmed and one shared destruction, resulting in him being recommended for a DFC – he received the award on 13 May 1941, by which time he had become a flight commander with 452 Squadron.

Flying Spitfire IIs and VBs, Finucane was to achieve outstanding success, adding a further 17 kills, a DSO and two bars to his DFC. Following an accident whilst running during the blackout, he was forced out of action from late October 1941 through to January 1942, whereupon he was posted to become OC of 602 squadron. Here, he added a further five kills and three shared to his score before being wounded in combat during a dogfight with a Fw 190.

By 27 June, Finucane's success was such that he was posted as Wing Leader of the Hornchurch Wing, but whilst flying his Spitfire VB he was shot down by machine gun fire from the French coast. Finucane tried to ditch his Spitfire on the sea, but it was seen by his colleagues to sink immediately. The affable Irishman was just 21 years of age when he died, and his score of 26 confirmed kills and a further six shared destroyed had made him (officially) the RAF's leading scorer by mid-1942. Like many geniuses, Finucane has been perceived very differently by others both during and after the war. Len Thorne, Finucane's wingman on several missions, provides an interesting insight into the ace's character:

On one occasion I travelled with Paddy on the train whilst going on leave. At this stage I was an undecorated NCO pilot, but of course Paddy was already a highly-decorated officer, and easily recognized. Rather than embarrass me, and perhaps also himself, Paddy wore a Mackintosh to ensure that whilst travelling, his decorations were not on display, and that he did not draw attention to himself.

Typhoon Pilot – Johnny Baldwin

At the beginning of the war Johnny Baldwin joined the RAFVR as an airman, and during the Battle for France he was a member of the ground crew for the AASF, before subsequently being involved on bomb disposal duties during the Blitz. In 1941, Baldwin became one of the earliest recruits to the newly-instigated, civilian-operated, British Flying Training Schools in the USA, and gained his 'wings' at No. 2 BFTS, Lancaster, California. On return to the UK, Baldwin undertook a course at 59 OTU and was then posted to 609 'West Riding' Squadron at Manston in November.

After initial teething problems with the Typhoon IA, the unit was re-equipped with Typhoon IBs, and Baldwin claimed his first combat success when he damaged a Fw 190. Three Bf 109Gs fell to his guns on 20 January 1943, after which he was awarded the DFC. By December 1943 Baldwin had scored at least eight confirmed aerial victories with the Typhoon IB, duly being promoted to command 198 Squadron, also based at Manston. He achieved a

Right *This rare, original, Intelligence 'K' report was hand-written by M.I.6 Intelligence Officer, P/O Norman Miller, who was himself a pilot on detachment to HQ RAF Fighter Command, Bentley Priory. In this report, Miller has written details of the Messerschmitt Bf 109E-1 Wk-Nr 3859 which crashed at Holmans Grove, Grayswood, near Haslemere, at 16.40 on 30 September 1940. The pilot, Lt Herbert Schmidt of 6./JG 27, bailed out but was seriously injured. Small fragments of this aircraft were found by the Wealden Aviation Group in 1977. Some 'K' reports were declassified circa 1972, but were then hurriedly reclassified and are now held in Washington. For the record, in 1941 P/O Miller did a lot of advance planning work for the subsequent invasion of Sardinia, before returning to become a flying instructor at 3 EFTS, Shellingford. In 1943 Miller was asked to return to Intelligence duties, but declined the invitation.* (via H. Morgan)

To be telephoned to A.I.1.(k).

1) Date and time down: 30.9.40   16.40

2) Place down: Holmens Grove - nr Grayswood - nr Haslemere   3655

3) Aircraft type: Me 109.

4) Aircraft marks: Yellow 3. + (?) Staffel Colour: nil.

5) Description of any Badge or Shield on aircraft:
   Crest shield outlined in red - with black bear rampant - long red tongue

6) Unit to which crew belong: —

7) Feldpostnummer: —

8) Ausweis (Colour, Place and Date
      of issue; Signature, if readable):

9) Place of start: —

10) Time of start (Our time): —

11) Course, Height and Speed: —

12) Details of Combat: Thinks he was attacked from below by fighter
    on return journey - engine suddenly went on fire + he baled out
    A/c complete wreck.

13) Mission: Bomber escort.

      (Lftn Schlichting
      shot down a month
      ago. Probably same
      Gruppe.)

14) Number and Weight of bombs: none.

15) Result of Mission:
       Shot down

16) Further attacks to be expected:
    ('Phone IMMEDIATELY to Fighter Command)

17) Morale and Reliability: Unable to judge owing to nervous condition

18) CREW: of P/W.

Function.	Rank.	Christian name(s).	Surname.	Identity Disc.	If wounded, etc.	Length of Service.
a) Pilot	Lt.	Herbert	Schmidt	(can't find)	yes.	—
b)						
c)						
d)						
e)						

      Haslemere Cottage Hospital. Tel. Haslemere 935.

19) Present Location and Telephone number of Survivors:

Wing Commander 'Johnnie' Johnson has long been officially recognised as the RAF's highest scoring fighter pilot of WWII with a confirmed score of 34 and several more shared destroyed. This photograph was taken in May 1944. At this time W/C Johnson commanded 144 Wing, and with his Spitfire IXb MK392 claimed the destruction of an Fw 190 on 5 May. (via Jerry Scutts)

further six confirmed kills with this unit, prior to taking-up a staff post with 2nd TAF in April, 1944.

After three months, Baldwin returned to operations as Wing Leader of 146 Wing, and before war's end he had risen to the rank of group captain and been placed in command of 123 Wing – a post he held until late 1945. During the war, Baldwin was credited with destroying at least 15 enemy aircraft, and was awarded both the DSO and Bar and DFC and Bar.

Postwar, he commanded the Fighter Test Squadron at Boscombe Down, prior to attachment to the Egyptian Air Force in 1948. He returned to the RAF in January 1949 and commanded 249 Squadron, which was equipped with Tempest 6s, in Iraq. By 1952, Baldwin had been posted on attachment to the USAF, flying F-86s in Korea, but he was lost – probably shot down – on just his ninth operational sortie with the 16th Fighter Interceptor Squadron of the 51st FIW on 16 March 1952. G/C Baldwin was 33 at the time, and believed to be destined for high air rank.

Tempest Pilot – David Fairbanks

David C. 'Foob' Fairbanks, who was to become the highest scoring Tempest pilot of 2nd TAF, was one of a number of US nationals who failed to gain acceptance, or were deferred from pilot training, in the massive USAAF aviation cadet programme, yet subsequently found the Empire Air Training Scheme operating in Canada a more receptive route by which to achieve their ambition of becoming fighter pilots. Fairbanks would have been in good company, for several American pilots including Chesley Peterson, Pierce McKennon, Don Gentile and John Godfrey – all later to become leading fighter pilots – also chose to train in Canada after being 'washed out' from the American programme.

Following training, David Fairbanks remained in Canada on instructional duties, prior to being posted to Britain. Fairbanks' first combat claims were obtained whilst flying the Spitfire VB with 501 Squadron from Manston on the 8 June 1944. During his time with the unit, he gained a reputation for being unimpressed by officialdom

– he was also a highly-accomplished jazz pianist. Fairbanks left 501 Squadron for 274 Squadron, located at West Malling, in July 1944, and claimed his first success with the Tempest V on 29 August when he shot down a V1 over south-east England. This was followed by the destruction of two Bf 109s and a further damaged in December 1944.

At the turn of the year, Fairbanks was posted to 3 Squadron, again equipped with the Tempest V, where he achieved a further four aerial victories, one shared, and a further two destroyed on the ground. He was then promoted to command his former unit, 274 Squadron, which, like other 2 TAF Tempest units, was based in Holland. In January 1945 Fairbanks was awarded the DFC, to which he subsequently was awarded two bars.

On 28 February 1945, whilst landing a flight of six Tempests, S/L David Fairbanks was attacked by a much larger force of Fw 190s and shot down, becoming a PoW for the remainder of the war. He returned to Canada in postwar years, becoming a test pilot for Avro Canada.

Hurricane Pilot – Paul Farnes

Paul C. P. Farnes joined the RAFVR in 1938, and shortly after the outbreak of war was posted to 501 Squadron at Filton. Equipped with Hurricane Is, the unit was kept busy taking part in convoy and anti-submarine patrols in the early months of the war. On 27 November it moved to Tangmere, followed some six months later by a posting to France to help support the beleaguered Battles and Blenheims of the AASF – indeed, 501 Squadron shared their first French base at Bethenville with the Battles of 103 Squadron.

On the morning of 12 May 1940, Sgt Paul Farnes scored the first of his aerial victories when he claimed one He 111 destroyed and a half-share in another with P/O E. J. H. Sylvester. Farnes also scored a further possible and a confirmed share in another before his unit was forced to hurriedly leave France, via Allemanche, Le Mans, Dinard, and St Helier, in the Channel Islands.

Farnes remained with 501 Squadron throughout the Battle of Britain, scoring a further six enemy aircraft destroyed, one shared and six damaged whilst flying from Middle Wallop, Gravesend and Kenley. He was awarded the DFM the following month and commissioned in November. His tour long expired, Farnes finally left 501 Squadron for instructional duties in February 1941, returning to operations with 229 Squadron, equipped with the Hurricane IICs, exactly a year later. He served initially as a flight commander with this unit during the defence of Malta, claiming no less than five enemy aircraft damaged, before eventually becoming OC of the squadron during its last days on the island.

Following the unit's relocation and temporary disbandment in Egypt, Farnes was posted to a staff appointment at Habbaniyah, in Iraq, where he remained until March 1945. In postwar years Paul Farnes continued to serve with the RAF in staff, flying and instructional posts until he finally returned to civilian life in 1958.

Chapter Two

Soviet Air Force

Around three-quarters of all aircraft lost by the Luftwaffe during the Second World War were destroyed in the battle with the Soviet Union. Some 57,200 Luftwaffe aircraft are believed to have fallen to all Soviet Air Forces on the Eastern Front alone, and Russian fighter pilots claimed 65 per cent of all aircraft lost by the Luftwaffe. Over 44,000 German aircraft were claimed to have been destroyed by the Soviet Air Force during air combat, and a further 13,000 after having been attacked from the air whilst still on their airfields.

The defence of the Soviet Union, and initially Byelorussia and the Ukraine, from the German invasion, which commenced with Operation *Barbarossa* on 22 June 1941, was a terrifyingly contested conflict. The Russian people, well aware that they were perceived by their attackers as 'Untermenschen', resisted uncompromisingly. Over the four years of the German campaign on the Eastern Front – known in the Soviet Union as the Great Patriotic War – the fighter pilots of both sides were engaged in the largest aerial battle ever to have taken place. The quantity of aeroplanes involved, and the number of aircrew participating, ensured that the opportunities for the Luftwaffe to meet the Soviet Air Force in the air were numerous.

Operation *Barbarossa* had demonstrated to the

Soviet Air Force the enormous value of airpower in modern warfare, but it was to be three years before they could extract revenge in kind during the Byelorussian Offensive in June 1944. Until the latter months of the war, when the battle was for Berlin, rather than Moscow or Stalingrad, the Soviet fighter pilots fought in the skies above their homeland.

Researching the Subject

Literature describing the history of the USSR after the 1917 revolution, and before *perestroika* and *Glasnost*, has been described as 'riddled with lies and myths'. Likewise, it seems that biographies of many of the Soviet air aces of the Second World War have been at the very least overly heroic in their content, rich in rhetoric about the fascist enemy, and ever-faithful to the Stalinist system. Whereas autobiographies by such pilots as Ivan Nikolaevich Kozhedub – the uncontested highest-scoring Allied ace of the conflict – found great favour postwar, by contrast, other fine fighter pilots received comparatively limited coverage because they lacked the backing of Joseph Stalin.

That Grigori A. Rechkalov achieved most of his 61 kills whilst flying the American-built P-39N proved to be something of an embarrassment to Soviet political leaders.

Another P-39N pilot who proved to be a truly great tactician of aerial combat was Alexandr Ivanovich Pokryshkin, the outspoken, but nevertheless loyal, ace downing 49 of his 59 kills with the Airacobra. He was one of only two fighter pilots decorated with the Hero of Soviet Union (HSU) on three occasions. Pokryshkin, who died in 1985, wrote a series of biographical articles, and later in life gave several interviews.

Interestingly, following *perestroika*, aviation publications within Russia appear to have focused more on aircraft from other countries like Germany, American and Britain, although journals like *Aeroplan*, *Aviatsiya/Kosmonavtika* and *Krylya Rodiny* do occasionally contain biographies, interviews and lists of aces of the Soviet Air Force, some of which have clearly been painstakingly researched. Even so, it is clear that no definitive history has been published, or indeed is likely ever to be, simply because of the unreliability of source material.

Red Air Force Experiences of Combat Prior to 1941

The primary function for the pilots of the Red Air Force during the Spanish Civil War was to provide support for the ground forces. The Soviet pilots were perceived by the Luftwaffe to be tactically naive, maintaining small, tight and defensive formations. They reportedly suffered from a general lack of personal fitness, limited skills in air gunnery, poor training, and a predilection for text book tactics that had been inculcated into the pilots to such an extent that they failed to show personal initiative in combat situations. As for the quality of the fighter aircraft flown, they lacked sufficient firepower to bring down enemy aircraft in air-to-air combat. The Soviet Air Force had entered Spain with high expectations, and for a while their 900+ I-15 and I-16 fighters performed well against the German He 51 and Arado fighters. However, by the summer of 1937 the Luftwaffe had begun to re-equip with the superior Bf 109, and German pilots sought to entice the Republican fighters into the air by strafing enemy airfields. Once aloft, the predominantly Soviet fighters were no match for the Bf 109.

Concurrently with the struggle in Spain, Soviet fighter pilots also became involved in combat with the Japanese over the disputed Mongolian border with northern China. Here,

Soviet fighter pilots in a relaxed mood during the Spanish Civil War. (via Russian Aviation Research Trust)

*This official photograph of the I-15 was issued by the
Ministry of Information. The caption read:*

NOT TO BE PUBLISHED BEFORE THE WEEKLY
PAPERS WEDNESDAY 27/5/42.
(Picture issued May 1942)
RED STAR OVER SEVASTOPOL.
Picture shows: A Soviet plane, the red star on her wings,
patrolling the skies above Sevastopol.

(via Russian Aviation Research Trust)

they seemed to fare rather better than in Europe.
For several years the Japanese had practised air
raid alerts in the area, and when the Sino-
Japanese War commenced in 1937, four I-15
fighter and two SB-2 bomber squadrons were

formed as part of the second Volunteer Air Group
and sent to defend Soviet bases in China, at
Lanchow, Nanking, Hankow and Chungking.
NII-VVS test pilots including Stepan Suprun,
who had already been awarded the Order of the
Red Star, were amongst those sent. Another
famed pilot in the form of Grigori Kravchenko
was sent to command the 22nd Fighter
Regiment, based at Khalkin Gol. Under his
leadership, the unit claimed 32 Japanese aircraft
destroyed for the loss of just one pilot.
Kravchenko went on to achieve both high
distinction and rank in the Second World War
prior to his death on the Volkhov Front in 1943.

The expansionist plans of the Japanese
government enabled the fighter regiments of the
Japanese Army Air Force (JAAF) and Imperial
Navy to cut their respective combat teeth in a
painful campaign against the Red Air Force in
Mongolia. The JAAF pilots, flying Nakajima
Ki-27 fighters, were forced to assume standing
patrols to intercept and repel the constant
offensives from Soviet SB-2 and TB-3 bombers.
The former suffered losses when, based upon
their previous experiences against the much
slower I-15*bis*, they made the error of
underrating the more modern I-153.

It has been recorded elsewhere that Russian
pilots deliberately flew their new aircraft with the
undercarriage lowered so as to appear to be
flying the obsolescent I-15*bis*, and then when the
Japanese pilots had fallen into the trap, quickly
retracted the undercarriage, rammed on the
power and turned to meet their adversaries.
However, as the undercarriage of the I-153 was
raised by means of a hand crank, the ability of
the pilot to quickly cycle in his landing gear in
the heat of combat, is open to debate.

The introduction by the Japanese of the early
Mark II version of the still-evolving Type A6M2
Zero fighter changed the face of the conflict in
China once and for all, and the Soviet-built I-16s
were decimated by the highly manoeuvrable,
long-range, 332 mph fighter.

For the VVS (*Voyenno-vozdushnyye sily* –
Soviet Air Forces), their employment as a 'tool'
of the ground forces left them tactically
unprepared for the Russo-Finnish War, otherwise
known as the Winter War. Despite the Soviets
attacking in bitterly cold weather on 30
November 1939, the Finnish Air Force putting up

sterling opposition against what was then the largest air force in the world.

Allied to their poor showing in support of the ground troops, the Soviet Air Force was also still reeling from Stalin's autocratic purges, which had seen tens of thousands of key personnel, aircrew, leaders, designers and engineers from the Soviet aviation industry savagely executed during the late 1930s. Such losses would severely curtail the operational performance of the air force in combat for some time to come – indeed, further purges still to cost the lives of several other key personnel in the Great Patriotic War.

Harsh lessons had been learned in Spain, and although senior officers sought to instigate change, by the outbreak of the Winter War the organization of the Red Air Force had not sufficiently improved to prevent another woeful showing in the Russo-Finnish War.

During this conflict, the Soviet Air Forces filed outlandish claims for the destruction of Finnish aircraft. Figures since meticulously researched by Finnish historians show that their air force suffered the loss of just 36 aircraft in aerial combat to Soviet fighters during the Winter War out of a total of 68 aircraft destroyed. By comparison, Soviet claims of 362 Finnish aircraft destroyed far outstripped the total number of aircraft flying in the whole Finnish Air Force! Pilots from the latter force, combined with Finnish anti-aircraft batteries, claimed a total of 490 Soviet aircraft destroyed during the short Winter War – Soviet losses of 579 aircraft have since been acknowledged in Russia. Today, many photographs exist of a variety of captured Soviet aircraft in Finnish markings, ready to fly against the very country in which they had been constructed.

Despite a poor showing by the Red Air Force during the Winter War, the Finns were compelled to accept Soviet terms of surrender on 30 March 1940, which changed the geographical line of the Finnish frontiers in favour of the aggressor. However, Finland, as an ally of Germany, declared war on the USSR again on 22 June 1941, and waged a bitter three-year campaign before finally accepting surrender terms on 4 September 1944.

Despite the Soviet Union having the largest air force in the world at the end of the first war with

A fighter pilot poses for the camera just before climbing into the cockpit of his I-15. (via Russian Aviation Research Trust)

A member of the ground crew is captured by the camera loading bombs onto a heavily-camouflaged Polikarpov I-15bis prior to it undertaking a ground attack sortie (via Russian Aviation Research Trust)

An abandoned I-153 photographed in 1941 by a German war photographer. (BAK 389)

Finland, in the weeks and months following the outbreak of the Great Patriotic War, it demonstrated that it was unquestionably an inferior air power when compared to the Luftwaffe, both in terms of the combat tactics employed by its pilots and the quality of equipment they had at their disposal.

Training

A typical VVS ace profile would reflect the experiences of a young Komsomol member who had learned to fly in an Osoaviakhim aeroclub in the late 1930s. This would be followed by military training as a VVS pilot just after the outbreak of war, becoming an instructor and then entering the fray in the spring of 1943. One example was Vladimir Orekhov (later Col V. A. Orekhov), a 19-kill fighter ace, and holder of the highest Soviet decoration, the HSU. An analysis of his training hours show that he flew a remarkably high total of just over 502 hours on aircraft like the antiquated Po-2, UT-1, UT-2, and UTI-4, prior to reaching operational status on a squadron. Like Orekhov, those former cadet pilots fortunate enough to end up in a leading fighter regiment, having displayed good innate abilities and received guidance from experienced and capable 'teachers', could go on to amass a

reasonable score by the conclusion of the war.

However, the bulk of new Soviet fighter pilots trained as replacements for those lost in the Russo-Finnish campaign were poorly prepared for Operation *Barbarossa*, for they had received instruction based on formation flying, rather than gunnery skills and modern combat tactics. Further, new pilots were posted to squadrons from operational training units having flown only docile trainers and obsolete I-15 fighters. In the frontline, they were issued with agile machines like the I-16 and I-153 'Tschaika', both of which proved difficult to master in an operational environment, thus resulting in many young pilots being killed in accidents.

Operational training units had been no substitute for exposure to real combat conditions, and bitter experience had taught the 'old hands' that different tactics needed to be employed on actual operations. The tactics of group, rather than individual, combat was instilled in the inexperienced pilots, and fighter leaders developed their own methods of teaching these skills. Pokryshkin, who had been in combat since the first day of the German invasion, set his pilots practical problems which they were to work out for themselves. He even held talks in an airfield dug-out, christened 'the classroom', as

A damaged I-16 Rata is over-flown by a Ju 52 on a captured Soviet airfield immediately following the commencement of Operation Barbarossa *at the end of June 1941. (BAK 389)*

its walls were festooned with diagrams, drawings, sketches, and model aircraft used for scale representation.

Tactics Employed in Combat

In this brief section some of the key concepts at the heart of Soviet fighter tactics will be explored, drawing upon the recollections of the great Russian fighter tactician, Pokryshkin, and then evaluating the effectiveness of the combat tactic of *'Taran'* – 'Ramming'.

Tactically, at the start of the conflict Soviet fighter pilots flew defensively and statistically, demonstrating that the lessons from Spain and

Deadly foes. A seemingly intact I-16 sits alongside a recently arrived Bf 109F of JG 54 in July 1941. (BAK 389)

the Winter War had not been learned. They displayed very little deviation from their normal horizontal flight patterns, their slow and poorly-armed aircraft proving easy prey for the quicker, lighter, and more heavily-armed German aircraft. By contrast, the Luftwaffe pilots displayed sound contemporary tactical awareness of the modern methods of air combat. It was only as time progressed, and surviving Soviet pilots gained in operational experience, that the knowledge accrued by the latter of air combat was passed onto new pilots.

An improvement in the quality of aircraft flown also had an impact on the confidence pilots took with them into battle. Gradually, the durable biplane fighters and the I-16 monoplane were replaced by aircraft that allowed their pilots to tackle the Bf 109s and Fw 190s on equal terms. In addition to modifying existing fighters, new designs sought to produce increasingly more heavily-armed, and faster, aircraft. Allied with the provision of new types, the Soviet Air Force finally began to adopt new tactics to effectively counter the Luftwaffe, developing the following techniques: 'zveno', 'etazherka', 'sokoliny udar', 'nozhnitsy', and 'kacheli'.

At the beginning of the war, Soviet fighter pilots flew their slow and poorly-armed aircraft in a horizontally static three-plane defensive formation known as a 'zveno'. As they quickly gained experience so the tactics altered to reflect the need to more aggressively counter the attacks of the Luftwaffe on Soviet territory. New tactical flight formations were developed, which saw Soviet fighter units belatedly catch up with the other national air forces by operating aircraft in pairs. Pokryshkin, with the special permission of his regimental commander, was one of those who pioneered this formation in the Soviet Air Force.

In the battle of Kharkov during the summer of 1942, the 'etazherka' ('stack') was born, in which pairs of aircraft were staggered in height and spacing – this tactic was later used extensively over the Kuban during the hot spring months of 1943. Pokryshkin described the first time that he applied the 'etazherka' with the air combat techniques of height, speed, manoeuvre and fire:

This was over the Kuban at Krymskaya (Krymskaya – west of Krasnodar, near the Kerch straits, the entrance to the Sea of Azov – in the spring of 1943 . . . Our group formation consisted of a 'stack' of pairs flying out of the sun, with a vertical separation of several hundred metres between each pair. We were at a height of 4,000 metres. With such a reserve of height we had no fear of being taken by surprise, as firstly we could see each other perfectly and each pilot could keep a look out for his comrades without worrying about himself, and secondly, we had been told by radio that we would only encounter enemy fighters over Krymskaya itself.

As our group of six fighters 'combed' the air space at lightning speed, we spotted aircraft over Krymskaya – these were our patrolling LaGG fighters. Our group again climbed to gain height. In a nutshell, we described a pendulum-like flight pattern – a shallow descent and then climb after flying through the region we were covering, and building up speed in the process. When we had gained enough height I gave the order, '180° turn', and once again we dived down towards Krymskaya.

We had only been out of the designated zone for a few minutes, but the picture had changed. Over a dozen Me 109s had appeared over Krymskaya and were diving on the four LaGGs still slowly circling. Now it was up to us. To the enemy's surprise I attacked the group leader and his Me 109 went down. Grigori Rechkalov[1], the number one in the top pair of our stack, also attacked one of the enemy fighters and brought it down. When we had gained height once more, we saw the enemy fighters making off – having unexpectedly lost two of their number.

Further Soviet tactical innovations included a surprise attack from a steep dive, christened the 'sokoliny udar' ('falcon blow'). Another, the 'nozhnitsy' ('scissors') was an attempt to provide cover for bombers, but at the same time permit the escorting pair of fighters to cover each other by alternating flying towards and then away from each other, thus enabling the pilots to obtain adequate views of the surrounding airspace. 'The swing', or 'kacheli', saw a large number of fighters adopt a pendulum-like flight pattern when undertaking fighter sweeps ahead of Soviet bombers, or providing cover for ground forces.

Today, Pokryshkin is credited in Russia as being the originator of the procedural tactic of 'height,   speed,   manoeuvre,   fire'.

Psychologically, he was a lateral thinker – a planner who recorded his experiences of each combat, drawing the figures flown, breaking each manoeuvre down into small stages, studying and evaluating his own, and his colleague's performance, and then developing increasingly efficient theories of combat which were verified by their employment in the frontline.

Interviewed in 1983, just two years before his death, Pokryshkin said:

The main thing is to have a creative approach to any air combat. Without speed you can't make that tricky turn, gain height, make the surprise attack or get in the decisive burst of fire. What do we achieve

This well-known photo shows women fighter aces in front of a Yak-1. Used in many publications in recent years, the image was accompanied by an interesting original caption when released by the Ministry of Information in December 1943. It read:

RUSSIAN GIRL AGED 22 IS RED AIR FORCE FIGHTER PILOT
Lily Litvyak, aged 22, fighter pilot and junior Lieutenant in the Red Air Force, has fought at Stalingrad and Rostiv. She has more than 130 operational flights and 66 aerial battles to her credit. She has shot down 7 enemy planes, capturing a number of German airmen including "one ace", a "Luftwaffe" officer wearing the Iron Cross. She started to study aviation in her teens and was barely 16 when she made her first solo flight. Before the war she was a flying instructress at an aeroclub and trained a number of new flyers most of whom have since been in action on the battle front. She is quite fearless and has often engaged several enemy planes single-handed. When helping to repulse a big enemy air-raid she was tackled by 6 Messerschmitts. Her ammunition ran out and a shell fragment pierced the radiator and wounded her in the leg. She managed to bring her plane, riddled with holes, safely home, and, herself, recovered to fight again.

Picture shows Litvyak (first from left) with Lieutenant Ekaterina Budanova, (centre), her best friend and splendid fighter pilot, and Vera Kusnetsove. This is Lily Lityvak's plane. The three girl fighter pilots have just received a new battle order and are studying the map before carrying it out.

It is believed that the pilot on the right should have read Mariya Kuznetsova, who, of the three, was the sole survivor from the war. Litvyak, who had 12 confirmed personal victories and two shared, was killed when she crash-landed, and was duly buried beneath the wing of her Yak-1. Budanova is reputed to have achieved 22 aerial kills and Kuznetsova, who died in 1991, shot down a Ju 88 and Ju 87, and was herself shot down several times. (via Russian Aviation Research Trust)

if we build up a good turn of speed? First of all suddenness of attack. In warfare, seconds can be priceless, and a split-second can decide an outcome. Speed enables all the attention to be concentrated on looking for the enemy ahead, speed resulting not only from engine power but from altitude.

After analysing dozens of air combats and having studied the outcome and the interrelationships between the elements of fighting on the dive and climb, I came to the conclusion that height gives you the opportunity to take up a more favourable position for your attack, improves your field of vision and enables you to build-up a high speed in a dive, which in turn assists you to carry out your 'vertical' manoeuvre. All this creates favourable conditions for a decisive surprise attack and makes it easier to break away afterwards.

As for firepower, then the essence of this component of the formula was its efficacy. You must hit the enemy from in close, thus ensuring a good chance of hitting without wasting ammunition. The dispersal of bullets and shells at a range of 300 metres was at that time so great that only a few got home, and then without any penetrating power. You had to get in close and open fire from around 100 metres, or often even closer . . . Faced with a real opponent in the heat of battle, a fighter pilot had to have willpower, stamina and an unshakeable determination to destroy his enemy. Only then could you hit the target.

Indeed, the Chief Administration for Operational Training, which came directly under the influence of the Chief of Air Staff, made considerable efforts to improve the combat

Official Ministry of Information photo circa 1941/42 shows a camouflaged I-16 serving as a backdrop for pilots receiving a post-mission debrief. The original caption read:

RUSSIAN PILOTS HAVE MET AND MEASURED THE GERMAN AIR FORCE
Shadows lengthen as Soviet pilots meet and discuss the day's experiences in air battles with the German Luftwaffe. From their experiences it would seem that they have nothing to fear from the Germans in the sky.

(via Russian Aviation Research Trust)

Another photo taken at the end of June 1941 by the Germans. Here, a Wehrmacht infantryman is seen as he is about to retrieve his rifle from the starboard wing of an unscathed MiG-3. With smoke billowing in the background, this view was taken just days after the commencement of the German invasion. (via BAK 136)

effectiveness of its fighter pilots. By February 1943, highly-experienced fighter pilots had been formed into a cadre, and charged with the responsibility of working with individual fighter divisions, or corps, in key sectors. During this first month the flight was attached to the 286th Fighter Division, 15th Air Army, on the Bryansk Front. The following month the cadre was posted to III Fighter Corps, 4th Air Army, in preparation for the Kuban air battles in the north Caucasus area. By the end of 1943 a manual was produced to prepare fighter pilots for the combat experiences in the year to come.

'Taran' was considered a legitimate, if comparatively uncommon, tactic of air combat by the fighter pilots of the Soviet Air Force, and was derived from the exploits of the Russian Air Force during the First World War. Demanding an extreme act of bravery, and no little flying skill, ramming was mostly employed during the Great Patriotic War between 1941–43, pre-dating the similar action of Kamikaze pilots of the JAAF by some almost two years. The similarity does not end at this point, for like the Japanese, the Soviet propaganda machine ensured the full and fervent support from the Soviet public, who viewed their pilots as heroes – they were dubbed Stalin's

'Falcons', opposing the Nazi 'Vultures'.

However, unlike the Japanese, both male and female Russian pilots engaged in the *Taran*, the decision to ram being made at their own discretion, but only when all ammunition had been expended, and when collision was the only option left through which to bring down the enemy aircraft – usually a bomber. It was therefore more of a pragmatic and rational approach to air combat rather than the emotional undertaking of the Japanese. The act of ramming was also not unknown – albeit a far rarer occurrence – in the western theatre, this form of attack only usually occurring after a pilot had run out of ammunition, and perhaps had suffered damage to his own aircraft. In sheer anger and frustration, he would then resort to ramming his foe.

For the Russian pilots it has been recorded that the following methods were employed:

1) To attack from the rear, probing the Soviet aircraft's propeller into the control surfaces of the e/a, which, with damage to rudder and/or elevator, would lose airworthiness and fall to the ground.

2) To ram a wing into the control surface of the e/a

or, at low level, to tip the wing into the wing of the e/a, so that it lost control.

3) To directly fly the a/c into the e/a, used only as an extreme and last resort.

The first act of *Taran* was achieved shortly after the opening of *Barbarossa* when, on 22 June 1941, Lt I. I. Ivanov lost his life when he rammed a He 111 with his I-16, and was posthumously awarded the HSU. Reported widely at the time was the *Taran* achieved by Victor Talalikhan of the 177th Fighter Air Regiment PVO. On 6 August 1941, whilst again

Ministry of Information photograph of a Yak-1. The original caption read:

RED AIR FORCE OPERATIONAL BASE.
A magnificent "Yakovliev (sic)" back from the skies. It has done a lot of flying today and is now being shunted into the hangar where the engine can have a rest.

(via Russian Aviation Research Trust)

flying an I-16 on a night patrol over Moscow, Talilikhan attacked a He 111 flying at approximately 15,000 ft. The Luftwaffe bomber dived to lower altitude with Talalikhan continuing in pursuit. At 7,500 ft, the Russian pilot had no further ammunition left, so he manoeuvred his aircraft to within 30 ft of the bomber with the intention of ramming. The gunner of the He 111 opened fire, hitting Talalikhan in his right arm just prior to the collision. Out of control, the bomber plummeted to the ground and crashed. Talalikhan managed to bale out, landing in a lake and surviving to fight again as a national hero. His mortal glory was to be short-lived, however, for Talilikhan was to lose his life just ten weeks later in an action over Moscow.

The top-scoring *Taran* pilot of the Second World War was HSU winner, Lt Boris Kobzan, of the 184th Fighter Air Regiment, who scored four victories through this method, whilst HSU Khlobystov made *Taran* attacks on three occasions. By 1942 it is clear that the Luftwaffe had acknowledged the possibility that some Soviet pilots might deliberately attempt to ram German aircraft. Even so, the general feeling amongst units on the Eastern Front was that this method of attack was not being used deliberately. A document compiled by Luftwaffe Air Command 3 on 2 October 1942 said:

Tactical experiences of combat units on the Eastern Front – the opinion on parts of the Eastern Front seems to be that Russian fighters are starting attempts to ram our aircraft in order to make them crash. This view has up to now not been confirmed, either through the questioning of prisoners of war nor through the known Russian orders. It must be a case of inadequate experience or training. It has been shown that keeping calm in a combat situation is the best solution. It is recommended that gunners hold their fire until the enemy is quite close.
(Air Command 3 dept 1a, op 1. No. 27 481/42)

It is possible that whilst *Taran* had a rational explanation for its use as a technique of aerial combat, it may also be that the physiological and psychological condition of Russian pilots may have, in some way, predisposed the pilots to employ such risky and extreme tactics. Russian pilots operated in severely stressful conditions,

Another Ministry of Information shot, this time of a Yak-1 production line. The caption read:

RUSSIAN FACTORY EXCEEDS PLANE OUTPUT PROGRAMME.
PICTURE SHOWS: Aircraft being turned out by the workers in excess of the output programme at the Soviet "X"
Aircraft factory. YAK-1 (1–26) fighters.

(via Russian Aviation Research Trust)

for they were either under attack or on the offensive themselves, having to constantly move bases in response to the fluidity of the frontline.

Facilities were primitive and improvised. Food was scarce for long periods of time, and a supplement called KOLA was given to operational pilots. The effect of suffering permanent physiological stress, and taking supplements to ward off starvation, may have resulted in light-headedness at altitude, predisposing pilots to take risks which normally they would not have considered. The relentless intensity of the Soviet peoples' opposition to the German invasion was apparent throughout the war, and in the spirit of nationalistic fervour, pilots were prepared to drive themselves to the extremes of their flying skill and bravery – and to pay the ultimate personal sacrifice in order to protect their country.

Bearing these factors in mind, there is a critical question to be answered – was *Taran* a formalized fighter tactic, or was it essentially an act which occurred in the heat of the moment, and was then elevated into aviation folklore by propaganda machinery keen to publicize supreme acts of individual heroism? The answer has yet to be firmly established.

Filing of Claims – the Process
Order No 0299
The overall process for the verification of claims followed the guidelines personally signed by Joseph Stalin, and issued to all fighter and ground attack units of the Red Army Air Force. The first edict, Order No 0299, was issued from Moscow on 19 August 1941. The purpose of these guidelines was to introduce standardization into the allocation of rewards for pilots who were viewed to have distinguished themselves in aerial combat. The word 'reward', rather than 'award',

Aerial shot of a Yak-3 adorned with eight kill markings. (via Russian Aviation Research Trust)

The nose of a crashed Yak-3, sporting a bent airscrew and exposed magazine. (via Russian Aviation Research Trust)

is used here simply because in addition to decorations being made, successful fighter pilots were provided with financial incentives for each enemy aircraft shot down.

The guidelines were as follows – a 'prize' of 1,000 roubles was made to each pilot for every one enemy aircraft shot down. With three enemy aircraft destroyed in combat, the pilot was to be recommended for an 'order' (citation and decoration), followed by a second 'order' if the total was doubled to six. After the destruction of ten enemy aircraft, the pilot was to be recommended for the highest 'order' which could be bestowed, the Hero of the Soviet Union.

For those few fighter units also making ground attack sorties against enemy airfields, there was added incentive. A 'prize' of 1,500 roubles was given if the pilot made five such sorties, and with fifteen sorties the pilot was recommended for an 'order' and a prize of 2,000 roubles – and so it continued, with a prize of 3,000 roubles being awarded for 25 sorties and the HSU and 5,000 roubles for those who successfully completed 50 ground attack sorties. *Taran* victories were also acknowledged by the recommendation for a decoration.

In Stalin's Order No 0299, claims needed to be supported by either the testimonies of the fighter pilot making the claim, ground troops

who witnessed the action, or the establishment of the location where the aircraft was shot down by Fighter Regiment Command. At this early stage (the summer of 1941), there was no mention of the role of partisans in providing evidence to support the claims of pilots, as was the case later in the war. Claims were held by the Air Regiment and/or Division Staffs, and were probably also deposited in political archives, for it is likely that there were two intelligence officers attached to every fighter regiment.

In addition to the unit's IO, an officer of the NKVD (the political and military police) played a role in reading pilots' combat reports, as well as the testimonies from other aircrew. Certainly, anomalies crept into the interpretation of fighter pilot claims. In China, for example, Gen A. S. Balgoveshchenski reported that the practice adopted in the final months of the Sino-Japanese war of 1939 saw any single JAAF aircraft fired upon by two Soviet fighters credited as a single kill to both pilots! This practice was continued on into the Second World War for a short period of time.

In the following extract, Col Vladimir A. Orekhov describes the process of accreditation for an aerial victory that was strictly adhered to in 1944:

Mistaken identity! Caption read:

THE SOVIET AIR FORCE AT WORK.
There is an incessant roar of engines as Soviet "Stormoviks" pass over the lakes and woods of the plains of Central Russia.

These aircraft are, of course, LaGG-3 fighters of the Red Air Fleet. (via Russian Aviation Research Trust)

La-5s of the 1st Czechoslovak Fighter Regiment on the Eastern Front. (via Russian Aviation Research Trust)

After the mission, pilots gathered together and everyone told about how many planes he shot down personally, and about the planes shot down by his comrades that he had observed. The squadron adjutant wrote down these facts. This document was named the 'Combat report of fulfilled mission'. The document had to be filled in after every mission, and contained data concerning the results of the mission, and pilots who claimed kills. At the end of the day, all such reports were collected in the regiment headquarters, where the regiment's own combat report was completed.

The kills were confirmed usually by the commander of the regiment. To get the confirmation, one of the following 'proofs' had to be available:

* confirmation from at least two other pilots who took part in the fight.
* confirmation from ground troops.
* confirmation from partisans.
* verification on the seized territory.

These forms of verification were equal, but some times – especially if the fight took place over enemy territory or there were only two fighters involved – the last two 'proofs' were obligatory.

FIGURE 1 – Extract from Vladimir Orehkov's log book

Mission 6/2/44 provides an example of an aerial victory recorded by pilot:

Date	6/2/44
Aircraft	La-5
Mission	Air cover of the ground troops in the vicinity of the lake Losvido
Number of flights	1
Time	0 hours 55 mins
Mission fulfilled	The group of 6 La-5 carried out aerial combat against 6 Fw 190 and 20 Ju 87. Personally shot down 1 Fw 190 that crashed in the vicinity of the village Turki.

A confirmed kill was noted in the pilot's flying logbook, and this served as the official recognition of the victory. Confirmation of the score would usually be given on the same day the

A Yak-9 pilot awaits for the signal to take-off from a rudimentary strip somewhere on the Eastern Front. (via Russian Aviation Research Trust)

A LaGG-3 series 35 is prepared for take-off in the harsh winter of 1942/43. The pilot of this aircraft, Capt I. A. Kaberov of 3 Gv IAP, was credited with eight personal kills and 18 shared victories. (via Russian Aviation Research Trust)

action took place if there were enough witnesses. However, weeks or even months could pass if confirmation from partisans on the ground was needed. At the beginning of the war the process of verification was much simpler because the Red Army was in retreat and confirmation from other pilots was deemed good enough. The practice of dividing claims either as 'personal' victories or as 'group' kills depended on the traditions of the regiment in question. In the 32nd GIAP (Guards Fighter Air Regiment), all the kills were 'personal', with every aircraft shot down 'belonging' to one pilot only.

Gun Camera

A. Shcherbakov, who won the HSU whilst serving as a fighter pilot during the Second World War and then went on to become a test pilot in postwar years, was interviewed about his experiences with gun camera confirmation of kills whilst serving with the 176th Proskurov FAR:

As a rule, gun camera film did not properly confirm victories. All our fighters in the 176th Proskurov FAR were fitted with camera guns . . . but even if the shells reached their targets, this might not be recorded immediately. A result could usually be

seen only after the attacker had stopped firing and left the victim. Such planes as our Il-2, LaGG-3, La-5 and La-7 were not particularly vulnerable. Being hit during a sortie, they often returned home and flew again after small repairs. Ground observers' testimonies and wreckage of destroyed aircraft were the best confirmation to an air victory.

Colour film was rarely used by the Soviet Air Force, and it is believed that the earliest surviving examples of colour footage of standard operational aircraft dates from 1946. Presumably, some colour film was employed earlier, but would only have been used in special circumstances – perhaps in experimental work, thus excluding operational pilots, and their aircraft.

Political Pressures

The threat of execution for failure was the ultimate price paid by senior Soviet Air Force officers, and this duly brought with it an overwhelming pressure for the units within their respective commands to succeed. Senior officers needed to present the best possible picture to their superiors, and thereafter to the Soviet public. Two notable examples were the highly distinguished generals Ivan I. Kopets and Yakov

V. Smushkevich. Kopets was commander of the Soviet Fighter Group in Spain from October 1936 to June 1937, becoming a HSU on 21 June 1937. In the Winter War with Finland, he commanded the Air Force of the 8th Army, then became the Commander of the Air Force of the Western Military District, which was hit by the German surprise attack on 22 June 1941, which resulted in the loss of some 528 aircraft on the ground and 210 in the air, out of total of 1,200 lost during the first day of Operation *Barbarossa*.

The disgrace felt by Kopets was so great that on the following day he committed suicide. Smushkevich, who had commanded the Soviet AF detachment in Spain from October 1936 through to June 1937 and had been awarded the HSU on 21 June 1937, rose to become Commander in Chief of the Soviet Air Force in September 1939, but was arrested in the Stalinist purges on 7 June 1941 for treacherous activity and executed on 28 October.

It is reasonable to propose that pressure from the political regime, and its thirst for propaganda, may have influenced the accreditation of kills – particularly of multiple victories. The question,

therefore, is, would some kills have been ascribed without adequate and objective verification? Indeed, would the situation have been any different to the over-claiming made by fighter pilots flying in any other national air force? The answer to the latter has to be no, for like other pilots, those in the Soviet Air Force were young, aggressive, men whose opposition to the enemy was such that motivation was never going to be a problem. They wanted to succeed, and would optimistically report their successes.

However, the tactic of *Taran* may have led to claims being made which resulted from unintentional collision with enemy aircraft. Indeed, *Taran*s may have been credited as victories by surviving squadron pilots who witnessed the action where the *Taran* pilot did not survive. It has been found that when Finnish records have recorded their aircraft being involved in the same action as that described by the Soviet foe, so the claim would also be made by, or on behalf, of the Finnish pilot involved.

Luftwaffe Victories versus Soviet Aerial Kills
The primary function of Soviet fighter regiments

The inscriptions on the two MiG-3s nearest to the camera in February 1942 read Za Rodinu *('For the Fatherland') and* Za Stalina *('For Stalin').* (via Russian Aviation Research Trust)

In the autumn of 1941 the RAF's 151 Wing was posted to an airfield near to the small village of Vayenga, in Murmansk. 151 Wing comprised 81 and 134 Squadrons, who had the dual tasks of both providing operational support to Soviet bomber squadrons in the defence of the port of Archangel, and teaching Soviet pilots to fly the Hurricane. Following 151 Wing's successful transfer of aircraft to the Russians, it returned home to the UK. In total, some 2,952 Hurricanes were transferred by Britain to the USSR under a lend-lease agreement. In this photograph, Boris Safonov (right) of the 72nd Regiment of the Russian Naval Air Fleet talks to RAF pilots Charlton 'Wag' Haw (left) and Kenneth Ward (centre). Safonov, who was later awarded the HSU, became only the second Russian pilot to go solo in the Hurricane, and Haw and Ward were themselves awarded the Order of Lenin. Haw scored three victories whilst in Russia to become the leading scorer of the RAF contingent.

was different from that of the Luftwaffe's fighter units, especially during the first two years of the Great Patriotic War. The task of providing air support for the land troops, as well as the ground attack and bombing forces, was the sole mission for fighter pilots during this phase of the war, and their successes in this sphere were more important than aerial victories. For example, when defending a ground attack or assault aircraft, Soviet fighters were instructed not to engage in dogfighting. When defending roads and bridge-heads for the ground forces, fighters had to operate at low-level for much of the time, making them vulnerable to German fighters holding the crucial advantages of height and speed. Further, 'free hunting' to seek out targets of opportunity, or pursuing an aircraft back over enemy lines, only became acceptable from 1943 onwards.

By comparison, from the very first day of the German invasion of the Soviet Union, the Luftwaffe had superior equipment to the Red Air Force, which was manned by highly-experienced combat pilots who had learned their skills fighting the RAF. Tactically, they were far more attuned to the combat requirements of modern warfare. Unlike their Soviet counterparts, the fighter pilots of the Luftwaffe had the capacity to choose the time and place of attack, and even when to avoid combat if the chances of being hit were too great. Soviet Air Force literature contains many references to the fact that the Luftwaffe knew the names and call-signs of Soviet aces, and were warned when these were flying in the vicinity[2].

The Luftwaffe's logistical support and technical maintenance was superior, whilst German pilots who were shot down often quickly returned to the fray. It has been variously recorded elsewhere in literature that Erich

Lend-lease aircraft played a highly significant part in equipping the Soviet air forces during the Second World War. This photograph, dated 10 September 1944, depicts the scene at Ladd Field, Fairbanks, Alaska, when the formal transfer of a P-63 Kingcobra by Col Russell Keillor (left) and Brig Gen Dale V. Gaffney (centre) to Col Peter S. Kisilev marked the occasion of the 5,000th aircraft transferred via the so-called 'Alsib' route – the Alaskan-Siberian ferry route. A total of 2,400 P-63s were sent to the Soviet Union as part of the agreement. (via Russian Aviation Research Trust)

Hartmann was shot down 14 times, Gerhard Barkhorn 9 and Günther Rall 7 (and seriously injured on two occasions). Kozhedub was never shot down, and neither was Skomorokhov, whilst Pokryshkin was 'bested' twice, as were Savitsky and Popkov. Part of the reason for this also lies in the fact that the less-armoured Soviet fighters were perhaps more vulnerable to fire than the well-protected Bf 109 which, in absorbing more punishment, allowed its pilot to either bail out or make it back to base to effect a crash-landing.

Soviet Women Fighter Pilots

The women who flew with the Soviet Air Force during the Second World War have been credited with being the first of their sex to see action in combat as an organized group. Following the ideological teachings of Marx, Soviet women were considered to have the same responsibilities and rights as men, and theoretically, the same opportunities to develop careers as military pilots. Rhetoric was one thing, however, and in

reality, it was not until the mid to late 1930s that women began to follow the example of epoch-making aircrew who, like navigator (and later pilot) Marina Raskova, had set numerous women's aviation records. She received high public acclaim, and a popular standing equivalent to that held by Amy Johnson in Britain. By 1940, almost one-third of all pilots trained in the Soviet Union were women.

Following Operation *Barbarossa*, Raskova was flooded with countless letters from Soviet women seeking to contribute to the war effort by learning to fly so as to combat the enemy in air. After being initially rebuffed, Raskova persuaded Stalin to permit the formation of women's air units. There was to be no distinction between the women's and the men's unit, with equipment, training and operational postings being allocated in the same way as the male units.

The 122nd Composite Air Group was initially formed, out of which three Air Regiments were subsequently developed. One of these, the 586th

Fighter Regiment, had become operational by April 1942, and was to play a significant role in the defence of Stalingrad. In addition to these all female regiments, women pilots were seconded for combat service to male fighter regiments – eight were attached for service with the 73rd Fighter Regiment, two of whom, Lilya Litvyak and Katya Budanova, were to achieve a significant number of aerial victories.

No Soviet woman fighter pilot received the HSU during the war, however, although women aircrew in all-woman bomber regiments received 28 HSU awards. Nevertheless, Lily Litvyak (who, like Budanova, was to lose her life in the conflict) was belatedly awarded a posthumous HSU in 1990. Women pilots, and other aircrew, served both on bomber operations and as liaison pilots to the partisans. Ironically, Marina Raskova never made it into combat, being killed when piloting a Pe-2 dive-bomber on her way to the front to take assume command of the 587th Dive-Bomber Regiment.

Women fighter pilots faced an especially difficult task, as the high publicity they generated by the Soviet propaganda machine failed to impress their male counterparts. The record of Soviet women fighter pilots, however, speaks volumes for their bravery and skill. Employed on largely defensive operations, the pilots of 586th Fighter Regiment flew 4,419 combat missions and achieved an aerial victory rate of 38 enemy aircraft in 125 aerial combats. The regiment's primary task was to protect targets from attack by the Luftwaffe in the Stalingrad area. They were only to engage the enemy in order to defend the target, and were not to pursue aircraft after they had left the vicinity of the target. Interviewed by former American WASP pilot Anna Noggle in 1994, Yekaterina Polunina (the regiment's archivist) also gave an indication of the courage of the women pilots assigned to male fighter squadrons when she stated:

Some eight crews from our regiment were assigned to two male fighter squadrons on the Stalingrad front, and they flew in pairs with male pilots as their wingmen because they did not have as much experience.

The wingman's duty was to protect the tail of the lead fighter pilot. When one of the girls – Nechayeva – was protecting the squadron commander who was about to land, three German Me 109s attacked them. She had no fuel or ammunition, but she covered his aircraft with hers, and everyone there saw her killed. Budanova – another of our pilots sent to the male squadron – perished in July 1943, but not before she had shot down over 20 German aircraft, and Lilya Litvyak, who was also an ace, died in August 1943. Five of the eight pilots came back to our regiment.

Our pilots would dive as much as seven kilometres in a dogfight, and their blood vessels

Capt Naidenko (centre) gives instructions to Russian pilots. In the background is an American-constructed Tomahawk Mk IIB. Some 2,097 P-40s were supplied by the USA to the Soviet Union. (via Russian Aviation Research Trust)

were damaged.

AWARDS AND DECORATIONS

Personal Awards
Bestowed for the first time on 20 April 1934, the highest order of honour in the Soviet Union, the Gold Star of the Hero of the Soviet Union (*Geroi Sovietskogo Soyuza – GSS*) had been awarded to no fewer than 181 pilots by the commencement of Operation *Barbarossa* on 22 June 1941 – receipt of the HSU automatically brought with it the Order of Lenin. From this date until the end of the war, 895 fighter pilots received the award, its relationship with fighter aces being formalized by the People's Commissariat of Defence in August 1941 when it was ordained that the HSU would be automatically awarded after the scoring of ten victories. Clearly, differing criteria were levied against other arms of the Soviet Air Force, and the award of the HSU was made for widely-varied reasons, few of which seemed to be consistently applied.

Towards the end of the war the ruling for the award of the HSU could deviate. For the ground attack *Shturmovik* pilots, it would depend upon the number of operations they flew. Memories from the war remain fresh in Russia even half a century later, and in the early part of 1990 the HSU was posthumously awarded to a 25-year-old woman pilot of a Su-2 attack aircraft[3] which rammed and downed a Bf 109. Some 26 fighter pilots were to receive the HSU twice, whilst two pilots, Kozhedub and Pokryshkin, each received the award on three occasions. Those fighter pilots fortunate to receive the HSU would have the five-pointed gold star painted on the tail of their aircraft. Double HSUs were honoured with a statue in their home village, town or city. For several decades after receiving the HSU, the recipient could expect to be rewarded with free flats, free petrol and other privileges.

Unit Awards
Certain individual units within the Soviet Air Force received honorary titles, the most prestigious of which was the designation 'Guards', which was ascribed to units having displayed particularly meritorious service. Many fighter units of the VVS received this title, resulting in a change of unit number, prefixed by the title 'Guards' – this honorary sobriquet was first applied in December 1941. Members of these air units were permitted to wear 'Guards' insignia on their uniforms, and they were also allocated a special banner. By August 1945, 288 air units had been ascribed this elite status.

Pilot Profiles
Yak-1 Pilot – Lily Litvyak
By the end of her brief life, Lilya Litvyak was to become one of the great figures in the history of Soviet military aviation. Litvyak's mother was a shop worker and her father was employed on the state railway system. Neither were told by their teenage daughter that she was taking flying lessons at the tender age of 16. Litvyzak reputedly first went solo after only four hours of dual instruction on the Po-2 biplane trainer, and following graduation became an instructor. She then joined the 586th Fighter Regiment (Air Defence) as one of its founder members, the all-women fighter unit being employed in the defence of major targets for the Luftwaffe. As such, the Russian pilots were not permitted to pursue enemy aircraft once they had turned for home following their attack.

In September 1942, Litvyak, along with seven other women pilots and their ground crews, were temporarily assigned to two 'free-fighting', all-male, regiments during the Battle of Stalingrad. The term 'free-fighters' was applied to these pilots for they had the specific task of actively seeking out and engaging the enemy. Litvyak and her colleague Budanova achieved several combat victories whilst flying with the male regiments, and both were to be killed in action during the summer of 1943. The former gained 12 confirmed personal and 2 shared victories, but was downed when she attempted to crash-land her stricken Yak-1 – Litvyak was buried where she fell, beneath the wing of her aircraft. When the aeroplane was later dismantled and removed, it was not realized that her remains still lay beneath the ground. Only many years later, and after considerable effort, was the body found and recovered for official burial in 1989. Lily Litvyak was posthumously awarded the Gold Star and the HSU by then President, Mikhail Gorbachev, in May 1990, although a monument had been erected to her memory at Krasy Luch, in the Donetsk region, many years previously.

Spitfires of various marks were also supplied in large numbers to the Soviet Union. Here, a No. 1 Aircraft Depot, Leningrad, two-seat Spitfire IX conversion is surrounded by a group of pilots under training. (via Russian Aviation Research Trust)

LaGG-3 Pilot – Vladimir Orekhov

Vladimir Orekhov joined the Red Banner Flying School at Kacha in January 1939 – he was just 18 years old. By March 1940 he had graduated, receiving a posting to the Ukraine, whereupon he continued to fly a variety of training aircraft before completing a further 75 hours in the I-16. His personal aircraft ('33') was destroyed on the first day of the war, and for the next ten days, Orekhov and his fellow pilots tried to fly whatever machines were available, but such were the losses of equipment that those without allocated aircraft were sent to the reserve air regiment to collect new fighters.

It was at this time that Orekhov was posted to the newly-formed 434 IAP, whose two squadrons were equipped with the LaGG-3, which was fitted with ShKAS and ShVAK guns. Orekhov achieved some success with the LaGG, his first combat victory being over a Bf 109E which he pounced upon when taking off from Lyuban

aerodrome – he went on to score a further three personal kills and one shared claim with this aircraft. By October 1941 Orekhov had been promoted to the rank of lieutenant, and made a flight commander. On New Year's Day, 1942, he was decorated with the Order of the Red Banner. In the spring of 1942 the squadron changed their LaGG-3s for Yak-1s, which were duly replaced in September by Yak-7Bs. Flying Yak-1s, -7Bs and finally -9s, Orekhov destroyed a further seven aircraft.

In July 1942 he was severely injured in combat when he was hit in the left arm and left leg by a burst from an enemy aircraft. In November 1942, 434 IAP became one of three squadrons of 32 GIAP (Guards Fighter Regiment), a reflection of the considerable success it had achieved during the battles of Kharkov and Stalingrad. 32 GIAP was considered to be an elite fighter regiment, commanded by Ivan Kleshchev, who had already been awarded with the HSU – the unit moved to

Photo-reconnaissance equipment as fitted to a small number of Spitfires used on the Eastern Front by Soviet air forces. (via Russian Research Trust)

marked with a '3'. Vladimir Orekhov was made a HSU in May 1943, by which time he had achieved 11 personal kills and 1 shared.

By the end of the war, he had gained 19 personal victories, two shared claims, four enemy aircraft destroyed on the ground and the destruction of two balloons – Orekhov had also attained the rank of major. In the postwar years, Vladimir Orekhov continued to serve in the Soviet Air Force as a specialist in navigation, and by the time of his retirement and transfer to the reserve, he had become the Chief Navigation Officer of 1 GIAK of the Western Group of the Soviet Forces. He today lives in Minsk.

Yak-3 Pilot – Aleksandr I. Koldunov

In 1943, at the age of 20, Aleksandr I. Koldunov qualified as a pilot from the Kacha Air Force Pilots' School and joined the Reserve Air Regiment. His operational career started in April 1944, flying the Yak-1 in the 17th Air Army on the 3rd Ukrainian Front. By August 1944, Koldunov had become the first pilot of his regiment to fly the Yak-3, a type in which he was

the Kalinin frontline sector soon after its formation.

In March 1943, 32 GIAP converted onto La-5FN fighters, Orekhov flying numbers '93' and '23' over the next 15 months, before re-equipping with the La-7 – he again flew an aircraft adorned with the number '23', as he was superstitious and always sought to fly a machine to achieve considerable success. Although Koldunov flew a total of 358 operational sorties by the end of the war, he engaged the enemy on only 96 occasions, during which he destroyed 46 personal victories. Koldunov was a double holder of the HSU, the being first awarded on 2 August 1944 whilst he was serving as a squadron leader with the 866th Fighter Regiment, and the second on 23 February 1948, again as a squadron leader with the same regiment.

In postwar years Koldunov was to obtain high Air Rank, before suffering a disastrous, and humiliating, end to his career. After graduating firstly from the Air Force Academy in 1952 and then the General Staff Academy in 1960, Koldunov rose through the ranks to become the Commander in Chief of the Air Defence Command in 1978, followed by his appointment as Deputy Defence Minister. He was promoted yet again to the position of Chief Air Marshal in 1984, but Aleksandr Koldunov became the very public, and political, casualty of the daring May 1987 flight by 19-year-old Mathias Rust from Helsinki to Red Square, Moscow, in a Cessna 172. Despite having detected the German pilot early on in his unauthorized flight, Soviet Air Force authorities failed to act, and Koldunov was duly dismissed because of it.

La-5 Pilot – Kirill A. Yevstigeyev
Kirill A. Yevstigeyev was born in 1917 in the village of Khokhly, Kurgan obl, and was employed as a lathe operator at an aircraft repair base prior to learning to fly as a young Komsomal at Chelyabinsk Aeroclub and the Biisk Air Force Pilots' School. Yevstigeyev joined the 240th Fighter Regiment in 1943, and was shot down and wounded during the Battle of Kursk. He subsequently returned to operations and achieved a formidable combat record as a La-5 pilot, completing over 300 operational sorties, during which he gained 53 personal

victories and 3 shared. During five days in June 1945 he shot down eight enemy aircraft, including three Bf 109s, three Fw 190s, one Ju 87 and one Hs 129.

In postwar years, Yevstigeyev made military aviation his career, and by 1984 he had become a major-general of Aviation. He was awarded the HSU on two occasions, the first whilst serving as a senior lieutenant/squadron leader in the 240th Fighter Regiment, and the second as a captain/squadron leader in the 178th Guards Fighter Regiment.

Footnotes
1. Grigori A. Rechkalov became the second-highest scoring Soviet 'ace' of the Second World War, meeting the enemy in combat on 122 occasions, gaining 56 personal and 5 shared kills, most of which were made with the lend-lease P-39N. Awarded the HSU in 1943, and then again a year later, Rechkalov had by then become the Deputy Commander of the 16th Guards Fighter Regiment.
2. Several biographers in the west have conveyed that leading Luftwaffe pilots were given 'nicknames' by Soviet pilots. Thus, Hartmann is reputed to have been known as the 'Black Devil of the Ukraine' and Johannes Wiese (with 133 victories), the 'Kuban Lion'. In reality, it is unlikely that the Soviet Air Force had, a) the ability to identify when these 'aces' were flying and, b) the inclination to do so as the animosity felt towards the Germans was such that it would have been extremely unlikely that Luftwaffe fighter pilots would be ascribed such romantic names by their Soviet counterparts.
3. The Su-2 was a short-range ground attack aircraft of sluggish performance, and was subsequently replaced by the Il-2 *Shturmovik* as the standard ground attack machine.

Chapter Three

United States Army Air Force

If I understand our greatest aces of the Second World War, their sole purpose was to destroy as many enemy aircraft as they could. They weren't carrying the extra baggage of worrying about encounter reports, victory symbols on their airplane, confirmation reports, or gun cameras . . . they were intent on the job of destroying enemy aircraft in the air or on the ground. You just can't be thinking about such things when you are over enemy territory . . . you are dead meat if you dwell on it. The whole system of victory confirmations is of no significance until you get back to your home airfield, and even then it is not top priority. Sure you want a victory awarded, but you take what the Air Force gives you. Its simple. No big deal. Just go out and do it, come back and report it.

Bob Strobell, P-47 pilot

Introduction

Much has been written about USAAF fighter aces, the process of comprehensive, retro-spective, analysis of their claims beginning in the late 1950s. In this account, a former fighter pilot vividly describes what it was like to prepare and take part in a combat mission, whilst the task of the squadron IO in the process of claim submission is also detailed. However, the chapter is unusual in that it also explores areas not normally reported in accounts of the top scoring

pilots, looking especially at the training of fighter pilots and the role of the squadron flight surgeon in observing and recording the effects of combat stress amongst fighter pilots. Finally, the systems of awards and decorations to USAAF fighter pilots is detailed, with specific reference to the guidelines issued by the USAAF during the war.

USAAF theatres of operations

The USAAF operated in many theatres of operation during the worldwide conflict, including the south-west Pacific, central Pacific, north-western Europe, the Mediterranean, China-Burma-India, Alaska, and Iceland. Most pilots who subsequently achieved ace status were volunteers, impressed into service as part of the massive aircrew training programme instigated upon America's declaration of war in December 1941. Once in the frontline, the fighter pilots would discover that the various USAAF commands operated their own Victory Credit Boards (VCBs), which governed the criteria by which claims were assessed and victory credits allocated.

The first American ace of the war was Lt Boyd 'Buzz' Wagner, who had downed the prerequisite five kills within nine days of Pearl Harbor being bombed during the doomed defence of the

Philippines – Wagner, who scored a further three victories before rotating back to the US, was killed in a training accident in Florida in November 1942. The Pacific theatre was also the stomping ground of the two highest scoring US pilots of the Second World War in the form of Richard 'Dick' Bong and Thomas McGuire, Jr. Sadly, neither of these P-38 pilots survived the war either, although only McGuire was actually killed in action.

The 23rd Fighter Group (FG), which took over from the legendary 'Flying Tigers' – officially known as the American Volunteer Group – in China became the key outfit involved in aerial combat in the China-Burma-India theatre. The unit's first two commanding officers, Col R. L. Scott, Jr, followed by Lt Col B. K. Holloway, eventually became two of the highest scoring pilots in the Fourteenth Air Force. The latter became a general after the war, retiring from the USAF in 1972, whilst Scott parted company with the Air Force in 1967, having attained the rank of brigadier general.

Capt John Voll of the 308th FS/31st FG became the top scoring USAF pilot of the North African and Mediterranean campaigns, his 21 kills coming from combat over areas as diverse as Romania, Hungary, Bratislava and southern Italy. Voll's tally included an incredible four victories, two probables and two damaged in a fifteen-minute spell on the morning of 16 November 1944 near the Italian airfield at Aviano.

The first aerial victory achieved by a fighter pilot of the USAAF in Europe occurred on 14 August 1942 when a Fw 200 Condor convoy raider was reported as having been damaged during an attack by P-38s flown by Lt Elza Shahan of the 27th FS/1st FG and Lt Joseph Shaffer of the 33 FS, the latter unit being part of the Iceland Base Command – Shahan's squadron was actually staging through Iceland on its way to Britain as part of the Eighth AAF build-up. Seventeen days after the encounter, the wreckage of the Condor was found, and the credit was duly shared between the two pilots, and their respective commands.

The three fighter wings of the Eighth were eventually credited with the destruction no less than 9,275 enemy aircraft during the conflict in Europe. These claims were assessed by VCBs

The front page of The Pensacola News-Journal *on the afternoon of Sunday, 7 December 1941, just hours after the Japanese attack on Pearl Harbor. RAF aircrew were training at Pensacola on the day of the attack, the USNAS base in north-western Florida being the location of a large training facility throughout the Second World War. Basic and advanced training facilities were provided for cadet pilots, with, many, but not all, graduating into Coastal Command* (via British Pensacola Veterans Association)

(the formal reviewing authority for claim submissions), which consisted of experienced combat pilots. Notable aces within the Eighth included G. E. Preddy, Jnr, with 26 personal victories, J. C. Meyer with 24, D. S. Gentile with 21, R. A. Peterson with 15, and J. H. Powers with 14. In postwar years Meyer was promoted to general, and was to subsequently achieve a further two victory credits in F-86As over Korea. Other Eighth AF aces of note include great fighter leaders like Hubert Zemke, Francis S. Gabreski, David C. Schilling, and Robert S. Johnson, who became the first ETO pilot to beat Eddie Rickenbacker's First World War score of 19 enemy aircraft personally destroyed, three shared and four balloons downed over the final six months of the war.

The Vultee BT-13A Valiant was the standard basic trainer of both the USAAF and RAF in America – particularly during the 1941-43 period. The aircraft was aptly christened the 'Vultee Vibrator', being powered by a Pratt & Whitney R-985-AN-1 engine that gave it a maximum speed of 180 mph and service ceiling of 21,650 ft. Over 11,000 of the type were manufactured. From 1943 until war's end, basic training for USAAF pilots was generally phased out, replaced instead by a two-stage course which saw pilots move directly from primary training on Boeing PT-17 Stearmans to AT-6s for advanced training.

Yet prior to America's declaration of war, US nationals flying with the RAF's 'Eagle' Squadrons had already made a real impact in operational combat against the Luftwaffe. G. A. 'Gus' Daymond had scored seven confirmed victories on the Hurricane and Spitfire VB whilst flying with 71 'Eagle' Squadron, and he later went on to command the 334th FS when the RAF units were absorbed in to the Eighth AAF in late 1942. D. S. 'Don' Gentile had attained two victories with the Spitfire Vb as part of 133 'Eagle' Squadron, before going on to score heavily with the 336th FS.

It is also important not to overlook the contribution made by American flyers who remained with the RAF to war's end, or pilots who became US nationals later in the war so as to allow them to fly with the USAAF. Texan Lance Wade flew all of his operational sorties with the RAF in the North African campaign, where he had achieved 23 victories, prior to his death in January 1944 in southern Italy. Polish-born Witold Urbanowicz, who had scored heavily with the RAF's 145 and 303 Squadron RAF before becoming Assistant Air Attaché at the Polish Embassy in Washington D.C. in late 1942, managed to wangle his way out to the Fourteenth AF in China on attachment, and whilst in-theatre claimed two Zeros shot down flying a P-40 with the 75th FS. Upon his return to America he took out US citizenship.

Lists of victory credits

Like many other air forces involved in the Second World War, the USAAF compiled no single list of victory credits either during, or immediately following, the end of the conflict. Indeed, there were no uniform rules governing the awards of credits in the various theatres and air forces, which resulted in a significant variation in the authentication of victory credits. In 1957, the Historical Division of the Department of the Air Force was handed the task of retrospectively verifying aerial combat claims by analysis and evaluation of the historical data that had survived.

'Project Ace' commenced in May 1959 with the aim of producing a preliminary list of fighter 'aces' from 1917 through to 1953. In January 1962 the list was published, edited by Dr Maurer Maurer of the AFHRA, as *USAF Historical Study No 73*. A summary of the extent of those records that do exist, and those that are missing, is given in the introduction to *USAF Historical Study No 85* (1978). Other detailed studies included *USAF Historical Study No. 133 – USAF Air Service Victory Credits, World War 1*, published in 1969, which looked at the claims and victory credits of the US Air Service solely in the First World War, and *USAF Historical Study No. 81 – USAF Credits For The Destruction Of Enemy Aircraft in Korea*, published in 1975. In 1970, the USAF Office of Internal Information Division published an information document Air Forces Aces. Since then, other published works have contributed to the increasing knowledge of the USAAF's fighter claims, filling gaps in the literature.

Psychological insights into combat stress

The observation of the psychological impact of combat on aircrew operating in the USAAF during the Second World War appears to have been given a high priority at the time, and a rich body of relevant literature survives. It is apparent that a flight surgeon would normally be attached to a fighter squadron, and was encouraged to record his observations of the effect of combat upon the aircrew under his watchful gaze. His task was to observe, record, treat and refer those requiring clinical attention away from the base. Many of the subsequent reports were compiled into USAAF Surgeon General publications and distributed throughout the command for the attention of fellow flight surgeons.

The accounts given later in this chapter give a taste of the way in which the USAAF sought to describe, measure and treat combat stress in differing theatres. The initial study on the Eighth AAF was completed on the anniversary of its first full year in Britain, the second and third reports focused on the Tunisian campaign in North Africa from January through to May 1943, and the fourth covered the tropical combat zone of the New Guinea campaign from July to November 1942. A general conclusion that can be drawn is that the ability of individual pilots to control themselves under conditions of utmost stress marked them as stable flyers, and such individuals were usually able to psychologically absorb the strain of aerial combat longer than others.

Training

Fifty years have made a considerable difference to the duration of training required to enable a pilot to reach a combat unit. Today, hundreds of flying hours (plus many more in the flight simulator) are

Upon graduation from the vast USAAF flying cadet training programme, newly-qualified aircrew would receive an individual copy of the pictorial review of the station, which would inevitably feature class photographs.

THIS COPY OF THE

HISTORICAL AND PICTORIAL
REVIEW

GUNTER FIELD

SOUTHEAST ARMY AIR FORCES
TRAINING CENTER

of the

UNITED STATES ARMY AIR FORCES

IS PRESENTED

To

By

1942

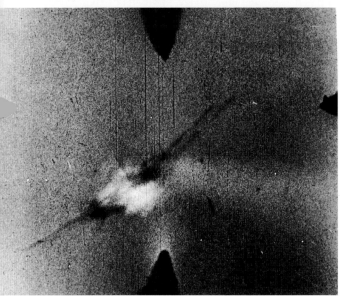

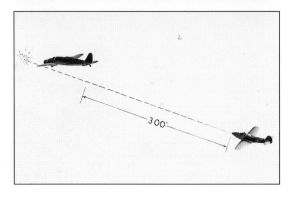

Gun camera action from the war in the Pacific. This sequence of photographs came from the gun camera of a P-39 Airacobra in New Guinea in the winter of 1943, and was used for the gunnery training of USAAF fighter pilots (bottom). The original caption accompanying the sequence read:

'Good Shooting' – A Jap 'Lily' at unusually close range is a perfect Bell P-39 target. Notice that the firing tab is visible. Results of this shooting are shown in the next picture of the Jap plane in flames, and the action is duplicated with models at the right. The four points at the side of every gun camera are for reference in gun camera harmonization.

(via NASM 26808 AC)

required before a pilot is considered to be prepared for a combat unit. During the Second World War the situation was very different, and American pilots reached frontline squadrons often after having gained less than 200 hours in the cockpit as a cadet pilot. Despite this paucity of flying time, USAAF cadets still had to manoeuvre their way though the massive, and challenging, pilot training programme, its demanding curriculum being infamous for its high 'wash out' (elimination) rate. For example, only three out of every five who started pilot training (as opposed to being selected for other aircrew duties) succeeded in receiving their wings at the end of the training. The much-hated Honor Code system, embodied in the practice of 'hazing', led to many potential pilots failing for disciplinary, rather than flying, reasons.

Surprisingly, a 'wash-out' on the USAAF aviation cadet programme did not necessarily mean that the cadet would fail to become a successful fighter pilot. Mistakes were clearly made by the Air Force, and of the 124,000 cadets who failed to succeed, there were many examples of those who subsequently trained as pilots with other Allied air arms, eventually becoming renowned in combat. This illustrious list includes Don S. Gentile, with 21 confirmed victories and John T. Godfrey, who flew as Gentile's wing man and scored 12 confirmed victories – unlike the RAF-trained Gentile, Godfrey found a suitable tuition in the RCAF. Chesley Peterson was 'washed-out' of the aviation cadet programme at basic training stage due to a 'lack of flying ability', yet after training with the Canadians, he achieved considerable success as a fighter pilot with both the RAF and,

'Good Shooting' – a Jap 'Lily' heads smack into the path of the bullets, although somewhat protected by the range. Despite the distance, the Bell P-39 scores a spectacular bull's eye. In the corresponding model (bottom), the Bell P-39 makes a dive at an 80° angle and aims slightly ahead in order to rip open the enemy plane's belly – a reverse of hari-kari'. (via NASM 26809 AC)

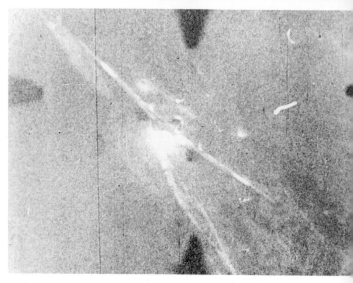

later, the USAAF. He was highly decorated by both, and eventually retired from the USAF as a major-general in 1970.

Following graduation after completing around 200 flying hours, the fighter pilot transitioned to an operational unit by way of the OTU-RTU training pattern. The American OTU system was founded upon their successful RAF counterparts, which had already been in operation for some time. Between December 1942 and August 1945, over 35,000 day fighter pilots were trained in the USAAF's OTU system, as opposed to only 485 nightfighter crews.

The OTU programme for fighter pilots had gradually evolved from its inception roughly a year after America's entry into the conflict, and by 1943 the trainee fighter pilot could expect to undertake simulated individual combat, instrument flying, and navigation exercises, focusing on high altitude operations, as part of the course. Pilots were also encouraged to develop combat vigilance and aggressiveness in the implementation of offensive and defensive tactics against air and surface threats. Considerable efforts were also made to enable the pilot to attain higher levels of proficiency during take-off, wing assembly, formation flying, and precision landings.

As unescorted bomber operations became increasingly vulnerable to attack, so training also focused on fighter-bomber co-operation. During the three years from 1942-45, a fighter pilot could expect to fly 40 hours at OTU in 1942, 60-80 hours by the end of 1943, and in late 1944 close to 100 hours. As the war progressed, fighter OTUs began to specialize in training for low-level offensive operations, or for long-range escort.

Filing of Claims

Bob Strobell, who flew P-47s with the 351st FS/353 FG, stationed at Metfield, Suffolk, in 1944, takes us vividly through a mission, and the subsequent claim that arose from it:

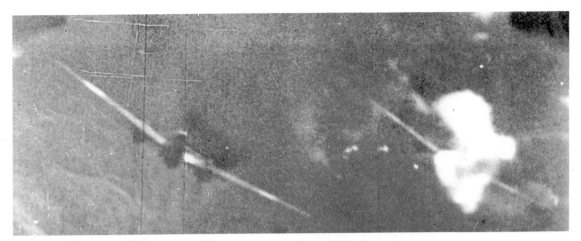

In this sequence of gun camera film, a P-39 attacks two Japanese aircraft on a sortie dated 15 August 1943. In the top photo the leading 'Lily' is hit by gun fire from the American fighter. In the middle picture, the second and nearest bombers are hit whilst the third falls away, mortally hit, and in the third photograph the second 'Lily' catches fire and, like his colleague, has no hope of survival. It is difficult to identify the individual USAAF pilot making this claim, although it is clear that all the kills made by P-39s on this day were by pilots of the 40th and 41st FSs, operating in the areas of Tsili Tsili and Marilinan. Fourteen confirmed claims were filed to P-39s on this day in the area. (via NASM 26815 AC)

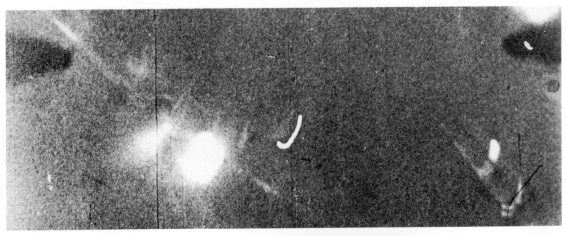

A typical mission usually starts with someone stomping into the Nissan hut and waking all those scheduled to fly that day. Most of the time the early morning call was in the dark. Off to the ready room and mess hall for a hot cross bun or breakfast, followed by a briefing in the briefing room. Here, the type of flight we were to make ('Ramrod', 'Sweep', 'Dive-Bomb', 'Circus', etc.) was detailed, and an explanation given as to where we were expected to fly, which included the compass headings to steer, weather en route, known flak sites, and any potential fighter opposition likely to be encountered. Time left to engine start and take-off was given at the end of the brief. Then to the latrine, grab a 'chute, hop on a jeep, or recon car, and be hauled out to your airplane (the one posted for your use in the ready room).

You know who you are flying with that day, and you know your position in the flight, with leader, wing name, element leader or 'tail-end Charlie'. The control tower either talks to you on the radio or fires a coloured flare, which means that you are to start engines, then you taxi out and enter the line of taxiing planes at your assigned position in the flight and stop short of the runway on the taxi strip. Check the mags and back it down to idle. Another flare goes up and the whole squadron takes off. Once off the ground you stay with your leader on his wing, or you lead the flight in a gradual turn that permits the other ships to catch up with you and take up position. When the group is assembled and the appointed minute arrives, all turn towards Europe, and you are off across the Channel, bound for enemy territory.

On this particular mission, 9 July 1944, I was flying 'Lawyer Red Two' as the wing man for the flight – Capt Frank Emory[1] was leading. We were on an area support mission deep in France, south of the beachheads at Cherbourg. We ran into a gaggle of enemy fighters and all hell broke loose. I stayed with Capt Emory right up to the time I saw Lt Tumlin diving away with a Bf 109 right on his tail. Tumlin was calling for help, unable to shake the enemy fighter. I waited for some reaction from Capt Emory but saw none and, after a few seconds more, I broke radio silence and told him I was going down after Tumlin. I split and drove on the Bf 109, fired a burst into it and watched it lose power and start into a glide earthward. Tumlin came around and followed it down with me and we saw it crash. He confirmed the crash.

At this time we were separated from the flight,

squadron, and group, with aircraft all over the skies, as other units came in to enjoy the party. We headed back home at the appointed hour and saw no other action either on the ground or in the air. Landed, relieved ourselves in the revetments, jumped in a jeep, went to the ready room, and filed an encounter report. We then went to the debriefing meeting with the Intelligence Officer, which usually lasted a few minutes, then off to the mess hall for a bite to eat. In the meantime the ground crew were removing the gun camera film from the airplane to be developed.

The Encounter Report
In the Eighth AAF it appears that a fighter pilot made a claim at group level by filing an encounter report on his return from combat. The rule was that a pilot must make an encounter

This Japanese Zero failed to gain sufficient height and speed after take-off and paid the ultimate price when hit by a USAAF fighter on a low-level strafing mission – date unknown. (via NASM 65375 AC)

report detailing a claim for an enemy aircraft as soon as was physically possible on return from a mission or, even if much later, he returned from a PoW camp.

The encounter report was then assessed at fighter wing headquarters and, if there was still doubt, at Fighter Command headquarters. In the autumn of 1944, VIII Fighter Command was replaced by the Eighth AAF's VCB[2].

Fred H. Lefebre of the 351st FS in 1944 recalled:

Fighter Command required a written report of any encounter resulting in a combat claim to substantiate the potential victory. Furthermore, the claim had to be substantiated additionally by an eyewitness, or by gun camera film. I recall no specific instruction with regard to the formulation of the written report. We just gave a narrative of what happened in our own words, gave it to the squadron Intelligence Officer, who passed it up the chain of Command, presumably along with his intelligence report of the mission.

Bob Strobell can confirm this as he was also flying with the 351st FS at the same time:

Part of flying a combat mission was the debriefing with the Intelligence Officer. We were required to file an encounter report when we engaged the enemy. There may have been a claim form, but I don't recall seeing one, meaning that I simply don't remember it. If you fired on an enemy aircraft it was considered an encounter, and you filed an encounter report. That report, along with gun camera film, and witnesses confirming reports, were all taken into consideration for your claim of a victory.

I never felt discouraged about filing an encounter report, and I was never limited by anything, or anyone, as to how much information, or how little, was included in it. I don't recall any pilot making an extravagant report. If it was done, it would have to cover an action that the pilot, himself alone, without witnesses, had concocted. My guess is that such a report would be dismissed out of hand. I don't know of any pilots that flew for the sole purpose of developing their personal, on the record, kill successes.

Claims made on behalf of other pilots
Within the Eighth AAF, claims could be filed by witnesses on behalf of pilots who did not return.

FIGURE 1 – Example of Encounter Report (Claim Later Confirmed)

Eighth AAF
1944

A Combat
B 22 December 1943
C 351st Fighter Squadron
D 13.43 hours
E Heerde Area (approximate because of overcast)
F Complete Overcast
G Me 109
H One Me 109 destroyed

I. I was leading 'Roughman Blue Flight'. At 29,000 ft 10+ Me 109s approached head on and passed to our right. I turned right back into them. They broke, but the first two pulled back up to the left. I closed to about 300 yards behind the second one and gave him a short burst from about 15 degrees astern. He snapped violently to the right as I saw strikes on left wing. I gave another short burst as he rolled to the inverted position, and saw many strikes on left wing root and fuselage and engine cowling. An instant later he burst into flames and trailed smoke as he disappeared into clouds. I saw no parachute. When I last saw the ship it appeared to be out of control.

Frederick H. Lefebre
Captain, Air Corps.

FIGURE 2 – Examples of Criteria for Claims

The USAAF had three main categories of claim:

A Destroyed – aircraft was observed to have been completely destroyed, or the pilot was observed to have bailed out.
B Probably destroyed – badly damaged aircraft, not expected to make it back to base.
C Damaged – Impacts observed but aircraft managed to get away.

Whilst this system was adopted by most USAAF air forces, inconsistencies did creep in as the war progressed – for example, the Ninth AAF introduced the concept of unconfirmed claims which appeared to have the same status as confirmed scores, even when it came to awarding decorations. So, the Ninth's VCB considered claims on the basis of unconfirmed destroyed, probably destroyed, and damaged. For example, comparisons can be made of two commands, one bombardment and the other fighter, in differing theatres of operations, namely the 2nd Bombardment Division and the US Army Air Forces operating in south-east Asia. It is clear from this example that the criteria for claims against enemy aircraft were more stringently (and obviously more frequently) applied to fighter command than to bomber forces, where defensive fire might damage or even bring down an enemy.

According to the 2nd Bombardment Division instructions (no's 55–5), dated 29 May 1944, pilots seeking to make a claim submitted encounter forms in triplicate to the Commanding General, 2nd Bombardment Division, Attention A-2 – the Assistant Chief of Staff of the relevant Air Unit. The submitted claim was then forwarded by courier so that they would reach the 2nd Bombardment Division Head-quarters by 12.00 hours the following day.

USSTAF Regulations No 80–6, clause 71, dated 8 May 1944, defined claims as follows:

a *Aircraft shall be considered destroyed when:*
1 Seen to crash.
2 Seen to disintegrate in the air or be enveloped in flames.
3 Seen to descend on friendly territory and be captured.
4 Pilot and entire crew seen to bail out.

b *Aircraft not in flight shall be considered destroyed when:*

1 Seen by photograph to have been blown apart or burned out.
2 Seen by strike photo to have been within unobserved lethal radius of a fragmentation bomb.
3 Seen to sink in deep water.
4 Known to have been aboard a carrier or other ship at time of confirmed sinking.

c *Aircraft shall be considered probably destroyed when:*
1 While in flight the enemy airplane is seen to break off combat under circumstances which lead to the conclusion that it must be lost, although it is not seen to crash.
2 So damaged by bombing or strafing as to require repair before becoming operational.

Whereas the February 1944 instructions issued to fighter pilots in the south-east Asia theatre offered additional specific definitions to aid in the submission of claims:

a *Enemy aircraft destroyed when:*
1 The aircraft is seen to crash into the ground or sea, or
2 It is seen to explode in the air or to be on fire all over and obviously out of control, or
3 The pilot (of a single-seater) is seen to bale out, or
4 Vital control or lifting surfaces, e.g. wing or complete tail unit, are seen to drop off, or
5 It collides and remains locked with another aircraft, or
6 An enemy aircraft is captured as result of a combat.

b *Probably destroyed when:*
1 The aircraft is seen to be on fire and losing height rapidly with engine(s) out of action, or
2 It is seen to be diving at such a great angle or speed that a successful pull-out appears improbable, or
3 On the ground it receives a near miss from a bomb or is set on fire by machine gun or cannon strikes.

c *Damaged when:*
1 Machine gun or cannon strikes are definitely seen, or
2 Small bits fly off the aircraft, or
3 Small fires are started in the aircraft, or
4 On the ground, bomb splinters are seen to strike.

For example, an encounter report was completed by Capt Frank N. Emory, who was flying a P-51 with the 351st FS on 16 April 1945 in an attack on the aerodrome at Reichersberg. He submitted the following comments:

I was leading 'Lawyer Red Flight' during an attack on Reichersberg A/D. On my next to last pass, I had just pulled up in a left turn through the smoke, when I saw one of our P-51s – later decided it to be Lt Risk – skidding along the ground on its back, and breaking up fast. The engine and parts of the fuselage went through a small clump of trees and clobbered a Fw 190 that was parked there beyond the trees, and the whole mess burned.

In fact, the claim was not confirmed. Just over one month beforehand, Lt Edward J Risk had gained his only combat victory on 14 March 1945.

The Eighth AAF, unlike many other USAAF commands, but following the example of the earlier American Volunteer Force, included ground claims as valid, therefore contributing towards a pilot's personal score.

Gun Camera

Gun cameras were essentially electrically-operated motion picture cameras, which were set up to produce visual records of aerial combat (as well as to record the results of gunnery training). The gun cameras used by the USAAF were manufactured and supplied by the Fairchild Camera and Instrument Corporation of Jamaica, New York. Fairchild produced varying types of gun camera including the N-6, AN-6N, N-9, and KB-3. The gun camera, officially known as the Gun Sight Aiming Point Camera, was initially manufactured to take a Type A-6 magazine of 16 mm film. Black and white stock was used until Gen 'Hap' Arnold reputedly learned that the US Navy was using colour, so the USAAF rapidly made the switch also!

The cameras had an overrun control, which automatically kept them operating for a period after the trigger control switch had been released.

FIGURE 3 – Gun Camera Film Evaluation Form 460, 1944

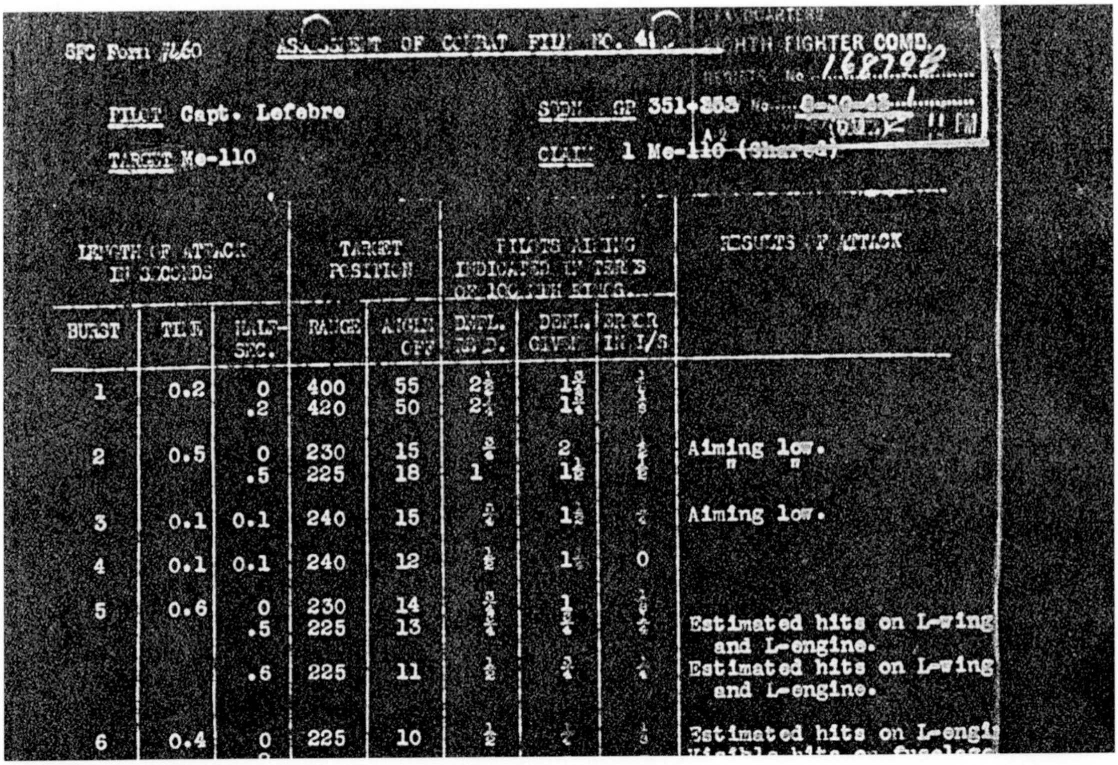

The Zero was the most feared of the Japanese fighter aircraft. It could, and did, cause havoc amongst the USAAF medium and heavier bomber forces and, as a result, the Americans made many attempts to destroy these fighters on their own airfields. This photograph was taken in late 1942 over the Japanese airfield at Lae, in New Guinea, at a height of just 100 ft. It shows a Douglas A-20 Havoc attack bomber skimming along a road as it makes a strafing attack on Japanese aircraft, which include a totally exposed 'Betty' bomber. Zeros can be seen on the right under a tree, on the upper right at the edge of the clearing and near the house at the centre, top. (via NASM 3088 AC)

This had the advantage of causing the portion of the film exposed during the period of overrun to be marked for identification. Exposure speeds on the N-6 and AN-6N could be set at 16, 32 or 64 exposures per second. Each unit did their own evaluation of the combat film, with the better clips being forwarded to higher HQ for disposition. The sequence for the evaluation of the film appears to have been as follows:

1) film processed
2) written report listing the angle, distance of each burst
3) identifying any observable results, and where film was effective rather than blurred, over- or under-exposed.

Bob Strobell recalls the significance of the gun camera film:

Part of the evidence in support of the claim for an enemy aircraft destroyed was the gun camera film. If you made a claim of a victory it had to be confirmed by other pilots witnessing the kill, or by the gun camera recording the kill. Gun cameras in the P-47 were 16 mm size. I think that the camera had to be pre-set before take-off to the light conditions expected to be encountered during the mission. The gun camera did play a big part in confirming a kill.

My recollection is that the gun camera had only two settings – one for bright sunlight and one for no sun (overcast, low light). If your mission took you above the clouds in bright sun, and you engaged the enemy and both of you went into or below the clouds, you had camera settings that would be effective for only one of these conditions. If set for low light it would be useless in bright sun above the clouds. This is not human misjudgement. It was the camera's inability to adjust to all light conditions while in flight. There was a lot of good combat footage lost because of this limitation.

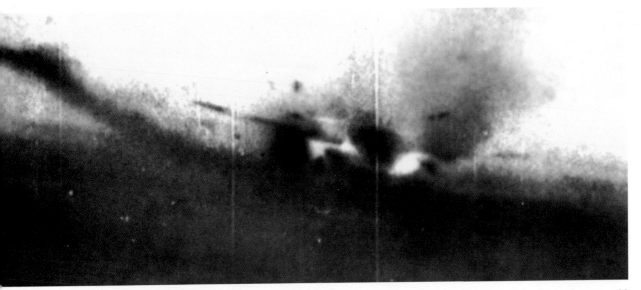

Gun camera shot from a P-47 taken over Lae as it hits a 'Dinah' reconnaissance aircraft in three places on 22 September 1943. P-47s of the 348th FG were in action on that day, and claims were confirmed for Lt Charles Cronk, Jnr, (two) and Capt John T. Moore, both of the 341st FS, plus one also for Capt Walter T. Benz, Jnr, of the 342nd FS. All were flying P-47D-2s on this day. (via NASM 26813 AC)

I claimed two kills during my tour, but got credit for only one, the second being classed as a probable. The probable was a kill, but because the camera was set for bright sunlight, it failed to record the enemy aircraft hitting the ground, even though I was filming the event as it was in low light below overcast.

Intelligence Officers

The task of the IO attached to fighter squadrons in the USAAF received definition in Army Air Force Field Manual 1-40, dated 9 September 1940, and called *Intelligence Procedures in Aviation Units*. The 'Bible' for the acquisition of combat intelligence was Field Manual 30–5. The

---

FIGURE 4 – Flight Commander's Report

Issuing unit

Place of issue

Date and hour of issue

1 Designation of the flight performing the mission.
2 Type and total number of airplanes involved.
3 Mission, type, and number.
4 Objective or purpose of mission.
5 Time of take-off.
6 Time of landing.
7 Flight Maps and Objective Maps used.
8 Routes out and back, or area covered, altitudes flown.
9 Visibility and weather conditions during flight.
10 Brief chronological account of items of information obtained visually; of any photographs taken; of messages sent and received; of enemy aircraft observed or encountered; and of enemy surface anti-aircraft fire observed or encountered.
11 Brief account of results of mission.
12 Ammunition, and pyrotechnics, expended.
13 Casualties suffered and airplanes or equipment lost or damaged.
14 Enemy casualties; enemy aircraft destroyed (damaged), and enemy surface material damaged, other than that listed in the objective of the mission.
15 Characteristics and tactics of enemy aircraft and of surface anti-aircraft units.

(signed) Flight Commander

This sequence of gun camera photographs shows a twin-engined 'Dinah' receiving hits from an attacking P-38H-1 Lightning. The victim's fuel tanks have ruptured and the wing has caught fire. This action took place on 16 September 1943, some 20 miles north-west of Hansa Bay, Wewak, New Guinea. The only claim made on this day within that area was by Maj Thomas J. Lynch, CO of the 39th FS – this kill was his 16th of the war to date. Lynch left the 39th just four days later for leave in the US, returning to the south-west Pacific area of operations with the 5th Fighter Command. Lynch continued to score aerial victories, raising his total to 20 confirmed before being shot down and killed by anti-aircraft fire over Tadji, Aitape Harbour, New Guinea, on 8 March 1944. (via NASM 26814)

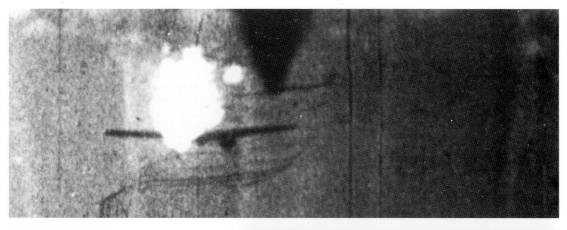

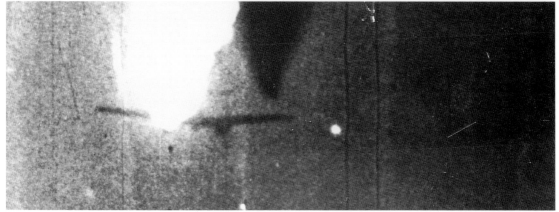

IO (or S-2 in Air Force parlance) who was new to the job had the responsibility of supplying the squadron CO with all information available on the enemy so as to aid the success of a projected mission. Following a sortie, the IO would receive a written report from the flight commander which would be made up of the combined observations and results of actions of the various pilots participating in that mission.

The report from the flight commander would include a description of the route flown, and a chronological account of the sequence of action. However, the IO was not perceived as being overly influential in the initial written encounter report, as Col Fred Lefebre remembers:

Intelligence Officers always conducted a thorough debriefing following a mission, which, of course, went into a detailed discussion of any claims, but I do not believe it had any major influence on the formulation of the pilot's claim. My reports, for example, were not in response to specific questioning by the IO.

It is clear, therefore, that in the Eighth AAF at least, the IO received individual encounter reports in which claims were filed directly after the pilot had returned from an operation. If the IO was satisfied that the pilot's written account of the action provided sufficient justification for a destroyed, probable or damaged claim, he would recommend that the report be checked against the gun camera film footage. The IO did not, as Fred Lefebre has indicated, seek to unduly influence the encounter report, for intense rivalry between units could have lead to squadron or group officers intentionally promoting suspect claims.

Psychological Stress of Combat Flying

My combat tour was based on the requirement of 300 combat hours. The 300-mark was in effect at the time I completed my tour in August 1944. Of a total of 165 flights, 85 were operational and 6 of this number were aborted – 60 of the 79 operational flights took place over a three-month period.

Bob Strobell

Flight surgeons were attached to USAAF fighter and bomber squadrons during the war, and many of them had the opportunity to closely observe, and gain insight into, the psychological impact of

The North American P-51 Mustang, powered by a Rolls-Royce Merlin engine, became arguably the finest generic fighter of the war. In this unusual shot, Mustang III FZ107 of the RAF's Air Fighting Development Unit at Wittering is seen in 1944 having just returned from dropping napalm canisters during evaluation tests. The pilot, Flt Lt Len Thorne, sits on the port wing. This test is believed to be the first time that napalm had been used by the RAF. (via Len Thorne)

The P-38 Lightning was employed by the USAAF in modest numbers in the south-west Pacific, China-Burma-India and Aleutian theatres of operation, with more aircraft actually seeing service in the European and Mediterranean sectors. Equipped with 20 mm cannon and four .50 calibre machine guns, the P-38 served throughout the war. This German photograph was taken after the forced landing and capture of an Eighth Air Force P-38 during 1944 somewhere in north-west Europe. (via BAK 1815)

combat flying upon aircrew. The Office of the Air Surgeon for the Army Air Forces produced a large number of reports documenting the effects of combat upon fighter pilots, and also sought to identify the psychological traits of successful pilots so as to influence basic and operational training. Unlike Italian and German pilots, USAAF fighter pilots were normally rested after an operational tour which might last, as in Bob Strobell's case in 1944, some 300 hours.

European Theatre
The Eighth AAF's first year of operation in combat gave flight surgeons the opportunity to observe the reactions of both bomber and fighter combat personnel at close quarters. Terms like 'Flak-happy' or the 'Focke-Wulf jitters' had already become common parlance amongst aircrew, and whilst applied as euphemisms to describe the symptoms of combat stress, such terms were very often used in the form of an aircrew in-joke to describe the small errors and eccentricities of everyday life in troubled times as experienced by otherwise sound young men.

In July 1943, Maj Donald Hastings MC

identified the different ways in which many aircrew displayed the tension of combat in the European theatre. He recorded that in some, tension was at its highest point during the night before a mission, and that such individuals would visualize their wing on fire, or their blood splattered over the cockpit windscreen. In many others, the greatest amount of tension was observed just prior to the operational mission, perhaps in the anticipation felt between briefing and take-off. For others the tension might be experienced when the enemy coast was about to be crossed, and was only relieved by action.

Hastings recorded that in a few the most marked response to combat was occasioned at the point of action itself, or even at the height of it. In such situations the pilot was unable to think, essentially freezing, and thus placing himself in the utmost mortal danger when his mind should have been at its most active. For some aircrew, the tension dissipated once the combat was over, and they began to think about what had actually occurred, almost obsessively go over and over again the sequence of events in their own minds. Hastings recorded that a very few displaced their attention away from the process of the preparation for combat, action and debriefing, and onto the personal relationships with others including wives, girlfriends and family.

In an extremely low number of aircrew, no tension was said to be experienced, or indeed observed, and these rare young men were seen to be highly aggressive both in combat and on the ground.

Hastings saw that there were significant factors which seemed to induce a condition of stress known as 'flying fatigue'. He identified three factors: high altitude missions; a sequence of missions on at least four consecutive days involving early morning briefings; and insufficient sleep, usually caused by apprehension, or by noise or confusion in the barracks on the night before the mission. Squadron flight surgeons were advised that flying fatigue was simply treated by prescribing the afflicted with two to five days' consecutive rest. Failure to recognize and treat this ailment led to inefficiency creeping into the air, with the pilot becoming dangerous to himself and others. This was called operational fatigue.

Recognizing the possibility of just such a problem early on in its ETO campaign, the USAAF had established a 60-bed ward located in a section of a general hospital within its first year of operations in England. Here, aircrew suffering from operational fatigue were given an intensive treatment programme lasting a month. During the first year, 36 officers and 33 enlisted men from across the command were treated. Eighteen of this number were pilots, although only two were fighter pilots. The first had already flown 11 to 15 sorties (exact number unknown), whilst the second had completed 20 operational missions.

Later in the war, the USAAF developed separate hospital sites both in England and Wales in prefabricated Nissan huts which accepted the rising toll of casualties from the frontline. These were often located only a short distance from airfields such as Broadwell (Bradwell Grove), in Oxfordshire, and their patients inevitably included those suffering from exhaustion or anxiety-related stress.

Pacific Theatre
Operating under very different conditions, Lt Col John E. Dougherty MC observed the stress of combat in pilots of an unnamed fighter squadron

The Republic P-47 Thunderbolt emerged primarily as a potent ground attack fighter in 1943, being used extensively in this role in the European, Mediterranean and Pacific theatres. Pilots like Neel Kearby and 'Gabby' Gabreski used the heavy fighter to great effect on bomber escort missions. This German photo shows a captured P-47 that was used for comparative evaluation by the Luftwaffe in Italy in 1944. (via BAK 484)

"FLYER'S MICKEY FINN"

FORMULA: MIX THOROUGHLY ONE PILOT OR
AVIATION CADET WITH TWO OR MORE
GLASSES ALCOHOL. CREAM IN ONE
VOLUPTUOUS BLONDE... ALLOW 2 TO 6
WEEKS FOR FERMENTATION.

RESULT: ONE LARGE PORTION SYPHILIS.
(A sure cure for flying)

MOST VENEREAL INFECTION BEGINS WITH A "HARMLESS" DRINK

Cautionary signs like "Flyer's Mickey Finn" aimed to warn young, energetic, American males who lived every day as if it were their last, of their vulnerability to venereal disease. Squadron flight surgeons were very aware that this scourge presented a threat to both the physical and mental health of fighter pilots.

flying P-38s and P-40s within the Fifth Air Force from July to November 1942 in New Guinea. The squadron undertook escort missions for transports, bombers and ground attack aircraft, and flew continuous patrols over the Buna – Cape Ward Hunt area. The tropical climate under which the campaign was fought played a big part, offering little assistance to the American fighter pilots in their campaign of sustained aerial warfare with their Japanese foes.

The inherent humidity, heat and frequent rainfall synonymous with the region badly affected the physical fitness of the American pilots, sapping their energy supply. A lack of modern sanitary facilities also led to highly-contaminated soil at the makeshift bases established by the USAAF, and mosquitoes and vermin were rife. Dysentery, malaria, hook worm, various types of fungal infections and tropical ulcers were widespread. Due to the theatre's geographical location, supplies of fresh fruit, meat, vegetables and milk were often not available. Vitamin supplements were given to the pilots, but still they suffered from a lack of vitamin C.

Fighter pilots flew a combined total of 5,055 combat hours in 3,047 combat sorties during the survey period, those pilots who survived during

this phase of the war, completing an average of 210 combat flying hours. Between 19 August and 31 December 1942, a total of 45 pilots had flown with the squadron under observation, six of whom were reported missing in action. A total of 282 flying days had been lost due to ill health during this period.

Dougherty recognized that the combination of the physical deprivations of the environment and the psychological stress of combat placed pilots in an especially vulnerable situation. Yet his study was paradoxical in that all but two pilots received medical treatment for ailments that appeared to be physical in origin like gastro-intestinal complaints (which were directly blamed upon the constant repetition of a highly-seasoned stew which contained considerable gas-forming elements!), and only two pilots were treated for anxiety reactions to combat flying.

The Mediterranean and North African Theatre
Lt Col Roy R. Grinker MC and Capt John P. Spiegel MC produced several reports on the emotional stresses and treatment procedures in relation to USAAF aircrew at various points during the war. They observed aircrew in general who were operating in the Tunisian campaign and the tense aerial warfare over Sicily, Sardinia

and southern Italy between January and May 1943. Their report specifically focused on war neuroses, (i.e. an acute and debilitating anxiety of combat flying). For the purposes of this chapter, their paper describes the physical conditions under which fighter and bomber aircrew were to operate.

Living conditions were portrayed as primitive, with monotonously repetitive food which the cook failed to make efforts to improve. Homes were pup tents with bedding rolls, no lighting after dark, no recreational facilities, dust everywhere and stubborn insect infestations. For those aircrew requiring psychiatric treatment off-base, this would effectively mean evacuation by air to a field hospital some 300 to 550 miles behind the ground frontlines. Remarkably, on average the journey would take from breakdown to arrival for treatment some two-and-a-half days, with the patient passing through casualty clearing stations and forward evacuation hospitals during this time.

Italian Campaign
A second earlier study by Maj Gerald Krosnick MC had focused specifically on USAAF fighter pilots in the Italian campaign, looking at the development of stress in this theatre. The pilots observed throughout 1942 flew missions which lasted from three-quarters to two-and-a-half hours, depending on whether they were bomber escorts, fighter sweeps, fighter-bombing, ground strafing attacks, or the less prevalent long-range bomber escorts. The fighter groups were usually stationed no more than 20 to 40 miles behind the lines. In the desert war, the USAAF had to keep

Lt. Arthur W. Heiden of 79th FS, 20th FG, 8th Air Force, in front of his P-38J "Lucky Lady" which had just completed its 65th operational sortie. Shaking Heiden's hand is crew chief M/Sgt Max Pyles. Although this P-38's marking depict two victories over Luftwaffe aircraft, Heiden had a confirmed total of .50 (ie a half share in a victory) which occurred in an action on 18 March, 1944 over Germany. Just over three weeks later, the 20th FG was awarded a Distinguished Unit Citation for its actions on 8 April. (via Jerry Scutts)

A P-47D of 352nd FS, 353rd FG. Leading ace of the 353rd FG was their commanding officer, Col Glenn E. Duncan who gained 19.5 combat victories with the P-47D. Duncan was shot down over Germany in July 1944 but managed to evade capture, remaining with the Dutch underground in Holland, until liberated by the Allies in Arnhem on 14 April 1945. (via Jerry Scutts)

pace with the advance on the ground, and their existence was hand-to-mouth under canvas.

Life for the fighter pilot was spent totally on the base, for there were usually no nearby towns or cities for relaxation. The airfields were frequently bombed or strafed during the day by fighter-bombers, and again at night by heavy bombers. There were long periods of inactivity, and Krosnick recorded that these seemed to increase the stress felt by the pilots.

He saw that the process of combat stress lasted from the briefing through to the debriefing at the completion of the mission, and that combat hours from a stress perspective had to include the time spent at operational readiness. He recorded the following early signs of fatigue for fighter pilots who were finding combat increasingly stressful. The first indication was that the pilot would often become reserved to the point of being non-communicative and morose. He observed that young fighter pilots seemed to 'age quickly'. The old adage that when a fighter pilot had something to gripe about he was obviously well, but when he stopped griping he was in some difficulty, seemed to be true. His physical state would change and his speech characteristics – the

mannerisms and mode of speech – would significantly alter.

At briefing for the mission, and on return at debriefing, the operationally tired pilot listened without comment. His capacity to joke, and express youthful humour, evaporated as he became accustomed to his task, but tired of his job. Krosnick commented that such individual fighter pilots frequently returned early from missions, with complaints of engine, or similar, problems.

LMF (Lack of Moral Fibre) was considered to be a significant challenge, despite few examples actually being cited in the doctor's report. Hastings described the response:

If a man must be removed from combat flying because of his fear of it, he should not be given easy, non-combat, flying duties – not assigned to a position which might permit more rapid promotion than his fellows who remain behind to do the fighting. Such situations create serious discontent amongst combat personnel when they learn of it.

In the Tunisian campaign Grinker and Spiegel saw that there were very few cases of genuine malingering, and many of those who were diagnosed as 'exhaustion states' were in fact labelled with the term LMF.

Awards and Decorations

The awards made to USAAF fighter pilots and other air personnel were predicted by the adoption of criteria specific to each command. In practice, these criteria were fairly consistently applied throughout the USAAF, and any significant changes to them can be traced on at least one occasion to orders given directly by Gen H. H. 'Hap' Arnold, Chief of the USAAF.

The Distinguished Flying Cross (DFC) had been instituted in 1926, and the Air Medal (AM) some six years later. During the first 18 months of America's official involvement in the Second World War, both the AM and DFC were automatically awarded following the completion of a set number of operational sorties and/or strike rate (the number of confirmed kills awarded).

Investigations reputedly prompted by Arnold led to an alteration to the guidelines of the award of the DFC in particular. The new criteria stipulated that an award made for heroism (stated in the 29 November 1942 guidelines) must be evidenced by voluntary action in the face of great danger above and beyond the call of duty when participating in aerial flight. For the DFC, the additional qualification needed was that the results of achievement while participating in aerial flight must be so exceptional and outstanding as to clearly set the perpetrator apart from other aircrew who have not been so recognized. From that point on, the DFC was only awarded after the recommendation (rather than nomination) detailed the extraordinary achievements, or act of heroism, which were identified as deserving of the award.

In 1944, these new revisions – particularly in respect to the AM – were deemed still to be not sweeping enough for Gen Arnold, who was quoted as saying that he did not want to read any more accounts of returning heroes who 'wear the

---

TABLE 1 – Criteria for Awards and Decorations as of 29 November 1942

Note: It should be remembered that these guidelines were subject to considerable review following Gen Arnold's prompting, which led, especially, to changed award criteria for the DFC and AM from 14 August 1943.

The award of the AM or DFC was based upon the destruction of enemy aircraft, or the number of sorties flown. In some cases strike/sortie were combined to provide sufficient composite evidence to justify the recommendation of an award. In its simplest form it can be seen that the destruction of a first enemy aircraft (E/A) would have the same value, in terms of award, as the completion of ten fighter sorties.

Destruction of enemy aircraft

For	Award
First e/a destroyed	Air Medal
Second e/a destroyed	Oak Leaf Cluster (worn on AM Ribbon)
Third e/a destroyed	Second Oak Leaf Cluster (worn on AM Ribbon)
Fourth e/a destroyed	Third Oak leaf Cluster (worn on AM Ribbon)
Fifth e/a destroyed	DFC
Tenth e/a destroyed	Oak Leaf Cluster (worn on DFC Ribbon)
Fifteenth e/a destroyed	Second Oak leaf Cluster (worn on DFC Ribbon)

Sorties	Award
10 Fighter Sorties	AM
20 Fighter Sorties	Oak Leaf Cluster (worn on AM Ribbon)
50 Fighter Sorties	DFC

Recommendations for awards were submitted to Eighth AAF headquarters in triplicate. Recommendations for the Purple Heart (where the pilot had received wounds as the result of enemy action) needed to be supported by a medical certificate completed by the Flight Surgeon detailing the treatment given to wounds. The posthumous award of the Purple Heart did not, unsurprisingly, require any recommendation. Simply, the award was made by the War Department upon receipt of notice of death.

Air Medal and six Oak Leaf Clusters because they had 35 combat missions'. The instruction signed by Arnold following Maj Gen Kuter's suggestion, prohibited all USAAF Commands from continuing to award AM, DFCs or any other award on a mechanical basis. Whilst Arnold was not seeking to inhibit the volume of awards made, he remained insistent that awards like the DFC and AM should only be made for 'worthy' acts. In the event, the AM tended to be given primarily in recognition for service, and was issued at around ten times the frequency of the DFC.

Other awards and decorations

Other decorations made to USAAF fighter personnel included the Distinguished Service Cross, instituted in 1918, the Silver Star (SS) in 1932, the Legion of Merit, which was offered in differing classes and, of course, the Purple Heart (PH), established by President Washington in 1782 – from 1932 the latter was issued solely to those individuals wounded or killed as a result of enemy action. The highest award for bravery issued by the United States was the Medal of Honor, which has been presented only rarely during the various conflicts involving American serviceman this century – just 466 personnel have received the award. USAAF pilots to receive this award as the result of their actions in the Second World War included fighter pilots 'Dick' Bong, Tommy McGuire and Neel Kearby.

USAAF fighter pilots were also decorated with awards from other friendly nations, although in theory these could only be accepted following approval by Congress. In practice, the latter gave their blanket consent to foreign decorations being made to members of the US

TABLE 2 – Eighth AAF – 29 November 1942

Guidelines for Awards and Decorations

Medal of Honor
Any officer or enlisted man who while in action involving actual conflict with an enemy distinguishes himself conspicuously by gallantry and intrepidity at the risk of his own life above and beyond the call of duty.

Distinguished Service Cross
To persons serving in any capacity who distinguish themselves by extraordinary heroism in connection with military operations.

Distinguished Service Medal
To persons serving in any capacity . . . who distinguish themselves by exceptionally meritorious service to the Government in a duty of great responsibility, and to enlisted men of the army to whom the Certificate of Merit had been granted on or before 9 July 1918 (in lieu of Certificate of Merit).

Silver Star
To each officer or enlisted man who is cited for gallantry in action in orders published by Eighth Air Force HQ or a Higher Headquarters, which citation does not warrant the award of the Medal of Honor or the Distinguished Service Cross.

Purple Heart
To persons serving in any capacity . . . who are wounded in action against an enemy of the United States or as the result of acts of such enemy, provided such wound necessitates treatment by a Medical Officer.

Oak Leaf Cluster
Not more than one MH or one DSC, or one SS, or one DFC, or one AM, shall be issued to any one person, but for each succeeding deed, act or achievement sufficient to justify the award of either one of the above listed decorations, a bronze Oak Leaf Cluster will be awarded in lieu thereof.

Distinguished Flying Cross
Awarded to any person who, while serving in any capacity with the Air Corps of the Army of the US subsequent to 6 April 6 1917, has distinguished or shall distinguish himself by heroism or extraordinary achievement while participating in aerial flight.

Air Medal
Awarded to any person who, while serving in any capacity in the Army, Navy or Marine Corps subsequent to 8 September 1939, has distinguished himself by meritorious achievement while participating in aerial flight.

armed forces. It not unusual to find USAAF fighter pilots from the European theatre, in particular, decorated with awards from the RAF, Belgian and French governments.

Unit Citations

The Distinguished Unit Citation (DUC) was awarded to USAAF groups/squadrons that had demonstrated acts of extraordinary heroism which were deemed to be equivalent to acts that would warrant the award of the DSC to an individual. The unit would be issued with a Distinguished Unit streamer with the name of the action embroidered in white. Each member of the outfit present, or assigned for duty in the action which led to the award being made, was entitled to permanently wear the DUC emblem. Those joining the unit at a later date were entitled to wear the DUC emblem only whilst serving with the unit.

A higher unit decoration in the form of the Meritorious Unit Citation was instigated for action occurring on, or after, January 1944. This decoration was to have equivalent status to the award of the Legion of Honor to an individual. Whilst several USAAF fighter groups received the DUC (some on more than one occasion,

marked by bronze oak leaf cluster), it was not discovered during the research for this chapter whether any USAAF fighter units received the Meritorious Unit Citation.

Pilot Profiles

P-36 pilot – Harry W. Brown

Harry W. Brown was one of the few USAAF pilots to achieve a victory whilst flying the Curtiss P-36A Hawk, this essentially pre-war fighter aircraft enjoying far more success with both the Finnish Air Force and the RAF in Burma. Brown had graduated as a pilot and been commissioned as a lieutenant just four months prior to the Japanese attack on Pearl Harbor. During the morning of the raid he claimed a Japanese 'Val' dive-bomber destroyed and a second damaged whilst flying with 47th Pursuit Squadron/15th Pursuit Group.

Brown was subsequently posted to the 9th FS/49th FG, operating over New Guinea in the P-38G. He claimed an 'Oscar' destroyed and one other enemy aircraft as a probable whilst attached to this group, before achieving ace status with the 475th FG's 431st FS. Brown brought up his fifth kill in style by downing three Zekes whilst flying a P-38H on 16 August 1943,

cont. p.105

Gun patches intact, this P-51D belonged to the 361st FS, 356th FG, 8th Air Force, based at Martlesham Heath. The 356th FG replaced its P-47s with P-51s in November 1944 and its leading ace on the P-51D was Major (later Maj Gen) Don J. Strait. Strait achieved 10.5 victories to add to the earlier three he gained with the P-47D. (via Jerry Scutts)

Supermarine Spitfire VB (LO-Y/BM113) of No. 602 'City of Glasgow' Squadron, RAF, flown by Flt Sgt Len Thorne, Kenley, April 1942.

1:72 scale

**Hawker Tempest V
Series I (R-B/JN751)**
flown by Wg Cdr R. P.
Beamont, Wing Leader,
Newchurch Tempest Wing,
Newchurch, June 1944.

1:72 scale

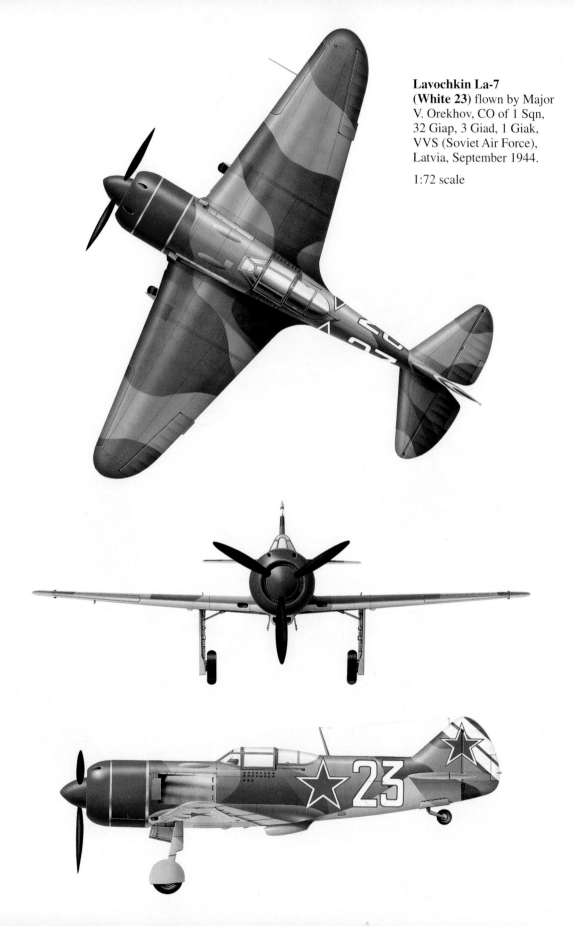

Lavochkin La-7
(White 23) flown by Major V. Orekhov, CO of 1 Sqn, 32 Giap, 3 Giad, 1 Giak, VVS (Soviet Air Force), Latvia, September 1944.

1:72 scale

Republic P-47D-5 Thunderbolt (YJ-K/serial unknown) of 351 Fighter Squadron, 353 Fighter Group, USAF, flown by Ltn Robert C. Strobell, Raydon, June 1944.

1:72 scale

**Fokker D.XXI
(Blue 7/FR-110)** of
3/LLv 24, Ilmavoitot
(Finnish Air Force), flown
by Ltn V. Pyotsiä,
Tammikuu, early 1940.

1:72 scale

**Curtiss Hawk 75A
(Yellow 0/CUw-560)** of 1st
Flight, LeLv 32, Ilmavoitot
(Finnish Air Force), flown
by 2nd Ltn K. Karhila,
Suulajärvi, May 1942.

1:72 scale

Messerschmitt Bf 109G-10/AS (Black 7/Werk-Nr. 491353) flown by Cap. Ugo Drago, CO of 4ª Sq., II° Gr.C., ANR (Italian Republican Air Force), Aviano, February 1945.

1:72 scale

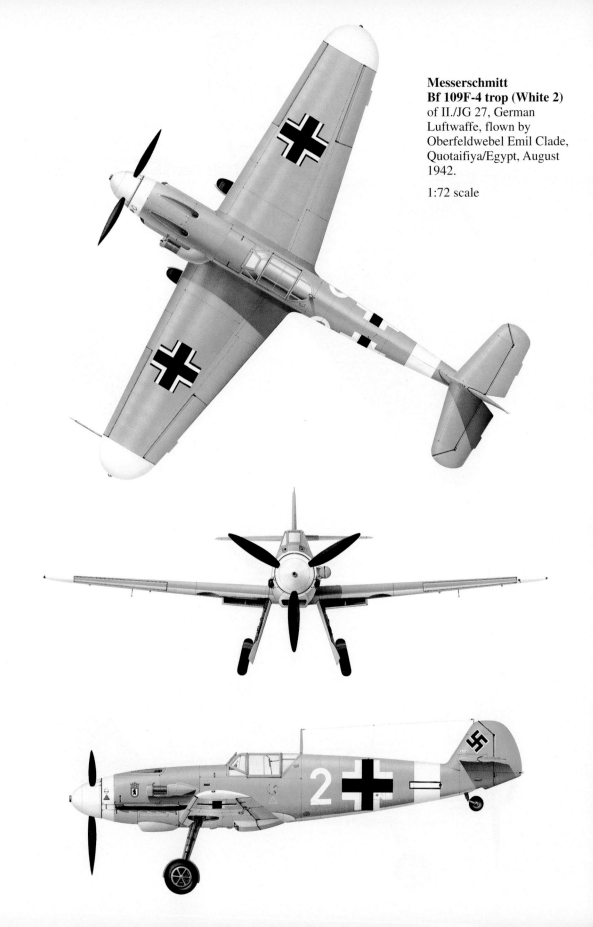

**Messerschmitt
Bf 109F-4 trop (White 2)**
of II./JG 27, German
Luftwaffe, flown by
Oberfeldwebel Emil Clade,
Quotaifiya/Egypt, August
1942.

1:72 scale

followed by a further Zeke on 24 October. Rising to the rank of lieutenant colonel after the war, Brown was discharged from the USAF in 1948. He died in 1991 at the age of 70.

P-38 Pilot – Thomas B. McGuire, Jnr

Graduating from aviation cadet training programme Class 42B in February 1942, Thomas B. McGuire, Jnr, was to become the second highest scoring American pilot in the Second World War. Like his great rival 'Dick' Bong, McGuire scored all 38 of his confirmed aerial victories in the Lockheed P-38 Lightning (thought by many fighter pilots to be an inferior fighter to both the P-51 Mustang and P-47 Thunderbolt). The similarity with Bong did not end there, for McGuire achieved all his combat successes in the South Pacific theatre of operations and, like Bong, was to lose his life in the final months of the war.

However, unlike Bong, McGuire had gained operational experience in the Aleutians prior to his posting to the Pacific on 14 March 1943. His most successful day in combat was on 26 December 1944 when on a single morning sweep near Clark Field, in the Philippines, he downed four Zeke 52s. The previous day he had destroyed three Zekes whilst escorting a heavy bomber formation. Less than two weeks later McGuire was dead, having been lost in action during a sweep over Los Negros Island whilst attempting to turn with a Japanese foe with external tanks still attached to his P-38L. His fighter stalled at low altitude, spun into the jungle floor below with fatal results.

In addition to being an exceptional fighter pilot, McGuire developed a reputation as a combat leader due to his ability to impart his experience and knowledge onto pilots posted into the frontline for the first time. Maj McGuire was posthumously awarded the Medal of Honor in 1946, and also received the DSC, three SSs, five DFCs, fifteen AMs and two PHs. The large air force base of Fort Dix, New Jersey, was renamed McGuire AFB in 1949 in honour of this great ace.

P-39 Airacobra Pilot – William F. Fiedler, Jnr

William F. Fiedler became the sole USAAF P-39 pilot to gain five aerial victories., despite his time in action being very brief. Qualifying as a pilot and gaining a commission in Florida in June 1942, Fiedler added to his 211 flying training hours with a further 241.25 pursuit hours before becoming a pilot with the 70th FS/347th FG, which was based in New Caledonia, with outposts at Guadalcanal. Fiedler claimed his first aerial success on 26 January 1943 by downing a Zero, followed by a second kill over a similar foe some nine days later. He was then posted to the 68th FS, with whom he gained a confirmed Zeke and two 'Vals' in mid-June. However, shortly after achieving his fifth victory, he was killed in an accident at Guadalcanal when his P-39K was struck by a P-38 in the process of taking off.

P-40 pilot – Levi R. Chase, Jnr

At the age of 23 Levi R. Chase, Jnr, graduated from class 41-G of the aviation cadet programme in June 1941 – he was destined to see considerable combat action in North Africa during 1942–43. Chase achieved four confirmed kills with the P-40F in the space of six weeks between December 1942 and February 1943, by which time he had become commanding officer of the 60th FS 'Fighting Crows'/33rd FG. He continued to score prolifically until he was transferred back to America in July 1943, his final six kills being achieved with the P-40L against Bf 109Gs and MC.202s.

A posting as deputy commander of the 2nd Air Commando Group led Chase to India at the end of 1944, and in February of the following year he became CO of the newly-formed 1st Provisional Fighter Group. This outfit was equipped with P-51Ds, and Chase had the opportunity to test his mettle against the Japanese, scoring a further two victories – both 'Oscars'. He had marked himself out as a fine leader of men early on his career, and it soon became clear that he was destined for high military air rank judging by his rapid promotions during the war.

Chase's distinguished flying career continued into the postwar years, and he subsequently flew F-80s and F-86s during the Korean War and later active saw service in Vietnam. Chase retired from the USAF in 1973 having attained the rank of major-general and been awarded with three Silver Stars, five American DFCs, one RAF DFC, twenty-one Air Medals, one Bronze Star Medal and one Legion of Merit from the various theatres of operations in which he had served.

Maj-Gen Chase died in 1994.

P-47 Pilot – Robert S. Johnson
By the time that Robert S. Johnson entered pilot training with the USAAF he already held a degree in engineering, but despite this, he showed a weakness in air gunnery during basic flying training and he was allocated to twin- rather than single-engined aircraft at the advanced stage of his course. Showing considerable guile and perseverance, Johnson persuaded the USAAF to transfer him to the 56th FG shortly after gaining his wings and commission. With the 61st FS, Johnson was to achieve outstanding success in the ETO, which was made all the more remarkable considering his previous difficulties with the gunnery aspect of his basic training.

Flying C- and D-model P-47s, Johnson was a key member of Col Hubert Zemke's 'Wolfpack', which also included such notable aces as Francis S. 'Gabby' Gabreski and David Schilling. At one point, Johnson became the highest scoring American fighter pilot in the ETO, and was the first USAAF pilot to equal Eddie Rickenbacker's score from the First World War. Having scored his 26th and 27th victories on 8 May 1944 to put him one behind 'Dick' Bong's score, Johnson was posted back to the US to promote the sale of war bonds, joining the recently-returned Pacific ace Bong on a nation-wide tour – the latter flew a P-38 and Johnson was issued with a P-47.

Unlike Bong, Johnson did not return to operational flying, instead joining the Army reserve in 1945 and rising to the rank of lieutenant colonel in 1949. Robert S. Johnson was inducted into the Oklahoma Aviation and Space Hall of Fame in 1983.

P-51 Pilot – George E. Preddy, Jnr
George Earl Preddy, Jnr, became the sixth- highest scoring AAF pilot of the Second World War, and had he not been shot down by 'friendly' anti-aircraft fire on Christmas Day 1944 (his 143rd mission), he may well have become the top scoring American pilot of the war. Preddy had qualified as a pilot and been awarded his commission just five days after the Japanese attack on Pearl Harbor. Initially posted to Australia to fly P-40s with the 49th FG in the defence of Darwin, Preddy claimed two Japanese aircraft as damaged during his time in the southern hemisphere. Following a mid-air collision, and subsequent hospitalization, in July 1942, he returned to the US, before being posted to England and eventually the 487th FS/352nd FG, based at Bodney. Here, he initially flew P-47Ds, a type with which he claimed his first two victories in December 1943, but it was when the squadron re-equipped with the P-51 Mustang that Preddy really showed what he could do.

Around lunch time on 6 August 1944 between Lüneburg and Havelburg, on the German coast, Preddy destroyed no less than six Bf 109Gs. Soon after this action he was promoted to command the 328th FS, scoring a further three confirmed kills, one probable and one damaged with the unit. Maj George Preddy, Jnr, was just 26 years old when he was killed, having scored 26.8 aerial victories and been awarded the DSC, two Silver Stars, nine DFCs and eight Air Medals.

Footnotes
1. Capt Frank N. Emory gained two confirmed victories with the 351st FS. Rupert M. Tumlin already had one destroyed prior to this mission.
2. In September 1945, the Eighth AAF Fighter Command produced the document *Eighth Air Force Final Report of Assessed Fighter Claims Against Enemy Aircraft*, which was revised for inclusion in USAF Historical Study No 85.
3. Fred Lefebre achieved three confirmed victories with the 351st FS, the first on 8 October 1943 and the third over a year later on 5 December 1944.

Chapter Four

Italy

The Regia Aeronautica (1940-43) and the Aeronautica Nazionale Repubblicana (1943-45)

I shot down ten enemy aircraft and quite a few which were not confirmed. As was usual in the Italian Air Force, the shot down aircraft were not accredited to the individual pilot but to the group, although a claims certificate was issued by the air force and handed to the pilot giving details of the action and any awards that were given . . . when I shot down an enemy aircraft I felt euphoria, but afterwards extreme sorrow for the enemy pilot.

Gen (ret) Giuseppe Biron

Introduction
Regia Aeronautica (RA)
Italian fighter pilots of the Regia Aeronautica claimed many successes in aerial combat during the Spanish Civil War against the Soviet and Republican Air Forces. A dozen fighter pilots managed to acquire scores that accorded them 'ace' status, whilst others continued to fly well into the Second World War gradually developing scores which would lead them to achieve five victories or more.

From 1923 to 8 September 1943, the Italian Air Force was known as the Regia Aeronautica, but in the wake of the armistice on the latter date, the ANR and the Italian Co-Belligerent Air Force were formed. Between 1940 and 1943, the RA's main theatres of operations were in North Africa and the Mediterranean, but it also fought on

many other fronts including Britain, Greece, Yugoslavia, Russia, Africa and, finally, mainland Italy itself.

Losses suffered by the RA during the conflict consisted of 3,007 dead or missing, 2,731 wounded with a further 9,873 made PoWs. During this period fighter pilots of the RA claimed a total of 4,586 aircraft shot down, or destroyed on the ground, whilst Italian losses totalled some 5,201 aircraft, although it is not clear how many of these were fighters. Italian pilots flew on several fronts, with many of the veterans of the Spanish Civil War flying Macchi C.200 and C.202 fighters on the Eastern Front with 22° Group alongside the Luftwaffe in the battle against the Soviets.

At the point at which the armistice was signed, the RA had claimed a total of 2,522 aircraft destroyed, including those downed by anti-aircraft batteries and air-gunners flying as crewmembers in Italian bombers.

The Italian Co-Belligerent Air Force and the Aeronautica Nazionale Repubblicana
The sudden cessation of hostilities in September 1943 divided Italy both geographically and militarily. A part of the RA followed King Victor Emanuelle's orders and surrendered to the Allies at their airfields in southern Italy. Now operating

A rare photograph of combined Luftwaffe and RA operations over North Africa in 1942. The photograph was taken from the cockpit of a Bf 110 of ZG 26, which was in a formation being escorted by a G.50 with no immediately identifiable unit markings. The white band was the RA's most conspicuous marking from late 1940 to September 1943. (via BAK 425)

alongside their former enemies, the RA was renamed the Italian Co-Belligerent Air Force – their exploits are not detailed within this text as they were mainly employed in ground support duties, and no pilots attained ace status.

In northern Italy, the armistice had become a focal point for the considerable resentment festering amongst the ranks of the fighter pilots within the RA, who continued to maintain their support for the fascist regime. The rescue of Mussolini from his mountain prison gave fresh impetus to the fascist cause, and on 10 October *Il Duce* announced the formation of the Aeronautica Nazionale Repubblicana. The primary role for the ANR's fighter units was to provide fighter defence for the heavily industrialized areas of northern Italy.

Former RA aircrew mustered at local airfields in the region on 15 October and were subsequently allocated to various units, with fighter pilots being based at Bresso Airport in Milan. This aerodrome eventually became home for the Fiat G.55-equipped II° *Gruppo Caccia* (the second ANR fighter group to be formed), which first saw action on 30 April 1944 under the command of T/Col Alessandrini – several of the unit's pilots had flown the Bf 109G with 3° and

150° *Gruppo Autonomo* in the months leading up to the armistice.

The first ANR fighter unit to be formed was 101° *Gruppo Autonomo Caccia Terrestre*, which was initially based in Florence before transferring to Mirafiori, close to Turin. After its early disbanding, several of its pilots were posted to Germany, where they were trained in Luftwaffe combat tactics. In addition, *Squadriglia Complementare* 'Montefusco' was formed in late 1943 and equipped with C.205 Veltros and G.55s – the best Italian fighters of the war.

Aside from these unit formations, one of the most important results of the initial gathering of fighter pilots in the north was the creation of I° *Gruppo Caccia* on 15 November 1943, which was later officialized on 1 January 1944. Initially commanded by Maggiore Borgogno, and then famous ace Maggiore Adriano Visconti, the unit was equipped with C.205s and commenced operations from Lagnasco (Cuneo) on 3 January, before moving to Campoformido (Udine) airfield, where it operated alongside elements of the Luftwaffe's JG 77 against Fifteenth Air Force bombers.

Prior to the break up of the RA, combat losses

suffered by fighter pilots had been comparable to those suffered by both the RAF and Luftwaffe over the same period. By comparison (and despite more specific combat training methods), the ANR suffered high losses due to pilots being increasingly overwhelmed in combat by greater numbers of Allied aircraft.

Influence of the Luftwaffe

Combat training and tactics, claim criteria and appraisal, and the provision of equipment, including aeroplanes, were the main areas in which the Luftwaffe influenced the fighter operations of the ANR. The enthusiasm of Italian pilots was noted by their German colleagues, and training in combat tactics and collaboration on operational missions served to cement the relationship. Even so, the Luftwaffe became increasingly anxious to exert further influence on the ANR, although they were already essentially controlling its fighter operations. In August 1944, the Luftwaffe instructed every ANR unit (despite protest from Mussolini), to disband and reunite as an 'Italian Legion'. Mussolini's pleas

to Hitler, and the threat of mutiny from the ANR fighter pilots who refused to fly under such conditions, won the day.

Code-named Operation *Phoenix*, the Luftwaffe's take-over bid had in fact unintentionally re-established the credibility of the ANR as an independent air arm within the Axis alliance. This was shown in 1945 when 13 ANR pilots of Iº *Gruppo* that were in Germany to train on the Bf 109 were selected and posted to Liegnitz for training on the innovative, rocket-propelled, Me 163, although these pilots never became operational on type. Plans were also laid for Italian pilots to receive training on the turbojet-powered Me 262, but no such conversion had taken place by the end of the war.

From late 1943, the Luftwaffe's Italian command in the form of the *Jagdfliegerführer Oberitalien*, had been under the command of 34-year-old *Ritterkreuz* holder, Oberst Baron Günther von Maltzahn, who achieved a total 68 kills during the war. As the conflict progressed, so the Luftwaffe's ability to provide fighter support to defend Italy eroded, and units,

This press photograph of a G.50 is dated 5 December 1942. The contemporary, if bland, German caption reads 'On an Italian airfield. Maintenance crew re-arming machine guns'. (via BAK 96 3)

Ciampino, 1943, and a CR.42 of 300 Squadriglia *is seen about to take-off for a night interception. Although this mission was clearly staged for the propaganda purposes, the photo shows one of the several tasks assigned to the ageing biplane – on this occasion it is equipped with two small searchlights under the wings. The RA operated the CR.42 on frontline duties up to the armistice on 8 September 1943.* (via D'Amico-Valentini)

together with combat experienced personnel, were posted back to defend the Reich. By the end of June this process was virtually complete, and with the failure of Operation *Phoenix* two months later (a plan which von Maltzahn refused to support, resulting in his removal from the post), and the withdrawal from Italy of the last German fighters, just one ANR fighter unit was left under the control of *Jagdfliegerführer Oberitalien* from October 1944 – this number had increased to two by February 1945.

Thus, the Luftwaffe, while continuing to operate in Italy with its night assault and reconnaissance units, also continued to exercise its presence in fighter operations, and thus play a role in the accreditation of combat claims made by ANR pilots. The most notable figure involved in this process was Oberst Günther 'Frankel' Lutzow, who had essentially been sent to exile in Italy in late January 1945 as *Jagdfliegerführer* following his involvement with Oberst Johannes Steinhoff (amongst others) in the unsuccessful bid to solicit support from Generaloberst von Greim and Gen Roller in their efforts to have

Reichmarshall Hermann Göring removed from office.

Lutzow took over from his friend, Oberst 'Edu' Neumann, another member of the inner circle of the attempted coup, but his duties were primarily to liaise with the ANR. 'Frankel' Lutzow remained in Italy until March, 1945, when he returned to Germany to fly the turbojet-powered Me 262 with Adolf Galland's elite JV 44. He was killed in action a few weeks later.

The Literature

Initial interest in the combat claims of Italian fighter pilots began to surface in the 1950s when researchers and journalists from several countries contacted the Italian Air Ministry in an attempt to discover official figures on confirmed claims from the RA and ANR. The 'ace' factor was beginning to raise its head as an issue for researchers who were keen to identify the 'key' fighter pilots of the recent world war. It transpired that the Italian Air Ministry did not have sufficiently-collated material to be of much assistance. However, by the mid-1970s, the

Italian Air Force Historical Branch produced a 'semi-official' list of the top 19 Italian fighter pilots based upon decorations and awards for meritorious duty. There were notable absentees from this list, including Gorrini, Bordoni-Bisleri and the legendary fighter leader, Adriano Visconti, who was murdered by Italian partisans immediately after surrendering the Bf 109s of 1° *Gruppo* to the Allies on 29 April 1945.

Over the past 20 years various accounts have appeared in Italian books and aviation journals and magazines, including *Storia Militare*, which have sought to add to or amend the list of the top scoring pilots. There are significant difficulties, however, for several squadron Operational Records Books (ORBs) have been missing since the end of the war, with 1943 being particularly poorly represented in archival material. A further problem in collating definitive data relating to the RA was that most claims were reported only in pilot's personal log books and in the units' squadron operational records.

During the war, there was a certain lack of definition and official status in the RA combat claim forms, and this can be seen in several of those that do survive. Hence, there is an understandable difficulty in locating single Italian claims. However, as more documents, previously thought lost or destroyed, come to light like the recently discovered log book belonging to Visconti, so claims and lists of successful fighter pilots can be clarified with increasing likelihood, though without the absolute certainty of providing a definitive list.

Training of Italian Fighter Pilots

During the 1940-43 period, the training of Italian fighter pilots was broken down into three stages: basic, advanced and operational. What is particularly notable is that Italian fighter pilots throughout the conflict received far less flying training hours than did their contemporaries in the Luftwaffe, RAF and USAAF.

Basic
From 1938 to 1940, the initial training of RA pilots consisted of 30 flying hours on the Breda Ba.25, after which a flight certificate was issued, before they moved on to complete the military certificate by flying a further 25 hours on the IMAM Ro.41. The total period of training took

around nine months to complete, and intakes of around 1,600 flying cadets were normal at this time. It was planned to open around ten 1st *Periodo* (basic flying training schools), each with around 40 aircraft. The old Ba.25 and Ro.41 biplanes were still being used for 1° *Periodo* training through to 1943, and indeed, only two weeks before the armistice did the Italian Air Ministry begin to actively seek to replace the IMAM type.

Advanced
After successfully passing out with their military

Tail-fin of a C.202 Folgore sporting the white cross of Savoia and the royal coat of arms. The pilot of this aircraft remains a mystery, although his feat of claiming seven enemy aircraft destroyed makes him an ace. This is one of the very few examples of an individual victory tally on an RA aircraft. (via BAK 444)

The agile CR.42 was used by the RA on several operational fronts. In the autumn of 1940 they were used to escort Italian bombers on raids over England, flying from bases in Belgium, but were quickly out-fought by the superior RAF fighters. In this photograph, taken at Palermo airfield in 1942, the curious message written on the engine cowling of this CR.42 of 377 Squadriglia reads 'I can't sleep anymore at night' – a clear indication this was in fact a nightfighter, used during the final stages of the Mediterranean air war. (via BAK 415)

certificates, fighter pilots were posted to *Scuole di 2° Periodo* for advanced flying training on the Fiat CR.30 or CR.32. There were three *2° Periodo* schools. By October 1940 training requirements had begun to change, but these were gradually accommodated. The flying hours at *1 Periodo* commenced with 30 hours on the AVIA Fl.3, followed by 20 hours on the

SAIMAN 202, and 10 hours of acrobatics on the CANSA C.5, SAIMAN 200 or Caproni Ca.164.

Instrument training was not introduced until June 1941, and even then this comprised just five hours on the SAIMAN 202. By the summer of 1942 training hours at the advanced stage were increased to around 85 flying hours, but this was still not comparable with the total being flown by other Axis and Allied air forces at that time. Future fighter pilots at the *2nd Periodo* schools in 1942-43 flew the Fiat CR.30/.32/.42 and G.50 aircraft, as well as the Nardi FN.305/.315 and Macchi C.200.

Operational
The third stage of the flying training for a fighter pilot took place at an operational squadron, and new fighter pilots were supposed to receive around 30 hours tuition to master aerobatics. Up to mid-1943, Italian fighter pilots did not receive intensive training in combat tactics – simulated combat situations (*Finta Caccia*) were, however, extensively employed. This style of training placed a considerable emphasis on the leadership skills of the individual squadron commanders, who were left to implement these tactics as they saw best, and this inevitably meant that the ability of a unit to acquit itself well in combat wrested almost solely with the CO.

Gunnery training
Gunnery skills were considered much less important, and many Italian pilots first learned to use their guns only in the heat of direct combat! The training itself consisted of two exercises: strafing at fixed targets on the ground and shooting at a small bunch of balloons which were left to float freely in the air. There was no training in shooting at a moving target, let alone in defection shooting. Gen (ret) Biron, who trained as a pilot in pre-war years, recalled:

I joined the Italian Air force in 1933 as a volunteer when I did my civilian pilot's licence and then my military ticket on the A.S.1 Breda 25 and the CR.100. The first unit I was posted to did simulated aerial combat, which was considered to be of great value and was employed to familiarize fighter pilots for aerial combat.

Combat training on the squadron was generally

carried out in pairs or in sections consisting of two to four aircraft. Normally, the simulation exercise was led by an experienced, often veteran, pilot so that he could 'show the ropes' to an inexperienced novice. When interviewed for this chapter, *M.llo* Aldo Barbaglio remembered that around 50 hours of combat training was undertaken by the Italian pilots.

Allievo Pil. Rolando Ancillotti began his flying training on 21 January 1941. At the basic stage (*1st Periodo*) he flew 60 hours on the Ba.25 and Ro.41, followed by 22 hrs 40 mins on the CR.30/.32/.42. Having attained his military certificate, he then moved to an operational unit, flying a further 53 hrs 25 mins on various types. Ancillotti's gunnery training was included in this latter flying training period, which finished on 26 August 1942, and totalled just 1 hr 20 mins on the CR.42 and 45 mins on the C.200.

It can be seen that even at this comparatively late stage in the life of the RA, flying training from novice to combat fighter pilot totalled only 135 hrs 25 mins – a very low figure when compared to the fighter pilots of other Allied and Axis forces at this time. An RAF pilot, for example, could have expected to receive between 150 and 200 hours flying training prior to being posted to an operational training unit for combat training in 1942.

Training of ANR Fighter Pilots

A limited number of Italian pilots were trained during the 1944-45 period in Germany, but none in Italy itself. Forty pilots received training in Leignitz from the end of April to July 1944, but reports from the period indicate that the German instructors had problems with Italians' lack of flying discipline, and several accidents occurred. Even so, on return to Italy some of the pilots were posted to *IIº Gruppo Caccia*, and served with distinction.

On November 1944, *Iº* and *IIIº Gruppo Caccia* (*Gr.C*) were posted to Germany (Holzkirchen and Furth) to convert onto the Bf 109. Much to the concern of the Luftwaffe, it was found that many of the *IIIº Gr.C* pilots had failed to complete any more than basic training back in Italy, and that was back in 1943! Inevitably, the trainees failed to complete their conversion onto the Bf 109, and were duly sent home. *Iº Gr.C* did, however, manage to successfully transition onto the demanding Messerschmitt fighter, and they returned to Italy in February 1945, and

This C.200 was flown by Generale Raffaelli, Commander of Settore Aeronautico Est in North Africa. The photo, taken in Libya in the autumn of 1941 clearly shows the Generale di Brigata *insignia below the cockpit – a blue square with a red star – applied on a Macchi of 373 Squadron, 53* Stormo. (via BAK 436)

subsequently saw action for the next two months.

The Luftwaffe was also concerned at the lack of Italian gunnery training, and sent two Bücker Bü 181s, with training personnel, to tour ANR fighter units in March 1945 with the express purpose of establishing a flight gunnery training course. Today, films and reports survive of this fleeting attempt to instil a rigour into Italian fighter pilot gunnery training.

Tactics

The Italian predilection for individual fighter tactics founded upon aerobatic technique pervaded the whole ethos of the combat methodology employed by both the RA and the ANR. Today, little or no written documentation relating to combat tactics seems to have survived – if indeed, there was any in the first place. Those combat tactics that were implemented with any consistency had usually been developed by expert pilots responsible for leading the squadrons themselves.

Fighter formations sometimes consisted of patrols made up of three to twelve aircraft arranged in 'V' sections of three fighters each –

in preparation for combat, the aircraft usually moved into a 'right wing' abreast formation. Later in the war the leader-wingman formation became more common. In combat, Italian fighter pilots gained a reputation within the RAF for being unpredictable, but it is certainly very doubtful that this unpredictability would have heightened their prowess in aerial combat – rather, it would have aided their chances of survival.

The tactics employed by the ANR had to be changed in light of their equipment with the Bf 109. The latter's greatest asset in combat was its speed, and its much heavier wing-loading did not make it suitable for aerobatics. Despite this, the ANR failed to standardize combat tactics, again leaving instruction to each squadron commander. Thus, in *IIº Gruppo Caccia*, Capt Ugo Drago (1a Squadron) emphasized the need for co-ordination in the air as the safety of his pilots was of paramount importance. By contrast, Capt Bellagambi (2ª Squadron) considered it essential to attack enemy aircraft by closing to the shortest distance before firing.

The lack of training both in instrument flying

Pantelleria Island, 1941. A G.50 of 352 Squadron, 51 Stormo *is seen on the transfer route to the North African front. Clearly visible in the background on the right is the entrance to the huge underground hangar which safely accommodated many aircraft, making it almost invulnerable to bombing raids.* (via D'Amico-Valentini)

Posed portraits of unknown Italian fighter pilots supposedly returning from missions in their aircraft. (via BAK 466)

and gunnery severely hampered the operational capacity of the fighter pilots of the RA during the first years of the war. As a result, Italian fighter pilots gained a reputation for being 'fair weather' fighter pilots – they simply could not operate in inclement weather because they had not received adequate instrument training.

Stress

Following the example of the Luftwaffe, once an Italian pilot became a member of an operational fighter squadron, he was expected to remain on operations for long periods of time, interspersed with a short period of R&R. The operational period lasted either two to three or four to five months depending on the front on which the unit operated. Gen Biron recalled:

We were briefed for a mission by the CO and flew on average about one sortie a day. We were not rotated like the British and Americans, and flew like the Germans all the time. When I shot down an enemy aircraft I felt euphoria but afterwards

extreme sorrow for the enemy pilot. I must say I never had any problems with combat stress or any related symptoms, nor did I ever feel that I could not fly a mission. You could be pulled out of the line if things got bad for you, and would then be sent for R&R up in the mountains, but we did not have much illness, and our medical service was excellent. Morale was always very good until 8 September 1943. Morale again improved when the ANR was formed in 1943, and we fought on against the Allies.

Gen Biron also flew in the Spanish Civil War and later in 22 Group on the Eastern Front, and had the opportunity to experience very different operating conditions. Of Russia he recalled:

Regarding the supply of men and machines, we did have some problems in Russia because of the extreme weather conditions in relation to the supply of men and machines. We usually had five to ten aircraft operational, but our replacement pilots were of as good a quality at the beginning, as at the end

An atmospheric shot of three Italian fighter pilots of 155 Group, 51 Stormo in front of a C.202 Folgore belonging to Cap. Franchini (the little rabbit was his personal insignia) on the island of Sardinia in 1942. Clearly dress regulations were relaxed within this unit. (via BAK 415)

of the war – the same goes for our aircraft. We always had aircraft on constant standby and operational readiness. Supplies of food were good. The number of days leave we received very much depended on the war situation.

Filing of Claims – the Process
From the early years of the Second World War the RA sought to guard against the psychological effect of individuals being lauded as 'ace' pilots, and others (who would inevitably be in the majority) perceived, and indeed probably viewing themselves, as being less-able aviators. The method employed was to credit any claims that were made to the squadron or group – not to the individual pilot. Between 1940-42 pilots were permitted to report claims in their personal flying log books, but official accreditation and recognition of the claims was given to the unit. This procedure was a reflection of the stated philosophy in Order numbers' B/18671 of 25 August 1940, 5/22191 of 7 September 1942, and

10/S.53 dated 3 March 1943, that '. . . every kill, even if made by an individual pilot, is the result of the combined action of many other pilots'.

With hindsight, it seems slightly incongruous that with the emphasis placed on group victories, rather than individual scoring, combat training and tactics during the first three years of war was primarily based on individual flying technique, rather than operating as part of a team! Further, the accreditation of claims to the unit rather than its individual pilots was a major departure from the earlier practice of the First World War, for Italy had used the 'image value' derived from great aces like Scaroni, Baracca and others to boost morale within the Italian public.

By the time of Order number 10/S.53 of 3 March 1943, the Italians saw the need to revise the criteria for combat claims, thus permitting the award of confirmed claims to individual pilots. A commission was established to devise guidelines both on the process of combat claims, and the accreditation of those claims to

Yet another task performed by the CR.42 was ground attack. Equipped with two bombs under the wings, the Italian biplanes attacked British columns in North Africa, but enjoyed only limited success, losing a great number of aircraft in the process. An aircraft is seen here preparing for a bombing practice flight (as evidenced by the very small exercise bomb barely visible under the wing). (via D'Amico-Valentini)

A C.205 Veltro of 360 Squadron, 155 Group, 51 Stormo RA. The black cat and mice insignia was created just before the war when G.50s of 51 Stormo managed to intercept S.79s bombers of 12 Stormo 'Sorci Verdi' (the 'Green Mice') during an exercise. 51 Stormo thus adopted the insignia of a black cat catching the three green mice. (via BAK 468)

A C.205 of 72 Squadron, 17 Group, 1 Stormo RA displaying the archer insignia in late 1942. The Italian pilot is talking to two German air crew. Both men are wearing life jackets denoting operations over water. One crew member has the four-winged rank insignia on his right sleeve indicating that he is a Oberfeldwebel/ Oberfähnrich. (via BAK 466)

individual pilots. Like the Soviet Air Force, but unlike most other major air forces, the RA sought to actively encourage the filing of individual claims by issuing a financial bounty to its pilots.

Bounty

All confirmed claims for an enemy aircraft shot down or a ship sunk were to be rewarded with a bounty. The following criteria were:

1) 5,000 Lire for every single- or twin-engined aircraft shot down.
2) 15,000 Lire for every four-engined aircraft shot down.
3) 150,000 Lire for every Merchant Navy vessel sunk, or light military craft.
4) 250,000 Lire for every war vessel sunk of average tonnage.

The guidelines for the consideration of claims prior to the armistice were based upon three main criteria: shot down, probable (air), and probable (ground). These were described in Order number 10/S.53 of 3 March 1943 as:

Shot Down
An enemy aircraft is considered shot down in combat when it has been seen to fall, crash or burn, compelled to land, destroyed on the ground, or in water, during air combat.

Probable (air)
An enemy aircraft that loses height and abandons combat, leaving a trail of smoke that makes one conclude that there is fire on board, is considered shot down in combat.

Probable (ground)
An enemy aircraft that has been centrally hit by the guns of the attacking aircraft is considered probably destroyed on the ground or on water.

The three categories needed to be supported by statements from witnesses, who did not necessarily have to hail from the same squadron, and photographic evidence elicited from gun-camera film. The written claim was made on Form 1, to which was attached written testimony, photographs and other relevant documentation. The claim was verified at squadron level, but the

concurrence of the group commanding officer was required. Once the claim for the individual destruction of the enemy aircraft had been verified, the pilot was informed that he had been credited with an individual victory, and he received his bounty as reward for his efforts. He was also accredited with the kill, but not given the bounty, if the enemy aircraft or vessel had already been hit, but not shot down, by other

An Italian and a German pilot joke with a cockerel next to a C.200, which interestingly has a name painted on its cowling – the unit is unknown. (ECPA via D'Amico-Valentini)

An Italian pilot lounging in his deckchair next his CR.42 of the RA – again the unit is unknown. (via BAK 435)

Sicily 1942. Routine maintenance on an anonymous Re.2000 fighter of the RA. Its only discernible unit marking is the aircraft's tactical number '5' painted on the white fuselage band. (via BAK 415)

A heavily-dressed Italian pilot is seen wearing a parachute next to his C.202 Folgore before a morning flight over North Africa in early 1942. The fighter belongs to 81 Squadron, 1 Stormo, and shows the typical Italian desert camouflage, but no unit insignia. (via D'Amico-Valentini)

pilots, but that his action was seen as the determining factor in the kill. In this case, all the other pilots who had contributed to the kill would be mentioned or, when the other pilots were not identifiable, the unit was credited with kill.

M.llo Aldo Barbaglio describes the process which existed during 1940-43:

Our combat report to Ops was a verbal one. A combat claim was not always accredited, and it was sometimes left up to the discretion of the CO if you got it or not. Then again, if a pilot was not known for a claim, it would be accredited to the squadron. The Air Intelligence Officer played no part in our unit.

Following the armistice in September 1943, the ANR, in conjunction with the Luftwaffe, introduced changes to the criteria for combat claim accreditation. It would seem fair to say the ANR method of claim submission mirrored the Luftwaffe process, which is not surprising in

light of the fact that the Luftwaffe had taken over responsibility for issuing confirmation of ANR claims. Regulation numbers 8218 of 27 May 1944 and 14270 of 10 July 1944 sharpened the crediting criteria in terms of the supporting evidence required, but also altered the guidelines for the types of claim which could be submitted in order to take account of the operational fronts over which the ANR was operating. Claims could be put forward for consideration if:

1) The enemy aircraft was shot down after it had been seen to be hit and crash to the ground, or in water.
2) The enemy aircraft was hit and caught fire, although it was not possible to immediately locate where it had fallen.
3) The enemy aircraft was hit, seen to catch fire, but not observed to crash on territory controlled by the RSI/ANR.

Rare photos of Italian and German combined fighter operations over the Alps in late 1943. The aircraft are a C.205 Veltro of I Gruppo Caccia *ANR and a Bf 109G of JG 77.* (via BAK 47017)

A special commission was established to examine all combat claims, and to ascribe verification and bounties. The commission was based at the ANR headquarters, and consisted of the commanding officer of the ANR Headquarters, who was the president of the commission, his deputy and the operations chief. A special Luftwaffe unit controlled the claims, and assigned them to ANR Headquarters for consideration by the commission.

The commission used the following criteria to determine whether:

1) The enemy aircraft was found on RSI territory.
2) The enemy aircraft was shot down into the water as reported by witnesses.
3) The enemy aircraft was shot down after air combat in territory not controlled by the RSI/ANR.
4) The enemy aircraft was shot down in territory controlled by the enemy and witnessed by others.

The commission required the following witnesses and documentation:

1) Verbal declaration by persons who had not been involved in the combat.
2) Written declarations by at least two people who had witnessed the air combat.
3) Declarations by enemy PoWs who had witnessed the air combat.
4) Enemy radio reports.
5) Information gathered from the intelligence service.
6) Other evidence obtained after the declaration and location of the enemy aircraft.
7) Location of enemy aircraft wreckage at sea.
8) Other testimonials and documents relative to the enemy aircraft kill.

Yet, Italian researchers have often puzzled as to why so many of the aircraft reported and confirmed as having been destroyed during this period were so categorized without any real attempt being made at the time to trace the wreckage, even though the aircraft had been reported to have crashed on controlled soil. This criticism can also be applied to the claims made by the Luftwaffe, whose criteria and process of verification had been adopted by the ANR, and

A Bf 109G-4 of 364 Squadron, 150 Group is seen revving-up its engine at Sciacca in June 1943. 150 Group, together with 3 Group, operated in Sicily with the German fighter from May 1943 up to the Allied landings. The Italian fighters were decimated on the ground by the continuous Allied bombardments. (via D'Amico-Valentini)

A rare in-flight shot of the C.205s of I Gruppo Caccia ANR *about to intercept enemy bombers of the Fifteenth AAF during the Spring of 1944.* (via D'Amico-Valentini)

indeed issued confirmation of claims made by ANR fighter pilots.

Despite the nature of the evolving claim criteria, Giuseppe Biron, who had flown in action in Somalia, Spain, on the Eastern Front and then back in his homeland, felt that the criteria were stringently applied throughout:

After combat we had to report to Ops and fill out a combat report – this we did ourselves. The combat claim was usually confirmed by our fellow pilots, and these claims were filled out as meticulously at the beginning as at the end of the war.

Gun Camera
It is believed that gun cameras were rarely used in Italian fighters during the 1940-43 period. As a result, claims were often not supported by the investigation of combat footage. With the advent of the ANR, many German aircraft like the Bf 109G-6 and G-10 were flown in combat by Italian units. These aircraft had, at least, been originally equipped with the facility for a gun camera, but the ANR did not normally take advantage of this during the last months of the war.

Intelligence Officers
Neither the RA nor the ANR made use of the Intelligence Officer in the debriefing session following a mission – indeed there were few, if any, IOs attached to fighter units within either force. This meant that there was no filtering process in the immediate verbal report made by a pilot to his senior officer directly after a mission, and a written report was only made by a pilot when a claim was to be submitted.

Awards and Decorations
A search of *Gazzette Ufficiali* from June 1940 to September 1943 reveals the main awards to which Italian fighter pilots would be entitled during this period. The RA issued 52 Gold Medals, 1,838 Silver Medals (which included 20 awards made to units as a whole), 2,059 Bronze Medals, and 1,809 *Croci di Guerra* – the Cross of War for Military Valour.

The award of the Gold, Silver and Bronze Medals and the *Croci di Guerra* was established on 4 November 1932 with the *Regio Decreto* number 1423. The criteria included:

. . . the concession of such decorations can take place

only when the act can be considered under every aspect, worthy of example and in imitation . . .

. . . loss of life can be the proof of the seriousness of the risks, but is not enough to be considered to be the basis of a military award, as it can result from the combination of all the other circumstances . . .

For submission to be considered the following points had to be observed:

. . . for the military in service the initiative of the proposal can be taken by the immediate superior in rank. The proposals, accompanied with all the documents necessary to prove the facts and the circumstances and to evidence the gallantry of the acts, must be submitted through the proper channels, in order to allow the superior authorities to form their opinion. The papers must be submitted to the central administration within three months from the facts.

In the process that followed, it is clear that recommendations were then submitted to the *Commissione Militare Consultiva per la Concessione e la Perdita di Decorazioni al Valor Militare*, which convened periodically and examined the proposals. The RA's proposal was examined by three air force generals and one navy admiral.

Judging by the vast differences between the numbers of Gold and Silver Medals awarded, it is clear that the former was awarded only for the most meritorious acts of bravery, whereas the latter could be given for acts of bravery, an action, or as an award which resulted from several recommendations to an individual for the Bronze Medal. In such cases, it was subsequently decided by the examining board that the combination instead deserved the award of a single Silver Medal.

It is not currently known whether RSI operated a *Commissione Militare Consultiva* under which ANR recommendations for awards could be examined. It is possible that awards were examined and decreed by the Director of *Militari Personnel and Schools* (Discipline

Two Italian ground crew leaning on the wing of a C.205 of I Gruppo Caccia *ANR in northern Italy in 1944.* (via BAK 47020)

Above *Seen at Lagnasco (Cuneo) in December 1943, Italian and German fighter pilots exchange combat experiences by the tail of a C.205 just delivered by II./JG 77 to I Gruppo Caccia. (via BAK R71)*

Top right *The Italian fighter pilot Fausto Filippi was awarded German pilot's wings as well as the Iron Cross Second Class for his aerial victories gained under the leadership of Hans-Joachim Marseille over Tobruk. Tenente Fausto Filippi fought with 363 Squadron during the RA period, then became a member of 5 Squadron, 2 Fighter Group of the ANR after the armistice. He is credited with six victories in the RA and two in the ANR. He was shot down and killed near Padua on the 23 January 1945. (via D'Amico-Valentini)*

Below right *Maggiore Mario Bellagambi was one of the finest Italian pilots and unit leaders. Initially seeing combat in the Spanish Civil War, Bellagambi flew operationally from the beginning of the Second World War. He later commanded a squadron within 150 Group and was awarded three Silver Medals and one Iron Cross 2nd Class. After the armistice he joined the ANR and became the CO of 5 Squadron, 2 Fighter Group, gaining another Silver Medal and one Iron Cross 1st Class. He also became the highest-scoring ANR pilot, with ten victories. (via D'Amico-Valentini)*

Section). At least one Gold Medal was (posthumously) awarded to an ANR fighter pilot, Capt Giovanni Bonet, who was serving as the CO of *Squadriglia Montefusco* (*Montefusco-Bonet* after his death), being shot down and killed on 29 March 1944.

Many Italian fighter pilots received awards from the Germans, examples indicating that the Iron Cross Second and First Class, together with the *Frontflug-spange für Jäger* in bronze, was awarded as shown.

Pilot Profiles
Ca.309, C.202/.205 and Bf 109G-10 Pilot – Adriano Visconti

Adriano Visconti di Lampugnano was born in Tripoli on 11 November 1915. He enrolled in the air force academy as a cadet pilot officer in SPE 'Rex Course' in 1937. In 1939 Visconti was posted as a second lieutenant to 23a Sq. OA/2 Gr. Colonial Aviation, before being transferred to 159a Sqdn./12°/Gr./50° Stormo, with whom he had two flying accidents flying the Ba.65/K.14 at

Scoring nine victories in the ANR as CO of 4 Squadron, 2 Fighter Group, Cap. Ugo Drago ranked second among the Italian late-war aces. Quite possibly the finest ANR unit Commander, Drago served with the rank of Tenente in the RA, flying with 363 Squadron, 150 Group and obtaining a War Cross for operations against France and three Silver Medals for his achievements on the Greek front, in North Africa and Sicily. During his time in the ANR a fourth Silver medal was awarded to Drago. He was an exceptional fighter leader, losing only two pilots from his unit between May 1944 and March 1945! This photo was taken in Sicily in June 1943 while Ten. Drago was commanding 363 Squadron. (via D'Amico-Valentini)

Benghazi and then at Tobruk. He was also shot down in a Breda over Bir el Kruggat after his aircraft had been struck by fire from British tanks – he parachuted to safety. Promoted to lieutenant, Visconti was assigned in 1941 to 76a. Sq./16° Gr./54° *Stormo*, flying C.200s and .202s.

Here, he started to achieve some significant combat success, eventually being credited with six Allied fighters including Spitfires and P-40s, as well as a Blenheim. In March 1943 Visconti was sent to Tunisia as 76ª Sqdn CO, holding the rank of captain. Later in 1943 he was posted for photo-reconnaissance duties to 310ª, Sqdn again as CO. A few months after the armistice, Visconti returned to operational flying with the C.205-equipped 1ª, Sq./1° *Gruppo Caccia*. He claimed to have brought down a further four enemy aircraft with the Macchi.

Visconti had developed a reputation as a fine fighter leader, and his wingmen have since emphasized his ability to successfully lead his formation into aerial combat. Promoted directly to major in recognition of his valour over a prolonged period, Visconti's final operations were flown with the Bf 109G-10 – his last combat success occurred in March 1945 when he filed a claim for a P-47 after having parachuted to safety – this kill cannot be confirmed as, the US pilot he fought against on that day (Lt Charles C. Eddy of the 346th FS/350th FG, USAAF) was never actually shot down.

Adriano Visconti received many decorations for bravery and meritorious duty, including six silver medals and two bronze medals, plus he was awarded the Iron Cross (1st and 2nd Class) by the Luftwaffe. Notably, Visconti never received his country's highest award, the Gold

Medal for Military Valour – a fact which still rankles with many in the aviation fraternity in Italy to this day. He came to a brutal and ignominious end when, shortly after surrendering his unit's Bf 109s to Italian partisans on 29 April 1945, he was executed in Milan.

Visconti's claims were previously thought to have been much higher, and had never really been called into question until recently when his log books – previously thought to have been lost or destroyed at the end of the war – came to light. These showed that Visconti had received 10 individual credits, as opposed to the 25+ he had been credited with since the war. Whatever his final tally (and his logbook seems to close the chapter on this argument), Visconti had demonstrated that he was both a fine and courageous fighter pilot and a good leader and tactician.

Fiat CR.32 and Macchi C.200/.202 Pilot –
Franco Lucchini
Born in Rome on 24 December 1914, Franco Lucchini was to become the leading Italian fighter pilot of both the Spanish Civil War and the Second World War. As a volunteer with the Nationalists, Lucchini flew the CR.32 'Chirri' fighter with 19ª. *Squadriglia* 'Asso di Bastoni', 10°. *Gruppo*, 4°. *Stormo* CT. He achieved his first aerial victory on 12 October 1937, and his fifth, and final, victory of the Spanish Civil War on 22 July 1938.

As a member of 90ª. *Squadriglia*, 10° *Gruppo*, 4. *Stormo* CT, Lucchini claimed his first combat victory of the Second World War when he destroyed a Sunderland flying boat of RAF Coastal Command. Operating in the Axis attack on Malta, he flew both the C.200 Saetta and C.202 Folgore with considerable success, claiming the destruction of six RAF fighters. On 27 September Lucchini was hospitalized with severe injuries to his back after a heavy forced landing in the Ustica area. Whilst in hospital he met his future wife, whom he married in March of the following year. On return to operational flying, Lucchini was promoted to become the

Magg. Adriano Visconti with his Bf 109G10/AS in one of the last operations he flew as CO of 1 Fighter Group in March 1945. (via D'Amico-Valentini)

Ten. Mario Cavatore of 1 Squadron, 1 Fighter Group ANR poses for a photo in his C.205 at Campoformido airfield (Udine) on March 1944. (via D'Amico-Valentini)

CO of 84ª *Squadriglia*, which was equipped with the C.202. With his new unit, Lucchini returned to the conflict over Malta, claiming two Spitfires as destroyed.

84ª *Squadriglia* was posted to the airfield at Martuba to take part in the North African campaign at the end of May 1942, and over the next five months Lucchini filed claims for the destruction of ten enemy aircraft, plus shared claims for six more – many of these were against P-40 Kittyhawks. On 24 October 1942 Lucchini was again severely injured in a forced landing following action with P-40s, crashing in the desert some distance away from the airfield at El Daba. He then spent a number of months convalescing.

In March 1943 Franco Lucchini was promoted to become CO of 10° *Gruppo* of 4°, *Stormo* CT. Continuing to fly on operations, Lucchini was finally killed over Sicily on 5 July 1943 when, having already accounted for a Spitfire, he was

himself shot down by a second RAF fighter. Franco Lucchini was 28 years old at the time of his death, and in 1952 his leadership and courage as a fighter pilot was posthumously recognized when he was awarded the *Medaglia d'Oro*.

APPENDICES
Examples of the Process of Combat Claims of the Italian Air Force and supporting documentation

A. Retrospective Regia Aeronautica Claim report

This claim was submitted more than 16 months after the events which are described in the submission. The critical feature behind the report appears to be that the former RA pilot, who was at the time of the submission serving in the ANR, was belatedly attempting to obtain the bounty money which had been implemented subsequent to the original action in which he claimed to have shot down two B-17s over Sicily. His statement is significant in that it provides clear evidence that prize money existed, and that pilots were motivated to submit a claim in order to grasp that bounty. Further, the process of the claim submission seems to be less structured and formalized than that in place for ANR kill accreditation:

Declaration
On 25 May 1943 I scrambled and took-off from the airfield Reggio Calabria aboard a C.202. After I had reached a height of 6,000 metres, I joined the other members of my squadron, as well as fighters from 161 Group. I was soon engaged in aerial combat with about 40 American Boeing B-17 bombers over the Straits of Messina. I engaged a bomber to the front and right of this formation. After several attacks on this aircraft it started to trail smoke from its inner right-hand engine, the enemy bomber then started to loose height and lag behind the formation. I continued my attack and after several more bursts of fire I noticed that a fire had started near the wing root of the aircraft, which soon engulfed the wing and fuselage, the aircraft then went into a near vertical dive and crashed into a valley of the Peloritanni mountains. After I had verified that the bomber had crashed, I started to climb again, and noticed another formation of enemy bombers, as strong as the previous one, and of the same type.

As I had enough fuel and ammunition left, I decided to jump an aircraft which was flying a bit lower and slightly apart from the rest of the formation. I closed up and opened my fire in a head-on attack, after this attack I noticed thick smoke coming out of the inner section of the left wing. I then moved to the left side of the aircraft and attacked once more, coming in abreast of it and aiming at the point where dense smoke was pouring out. After a few more shots the aircraft caught fire and crashed near the shoreline, close to Milazzo. I returned to base at the very limit of my endurance.

P.B.C. 857, 21 October 1944.
Serg. Magg. pil. FORNACI Fausto

Declaration
The undersigned Sergente Maggiore Pilota FORNACI Fausto.
The undersigned is aware of the administrative and legal responsibilities that are involved in making this declaration, and states that he has not received in part or whole the 'DUCE Prize money' for shooting down two enemy Boeing B-17 aircraft over Sicily on 25 May 1943 at . . . hours.

P.B.C.857, 21 October 1944.
Serg. Magg. pil. FORNACI Fausto

Declaration
On 25 May 1943 at 11:10 hours I scrambled from the airfield Reggio Calabria as wingman to Cap. pil. GIUDICE Eber. After we had reached an altitude of 6,000 metres, we intercepted near Capo Spartivento a formation of twelve four-engined Liberators heading south after having bombed Messina. The commanding officer attacked the leading aircraft nearly head-on, I was flying slightly behind him during his attack. I engaged and opened my fire on an aircraft flying to the right of this formation, but with no apparent effect. I flew a new attack, this time coming in from behind the last aircraft in the formation. As I was turning away I was attacked by the escorting fighters who tried to get on my tail. In the meantime, the aircraft I had hit was losing height and trailing smoke. After I had shaken off the enemy fighters I went after the damaged bomber and fired the rest of my ammunition into it. The aircraft caught fire and crashed into the sea near Capo Passero (Sicily).

P.B.C.857, 21 October 1944.
Serg. Magg. pil. FORNACI Fausto

Declaration
The undersigned Serg. Magg. pil. PACINI Giuseppe, of 3rd Squadron, 2nd Fighter Group, describes the following events. On 25 May 1943 at 11:10 hours I scrambled from the airfield Reggio Calabria. After I had reached a height of 6,000 metres together with Cap. pil. GIUDICE Eber and Serg. Magg. pil. FORNACI Fausto, we attacked a formation of 12 Liberator bombers. During the engagement I saw the aircraft piloted by FORNACI Fausto attack and shoot down in flames an enemy aircraft which crashed near Capo Passero (Sicily).

P.B.C.857, 21 October 1944.
Serg. Magg. pil. PACINI Giuseppe

Declaration
The undersigned Cap. pil. GIUDICE Eber, squadron commander, describes the following

events. On 25 May 1943 at 11:10 hours I scrambled aboard a C.202 as commander of three aircraft. When we got to the Straits of Messina, I observed below us an enemy formation of 40 Boeing B-17 bombers returning from a raid on Messina. Together with my wingmen, we jumped this formation, and during the following combat I saw the aircraft piloted by Serg. Magg. pil. FORNACI Fausto engage an enemy aircraft and shoot it down. The same pilot then engaged an other aircraft of the same type with very accurate fire and at close quarters, the same aircraft was then again attacked by him and shot down. Both aircraft crashed, the first in a valley of the Peloritani mountains and the second on the shoreline near Milazzo.

P.B.C.857, 21 October 1944.
Cap. pil. GIUDICE Eber

Declaration

The undersigned Cap. pil. GIUDICE Eber, describes the following events. On 25 May 1943 at 11:10 hours I scrambled aboard a C.202 fighter with Serg. Magg. pil. FORNACI Fausto as my first wingman. After we had reached a height of 6,000 metres, we attacked a formation of 12 Liberator bombers. During the dogfight I saw my wingman (Serg. Magg. pil. FORNACI Fausto) shoot down in flames an enemy aircraft which crashed near Capo Passero (Sicily).

P.B.C.857, 21 October 1944.
Cap. pil. GIUDICE Eber

Declaration

The undersigned Serg. Magg. pil. PACINI Giuseppe, of 3rd Squadron, 2nd Fighter Group, describes the following events. On 25 May 1943 at 11:10 hours I scrambled from the airfield Reggio Calabria aboard a C.202 aircraft as a wingman in a formation led by Cap. pil. GIUDICE Eber. When we got to the Straits of Messina, we observed below us an enemy formation of 40 Boeing B-17 bombers returning from a raid on Messina. We attacked immediately and in the following combat I noticed a C.202 attack an enemy aircraft and shoot it down. After a while he flew another attack against a second aircraft which was shot down and crashed near the shoreline in the neighbourhood of Milazzo. After I had landed back at base, I noticed that the successful fighter was the mount of Serg.

Magg. pil. FORNACI Fausto.

P.B.C.857, 21 October 1944.
Serg. Magg. pil. PACINI Giuseppe.

B. ANR Report modelled on Luftwaffe claim procedure, with supporting witnesses.

II Fighter Group

Date: 26 July 1944

1a Squadron
Combat Claim Or Destruction Report

1   Date (day, hour, minute) and locality of crash
    26/7/1944 17 hrs 10 mins near Gropparello-SSE of Piacenza, altitude 4,000 metres
2   Name of claiming pilot   Ten. pil. Drago Ugo
3   Type of enemy aircraft   'Thunderbolt'
4   Nationality of aircraft shot down   markings American
5   How was it shot down:
    a – fire on board, *with dark, white smoke* (1)
    b – breaking of parts (specify), explosions: engine on fire
    c – forced to land: this side or other side of front, normal or emergency (1)
    d – on fire on the other side of the front, on ground
6   Details of crash
    a – this side or other side of front (1)
    b – dived gliding, caught fire on the ground, cloud of dust (1)
    c – not observed because: engaged in combat with other fighters
7   Crew fate: dead, bailed out with parachute, not observed (1)
8   *Claiming pilot report enclosed*
9   Witnesses
    a – in flight: Ten. pil. Valenzano Raffaele
    b – on ground
10 Number of attacks on enemy aircraft: one
11 Direction of attacks: from above, right wing and engine
12 Distance from which the a/c was shot at: short distance
13 Tactical position of enemy: last, in right turn
14 Enemy gunners shot
15 Type of ammunition used: incendiary, explosive
16 Shots fired: 40 of 20 mm and 160 of 13 mm
17 Number and type of own guns: 3 (1 of 20 mm and 2 of 13 mm)
18 Own aircraft type: Me 109G-6
19 Other tactical or technical observations

20 Number of hits received
21 Participation of other units

Squadron CO signature
Ten. pil. Drago Ugo
(1) underline applicable response

(Name and rank) Tenete DRAGO Ugo
(Unit)1st Squadron – 2nd Fighter Group
(date) 26 July 1944

Claiming Pilot Report
Shooting down of a Thunderbolt on 26/07/1944:
hours 1710

Locality	near Gropparello, SSE of Piacenza
Flight order	Free patrol in Mantua-Piacenza area
Take-off	1635 Locality Villafranca
Landing	1725 Locality Villafranca

Declaration
On 26 July 1944 at 16 hrs 35 mins I took off for a freelance patrol flight in the Mantua-Piacencza area as formation leader. At about 17 hr 10 min, Cap. Miani Carlo sighted south of Piacenza a formation of four Thunderbolt fighter-bombers and moved to attack from above astern.

I followed him with my section and when I closed on him I opened fire, aiming at tail-end aircraft, the enemy fighters being in line astern, turning right. With my third burst I shot the enemy plane between its right wing and the engine, which then started poring black smoke. Being engaged in combat with other enemy fighters, I wasn't able to follow the damaged plane. The combat occurred at 17 hrs 10 mins at an altitude of about 4,000 metres, near Gropparello, SSE of Piacenza.

Signature and rank
1st Squadron 'Gigi Caneppele'
CO Ten. pil. Drago Ugo

(Name and rank) Ten. VALENZANO Raffaele
(Unit) 1st Squadron – 2nd Fighter Group
(date) 26 July 1944

Evidence of the Witnesses
On the shooting down of a 'Thunderbolt' enemy aircraft on 26/7/1944 hours 1710 by Ten. pil. DRAGO Ugo

Declaration
On 26 July 1944 at 16 hrs 35 mins I took off for a freelance patrol flight in the Mantua-Piacenza area

as wingman to Ten. pil. DRAGO Ugo.

At 17 hr 10 mins, sighted a formation of four Thunderbolt fighter-bombers, we started an attack from above astern. I was closely following Ten. DRAGO, who machine-gunned the last fighter of the enemy formation.

The aircraft dived trailing black smoke near Gropparello.

Signature and rank

Ten. Valenzano Raffaele.
II Group
1st Squadron   (Date) 26 July 1944

Squadron Commander Assessment
(Blank)

Squadron CO

Group Commander Assessment

From examination of the declarations I consider the claim confirmed

Group CO
T.Col. Alessandrini Aldo.

C. Luftwaffe Combat Confirmation for the Italian Air Force
Two Claims on One Document

The Commanding General of the German Air Force in Italy
9/2/1945   No.29/45

For Oblt Ugo Drago
1.Flight / II, Italian Fighter Group,

Shot down one Liberator on the 21/7/44 at 10:50 (Area Fola)

Claim is herewith confirmed

Stamp
General der Flieger

The Commanding General of the German Air Force in Italy
9/2/1945   No.22/45

For Oblt Ugo Drago
1.Flight / II, Italian Fighter Group,

Shot down one Thunderbolt on the 25/7/44 at 17:10 (Gropparello)

Claim is herewith confirmed

Stamp
General der Flieger

COMMISSIONE MILITARE CONSULTIVA UNICA PER LA
CONCESSIONE E LA PERDITA DI DECORAZIONI AL V. M.

PROCESSO VERBALE DI SEDUTA

L'anno millenovecentotrent **otto XVI°**   addí   **30**   del

mese di _____ alle ore _____ **8** _____ si è riunita in Roma,
Agosto

nella sua sede, la Commissione Militare Consultiva composta dai Sigg.:

GABBA Cr.Cr.Melchiade Generale com- des. d'armata   Presidente

RAINERI BISCIA Comm. Giuseppe Ammiraglio di Divisione   Membro

CARNEVALI Comm.Luigi Generale di Divisione A.A.   "

TOCCOLINI Comm. Tullio Generale di Divisione A.A.   "Relatore

SABATINI Comm.Arnaldo Generale di brigata A.A.   "

DE SILVA Comm.Gioacchino colonnello di fanteria   Segretario

Esaminata la proposta di concessione di decorazione al V. M. pervenuta dal Ministero

dell _____ a favore del
'Aeronautica"S"

Sergente pilota MOTTET Giuseppe, di Giuseppe

la Commissione, poichè, a suo giudizio, ricorrono gli estremi previsti dal R. decreto n. 1423,

in data 4 novembre 1932.

Visto l'art. 9 della legge 24 marzo 1932, n. 453;

esprime a   parere FAVOREVOLE sull'accoglimento
d unanimità

della proposta stessa.

In conseguenza, ritiene il _____ sergente MOTTET Giuseppe _____

meritevole di MEDAGLIA D'ARGENTO e propone la seguente motivazione:

""Volontario in missione di guerra per l'affermazione degli ideali fascisti,

pilota da caccia di non comune abilità, partecipava attivamente alle operazio

ni sul fronte di Madrid.

Nei molteplici combattimenti sostenuti dimostrava le sue rare qualità

di valore audacia e aggressività, recando valido contributo alle vittorie con

te dal suo reparto e abbattendo diverse unità avversarie""

Cielo di Madrid: luglio 1937 XV°

Polistampa Ord. 1860 (2.000) Roma - 1938 XVI

This details the composition of the Commission and the award made to Sergente Giuseppe Mottet. Although this award was made in 1937, the RA continued to use this format throughout 1940-43. (via Ferdinando D'Amico)

SOTTOSEGRETARIATO PER L'AERONAUTICA
DEL MINISTERO DELLE FORZE ARMATE
Direzione Generale del Personale
MILITARE E DELLE SCUOLE

Posta da campo N. 875 lì 4 FEB 1945

Alla Signora

GHIMENTI Ainzara Ved. Bonet

DIVISIONE DISCIPLINA

Prot. N. 3890.30 PERS. Allegati

Risposta al foglio N.

del

OGGETTO: Comunicazione.=

= BAGNOLO DI S. PIETRO FELETTO=
(Treviso)

Si comunica che con Decreto in corso di firma é stata concessa al vostro compianto consorte, Capitano Pilota

BONET Giovanni,

la Medaglia d'Oro al Valor Militare "alla memoria„ con la seguente mo= tivazione :

""VALOROSO COMANDANTE DI SQUADRILIA DA CACCIA, COMBATTENTE DI DUE GUER RE, TORNAVA IN LINEA FRA I PRIMISSIMI DOPO GLI INFAUSTI EVENTI DEL SET TEMBRE.-
ANCORA CONVALESCENTE DA UNA GLORIOSA FERITA, DEDICAVA OGNI SUA ENER GIA ALLA RICOSTRUZIONE DEL SUO REPARTO.-
PARTITO SU ALLARME PER LA DIFESA DELLA SUA TERRA, SEGUITO DA POCHI VALOROSI CHE SI ERANO STRETTI INTORNO A LUI, SI SCAGLIAVA IMPETUOSAMEN TE CONTRO PODEROSE FORMAZIONI DI CENTINAIA DI QUADRIMOTORI E CACCIA NE MICI.-
DURANTE L'IMPARI LOTTA ABBATTEVA IN FIAMME UNO DEI BOMBARDIERI, FIN CHE' A SUA VOLTA, SOPRAFFATTO DAL NUMERO, CADEVA GLORIOSAMENTE NEL CIE LO DELLA BATTAGLIA, SACRIFICANDO LA SUA GIOVANE ESISTENZA PER LA SALVEZ ZA DELLA PATRIA MARTORIATA.-
LA SUA GRANDE ANIMA DI PURISSIMO EROE RIMANE PRESENTE IN OGNI CUORE PER GRIDARE, NEL ROMBO DEI MOTORI, NELLE RAFFICHE DELLE MITRAGLIERE, LA PAROLA DI OGGI E DI DOMANI : "ITALIA„.=

Cielo di Torino, 29 Marzo 1944-XXII.=

IL DIRETTORE GENERALE DEL PERSONALE
MILITARE E DELLE SCUOLE
(Colonnello Pilota-P. d'Ippolito)

The official letter written to Capt Giovanni Bonet's mother in which she is informed that her son, who was killed on 26 March 1944, had been posthumously awarded the Gold Medal – believed to be the only Gold Medal awarded to an ANR fighter pilot. Squadriglia Montefusco then became known as Montefusco-Bonet *in his honour. (via Ferdinando D'Amico)*

n° di Matricola	Cognome e nome Luogo di nascita (Comune e provincia	Grado	Corpo	Ricompensa proposta	MOTIVAZIONE	Luogo in cui avveniene il fatto.	Data del fatto
	AMAOTIGUITE			ASITUAMOMEA			
	VALENZANO Raffaele da TORINO	Tenente Pilota	2°Grup= po C.T.	Medaglia di Argento al Valor M. SUL CAMPO.		Fronte del= l'Italia Settentrio= nale.-	Periodo dal 18 1943 a 31/3/1

MOTIVAZIONE	Luogo in cui avveniene il fatto.	Data del fatto	n° d'ord. della relazione e del fatto.	Ricompense ottenute per fatti e benemerenze antecedenti	Annotazioni	Parere della Commissione sulla propo
DILA	Fronte del= l'Italia Settentrio= nale.-	Periodo dal 18/10/ 1943 al 31/3/1945	1	1 Medaglia di Argento al V.M. 1 Medaglia di Bronzo al V.M.		

These proposals and associated documents for the award of Silver Medals to pilots of II Gruppo Caccia were preserved by Capt Ugo Drago, formerly CO of 1 Squadron. (via Ferdinando D'Amico)

2° GRUPPO CACCIA
COMANDO

MOTIVAZIONE

3"INTREPIDO PILOTA DA CACCIA,FERMO NEL PROPOSITO DI RIVEN=
DICARE LA GLORIA E L'ONORE DELLA PATRIA,AFFRONTAVA RIPE=
TUTAMENTE IN CONDIZIONI DI STRAGRANDE INFERIORITA' POTEN
TI FORMAZIONI DI VALIVOLI NEMICI.

IN COMBATTIMENTI PARTICOLARMENTE RISCHIOSI E DIFFICILI
CONSEGUIVA BRILLANTI E NUMEROSE VITTORIE".-

IL COMANDANTE
(Magg. Pil. Carlo Miani)

2° GRUPPO CACCIA
COMANDO

Rapporto informativo n° 4 relativo al Tenente A.A.r.n. Pilota

V A L E N Z A N O   R a f f a e l e

R A P P O R T O   I N F O R M A T I V O
===

Ho alle mie dipendenze il Tenente A.A.r.n. Pilota

V A L E N Z A N O   R a f f a e l e

dal 18 ottobre 1943.

Prestante nel fisico,resistente a qualsiasi disagio sia a terra che
in volo.

Sano di carattere,sereno e ottimista per temperamento,disinvolto,si
curo,fortunato.

Volitivo e capace nutre sane ambizioni.

Ufficiale compito ed esemplare sente profondamente la sua missione.

Pilota di grande perizia e coraggio eccelle come combattente osti=
nato ed ardimentoso,come capo pattuglia intelligente e fidato.

Gode di un elevato prestigio sia tra gli inferiori che tra i supe=
riori.

Soldato d'onore è stato uno dei pionieri della ricostituzione del=
l'Aeronautica Repubblicana.

Ha prestato servizio in guerra dal 1° gennaio 1942 al 31 agosto 942
presso il 2° Stormo C.T. partecipando a numerose azioni di guerra
tra le quali:10 partenze su allarme,30 scorte a convogli navali,20
crociere di protezione ed a 15 mitragliamenti.

Dal 1° febbraio al 30 giugno 1943 in Sicilia-Tunisia col 153° Grup
po in 30 partenze su allarme durante le quali sosteneva 15 combat=
timenti e abbatteva 2 aerei nemici,in 40 scorte a convogli Aerei e
navali ed in rishiose ricognizioni sulla munita base nemica di Mal
ta,dava prova della sua rara perizia e del suo ardimento.

E' decorato di 1 medaglia d'Argento al V.M. e di 1 medaglia di Bron
zo al V.M.-

IL COMANDANTE
(Magg. Pil. Carlo Miani)

IM NAMEN DES FÜHRERS
UND OBERSTEN BEFEHLSHABERS
DER WEHRMACHT
VERLEIHE ICH
DEM

Major

Adriano Visconti
I. Italienische Jagdgruppe

DAS

EISERNE KREUZ
1. KLASSE

Hauptquartier   18. Mai   1944

Der Chef der Luftflotte 2

(DIENSTSIEGEL)

Generalfeldmarschall

(DIENSTGRAD UND DIENSTSTELLUNG)

Again rare – the certificate conveying award of the Iron Cross First Class made to Adriano Visconti on 18 May, 1944.
(via Ferdinando D'Amico)

Vorläufige

Verleihungsurkunde

Im Namen des
Oberbefehlshabers der Luftwaffe

verleihe ich dem

Major   Mario   Bellagambi

II.ital.Jagdgruppe,4.Staffel

die

Frontflug=Spange für Jäger
in Bronze

Gefechtsstand   , den 15.April 194 5

Jagdfliegerfuehrer   Gefechtsstand,5.1.45.

Oberitalien.

Vorlaeufige Verleihungsurkunde.

Dem Maggiore Mario Bellagambi,II.(ital.)/J.G. ist vom Fuehrer und

Obersten Befehlshaber der Wehrmacht das E.K.I verliehen worden.

Die Verleihungsurkunde wird nachgereicht.

Oberst u.Jagdfliegerfuehrer.

Certificate of Frontflug-Spange für Jäger *in Bronze made to Mario Bellagambi. Of particular interest is the signature of*
'Edu' Neumann, the Commanding Officer of the Luftwaffe Fighter Command in Italy. (via Ferdinando D'Amico)

Chapter Five

Finnish Air Force

I dived, shooting directly in front of the I-16s. 'Ivan' began to break his attack and dived to the south, twisting from side to side. I followed him, coming closer and closer, but held back from shooting again. 'Ivan' dived very steeply and when we were close to the top of the trees I held him in my gunsight and, at a distance, of less than 100 m, I fired. The burst was a full hit and the I-16*bis* burst into flames.

Kyostia K. E. Karhila, Hawk pilot, LeLv 30, FAF

During the period that Britain was engaged in the Second World War, fighting on several fronts across the globe, so Finland was also embroiled in conflict on two separate occasions with its huge neighbour, the Soviet Union. Yet, Finland and Britain were the only two countries involved in the European theatre of operations never to be occupied. From 1939 to 1944 there were three distinct periods in Finland's history: the Winter War against the USSR, which lasted from 30 November 1939 to 13 March 1940; the temporary peace period which followed immediately in its wake; and the Continuation War again against USSR, but this time with Germany as comrade-in-arms against a common enemy, between 25 June 1941 and the armistice signed on 4 September 1944.

Introduction

The Finnish Air Force (FAF) was founded on 6 March 1918. The blue swastika adorning its aircraft from this point onward held no political significance and, indeed, preceded by some 15 years the use of the swastika by the National Socialist party in Germany. The emblem was simply the personal insignia of Swedish Count Erik von Rosen, who had donated the first aircraft to the fledgling FAF in 1918.

Just prior to the outbreak of the Winter War (otherwise known as the first Russo-Finnish War) on 30 November 1939, the FAF was equipped with a small force of single-seat fighters and twin-engined fighter-bombers of mostly Dutch and British design. The FAF was composed of an air staff, a central flying school, three air regiments (*Lentorykmenti*), and also a naval co-operation squadron, together with associated support units. Two fighter squadrons, LeLv (*Lentolaivue*) 24 and LeLv 26, were equipped with fighter aircraft consisting of 36 Fokker D.XX, 10 Bristol Bulldogs and 14 Blenheim Is. On the eve of war, the FAF had just 116 combat aircraft, over half of which were obsolete aircraft including the Bulldog, Gloster Gamecock, Blackburn Rippon, Junkers K 43, Fokker C.X and C.VE. Only the Fokker D.XXs and Bristol Blenheims were considered to be modern equipment.

Lt Jorma Sarvanto became the highest-scoring Finnish fighter pilot of the Winter War, and here he proudly displays the 'Yellow 5' cut from the fuselage fabric of one of his victims. On 6 January 1940 he personally shot down six Russian DB-3 bombers in his D.XX in only 240 seconds of combat. During the Continuation War, Sarvanto flew the Model 239 Buffalo, again with LeLv 24. (via Finnish Defence Training Development Centre, photos nos 2828 and 104700)

There was clearly a need to dramatically increase both the quantity and quality of combat aircraft of the FAF, and the Finnish people enthusiastically donated valuable heirlooms to help to raise the finance necessary to purchase aircraft from Britain, America, France, Italy and Germany. Gold wedding rings were handed over in large numbers, and in return, the Finnish Air Force provided the generous populace with an aluminium ring engraved with the FAF emblem.

Prior to the start of the Winter War, the FAF sought to develop a high *esprit de corps* amongst its fighter pilots. High emphasis was placed upon physical fitness, including cross-country runs, hunting and shooting, and bunkers were dug by aircrew in tandem with ground personnel. Intense instruction and practice took place at summer gunnery camp. It was the quality of training of fighter pilots which became one of the benchmarks in determining the outstanding successes of Finnish fighter pilots in the Second World War.

The Winter War

On 30 November 1939, Soviet bombers operating from an airfield near the town of Paldiski, in Estonia, attacked Helsinki at 09.00, with a further attack on the Finnish capital being made some three hours later. The towns of Petsamo and Viipuri were also attacked, the total

This photograph was taken on 27 or 28 June 1944, and shows the 3rd Flight of LeLv 24 being inspected by the Commander in Chief, Lt Gen J. F. Lundquist. At the left end of line is Capt Hasse Wind, who was shot down and injured shortly after this photo was taken. On the right of the photo, awaiting to be introduced, is Viktor 'Vikki' Pyotsiä. Already 30 years old at the start of the Winter War, Pyotsiä achieved considerable combat success with his D.XXI (coded FR-110), and by the end of the war on 13 March 1940 he had scored seven personal and one shared kill, making him the third-highest scoring Finnish pilot of the brief conflict. Pyotsiä continued to fly with LeLv 24 during the inter-war and Continuation War years, scoring well with the American Buffalo and then the German-constructed Bf 109G-2/G-6. Pyotsiä survived these conflicts with an aggregate score of 17 personal and five shared aerial victories. (via Finnish Defence Training Development Centre, photo no. 155485)

Soviet force comprising around 900 aircraft. On the ground, a general invasion of Finland had begun when around one million Soviet soldiers crossed the border. The first war between Russia and Finland had started.

During the first phase of the Winter War, large numbers of Soviet Air Force bombers flew over Finnish territory without any fighter escort. They quickly realized the need for good fighter escort, however, as Finnish fighter pilots soon got amongst the lumbering bombers with considerable ease. In the air, the small FAF fighter force discovered easy pickings amongst the bombers, but found that the Soviet Polikarpov I-16 (Rata) and the I-153 Tschaika biplane, in particular, were remarkably agile opponents.

The first aerial victory was made by a D.XX on 1 December 1939. On this date, 'Eikka' Luukkanen took off from Immola and shot down a Soviet Ilyushin DB-3 bomber over Vuoksenlaakso. It was portent of events to come, for despite the Fokker D.XX's obsolescent fixed undercarriage (which was sometimes replaced with skis, thus enabling the Fokker to operate from ice), the fighter boasted some 2,200 rounds of ammunition for its quartet of 7.7 mm Browning machine guns which pilots used to achieve a remarkable 16-to-1 victory/loss ratio against the Soviet Air Force during the short Winter War.

The uncompromising nature of the conflict was graphically illustrated when D.XX pilot 'Illu' Juutilainen attacked and hit a Soviet bomber at 14,000 ft. The aircraft went into a vertical dive, yet the tail-gunner continued to fire at Juutilainen's aircraft which was in hot pursuit. The tail-gunner eventually bailed out at low altitude, pulling his rip cord and opening his parachute at an estimated 1,300 ft. As he hit the ground, Finnish soldiers ran over to him, but by the time they had reached the Soviet airman (who held the rank of Major), he had shot himself in the head so as to avoid being captured.

Operating in conditions of extreme cold (sometimes as low as –45° C), maintenance of aircraft always posed problems for FAF and Soviet Air Force ground crews alike. Finnish personnel had to undertake maintenance round the clock, one mechanic being allocated to keep the tools warm by heating them with a blow

Eino 'Eikka' Luukkanen flew the D.XX during the Winter War as leader of the 3rd Flight of LeLv 24. He achieved only moderate success with the Fokker, destroying two aircraft, plus a third as a shared victory. However, during the Continuation War Luukkanen discovered his touch, firstly with the Buffalo and then with the Bf 109. With the latter type he scored 39 confirmed victory kills, several of which were Russian-flown lend-lease aircraft including the Airacobra and Boston. Luukkanen's final tally amounted to 53 personal and six shared victories. (via Finnish Defence Training Development Centre, photo no. 153310)

torch whilst the others worked on the aircraft. When at combat readiness, aircraft were kept primed through the employment of electric radiators, whilst electrically-heated dipsticks were used in the oil tanks to retain low oil viscosity.

Foreign Nationals
Fortunately for the Finns, the Red Air Force was also equipped with largely antiquated aircraft, the critical difference between the two protagonists being that the Soviet aircraft were

flown by aircrew who were tactically naive and inadequately prepared for fighting over enemy territory. At this stage, the Finns were very much on their own, as the German/Soviet pact left the FAF relying on equipment supplied from distant countries including Britain, France and the USA. Nevertheless, the Finns permitted Danish personnel to join their squadrons, and eight pilots duly flew on operations during the Winter War period with LeLv 24, 26 and 28, four of whom lost their lives. Swedish volunteers also operated in Lapland with Gloster Gladiator and Hawker Hart biplane fighters. Even so, throughout this period Finland continued to trade with Germany, and this commercial relationship was to have increased significance when Germany later invaded the Soviet Union.

In early 1940, the cosmopolitan make-up of the fighter units within the FAF was further accentuated by the introduction of 44 Brewster Buffaloes, 10 Hawker Hurricanes, 33 Fiat G.50s, 30 Gladiators, 30 Morane MS 406s and several

examples of captured Soviet aircraft including I-153s, I-16s and I-15bis.

During the Winter War LeLv 24 became the leading fighter squadron of the Finnish Air Force, achieving some 120 victories with the D.XX and producing five aces. Originally formed in July 1933, LeLv 24 was based at Immola at the start of the Winter War. The unit was immediately ordered by FAF commander, Gen J. F. Lundquistat, to send its 31 pilots and aircraft to protect the vital power station at Imatra, some 30 miles north of Viipuri. The squadron's HQ moved to Joutseno at the end of the year, before eventually returning to Immola – LeLv 24 also spent short spells at Lemi and Ristiina.

Whilst the location of the squadron HQ remained reasonably static, the five flights of LeLv 24 found themselves operating from several different bases during the course of the war. The dispersed nature of FAF fighter squadron flights was also reflected in the

Second-highest scoring Finnish ace of the Winter War was Oiva 'Oippa' Tuominen with seven personal and two shared victories. His greatest success during this period was achieved with the Gladiator on 13 February 1940 when he destroyed three SB-2 bombers, and shared in the destruction of a fourth. Tuominen went on to later achieve considerable success with the G.50 'Freccia' and Bf 109G-2/G-6 during the Continuation War, finishing with a score of 42 personal and three shared victories. (via Finnish Defence Training Development Centre, photo no. 111686)

operations of LeLv 26, whose ten Bulldogs of the first flight flew from differing locations, and were eventually replaced by Gladiators for a short period, before the arrival of G.50s. The two remaining flights of LeLv 26, which were equipped with D.XXs, were placed under the command of LeLv 24.

It was during the Winter War that the Finnish Air Force suffered the biggest single defeat in an aerial combat it was ever to receive. On 19 February 1940, a large force of Soviet aircraft attacked the base on the frozen lake at Ruokolahti. Some 24 Polikarpov I-153 and I-16 fighters strafed the Finns, enticing the Gladiator and Fokker flights of LeLv 24 and 26 to attempt to take-off and engage the enemy force. The two flights made a valiant attempt to get off the ground, but lacking speed and height, the vulnerable Gladiators were easy prey for the Soviet fighters, who shot down three biplanes on take-off and a further two and one Fokker in the ensuing combat, all for the loss of just one Soviet I-16.

Claims and counter-claims

The FAF suffered the loss of 36 fighters in aerial combat to Soviet aircraft out of a total of 68 machines lost during the Winter War. Soviet claims for the same period were 362 Finnish aircraft destroyed filed during the 15 weeks of conflict, a figure which in fact far outstripped the total number of aircraft in service with the FAF! In return, the small Finnish fighter force wreaked havoc, and in recent years a Soviet loss of 579 aircraft during this short period has been acknowledged in Russia. This figure is likely to be a fair estimate of the actual Soviet losses, for it is reasonably in line with the claims made by the Finnish Air Force and anti-aircraft batteries, who claimed a total of 521 Soviet aircraft destroyed during the short Winter War. This conflict was to last only 15 weeks before the Finns were forced to accept terms under the Treaty of Moscow which changed the geographical line of the Finnish frontiers, making parts of Karelia Soviet territory.

Inter-war period

After the Winter War, Finland moved into the illusory phase of the Inter-War period. Having had its geographical boundaries severely affected

Ilmari Juutilainen joined the Finnish Air Force in 1935 and scored two personal (and one shared) combat victories during the Winter War, which lasted just 15 weeks. However, during the longer Continuation War 'Illu' Juutilainen, found outstanding success in both the Buffalo and the Bf 109G-2/G-6, rising to become the highest-scoring Finnish fighter pilot of all time with a score of 93 personal and one shared victories. (via Finnish Defence Training Development Centre, photo no. 155493)

by the Soviet Union under the imposing terms of the armistice agreement, an uneasy truce remained in operation that left the FAF standing vigilant in case of any surprise Soviet attack.

During this time the FAF managed to enter into financial arrangements with America that saw aircraft obtained from Britain, France, Italy and Germany. The breakdown of the German/Russian pact, and the alignment of the latter with the Allies, placed Finland in an extremely vulnerable position. They could no

All of Hans Wind's 72 personal and six shared combat victories were achieved during the Continuation War. For two-and-a-half years Wind flew LeLv 24's Buffalos before scoring prolifically with the Bf 109G-6 from April 1944. Whilst flying one of the latter on a reconnaissance mission on 28 June 1944, he was severely injured and was still in hospital at the time of the armistice on 4 September 1944. (via Finnish Defence Training Development Centre, photo no. 139511)

longer count on support from Britain and France, whilst Germany, who had established good trading links with Finland, offered some protection against the Soviet Union, who continued to view the small nation in terms of it being the 'Finnish problem'. The German invasion of Russia on 22 June 1941 precipitated Soviet raids on Finland by just three days. Bereft of allies, Finland was left with little choice but to align itself with Germany, and thus the Continuation War (as it was christened in Finland) commenced.

Continuation War

The war started again and the Russian bombers began to bomb many towns in South Finland. The order to enter service with the FAF arrived, and I returned to my squadron. We flew to a base in South Finland. In three weeks I flew 18 flights, not making the slightest sight of the enemy. We then received a surprising order – to change the whole fleet of Fokker D.XXIs, to Curtiss Hawk 75As.

We were really happy!

Kyostia Karhila

In June 1941 Nos 2 and 3 Wings of the FAF consisted of three and two fighter squadrons respectively. In No 2 Wing, LeLv 24 was equipped with Buffalos, LeLv 26 with G.50s, and LeLv 28 with MS 406s. In No 3 Wing, LeLv 30 and LeLv 32 flew the ageing D.XXs, which were eventually supplemented by Hurricanes. The recently-arrived 'hotch potch' of fighters from across the globe played a significant role in improving the effectiveness of the FAF. Kyostia Karhila describes a successful sortie with the American-built Hawk:

With two Curtiss Hawks, I was ordered to cover a Fokker C.X which was going to lead our artillery's attempt to shoot and destroy a Russian bridge near the frontline. The sky was clear when we took off, together with the Fokker, and climbed towards the bridge area. Within 30 minutes we were over the target, and the Fokker at this point was at 5,000 m whilst we were slightly higher. The Fokker's observer directed the aiming of the artillery by radio. All was OK, but about ten minutes later I saw one aircraft from the south (on the Russian side) diving towards our Fokker.

I rolled over and dived to counter the attack of the enemy. I identified the aircraft as a Russian I-16*bis* fighter. The Fokker, noticing also that the Russian fighter was moving into attack, put her nose down and dived for home. I was in a dive, shooting directly in front of the I-16. 'Ivan' began to break his attack and dived to the south, twisting from side to side. I followed him, coming closer and closer, but held back from shooting again. 'Ivan' dived very steeply, and when we were close to the top of the trees I held him in my gunsight and, at a distance, of less than 100 m, I fired. The burst was a full hit and the I-16*bis* burst into flames.

The pilot bailed out of the flaming cockpit, passing me on the left side, only 1–2 m from my left wing. The altitude was less than 50 m, and the I-16*bis* dived straight into the wood, the impact producing flames of around 300 m trailing in its wake on the ground. The pilot had no chance of survival, not even to open his parachute. We returned home to base where I made low pass, pulled up and landed. I then reported the details of what had just taken place to my Flight Commander, and filed a written claim for I-16*bis*.

Brewster Model 239

A highly significant aircraft purchased from America was the much-maligned Brewster Model 239 Buffalo. The first operational unit to receive the fighter was LeLv 24, which replaced its fleet of D.XXs on 19 April 1940 with 17 Model 239s at Helsinki-Malmi airport. Prior to this, these aircraft had been temporarily issued to *Lentolaivue* 22, located on a frozen lake at Hollola in southern Finland, commanded by Capt Erkki Heinilä. These Buffalos were part of the original order for 44 purchased from the Brewster Aeronautical Corporation on 16 December 1939 after they had been declared surplus to US Navy requirements.

The Brewsters had been shipped packed in crates from America to Stavanger, Norway, then sent on a train to the SAAB plant in Tollhattan, Sweden, where they were assembled, before being collected by Finnish fighter pilots and flown to Finland – the first four arrived on 1 March 1940 and the last on 1 May. All these aircraft were equipped with single examples of the 7.62 mm and 12.7 mm guns synchronized to fire in harmony, plus a further two free-firing 12.7 mm machine guns. Ascribed serial numbers BW-351 to -394, the Model 239s were to make a considerable impact during the next two years of aerial combat.

The Buffalos proved to be agile, well armed and quick, plus provided the pilot with protective armour beneath his seat and behind his back. During the first year of the Continuation War, the Brewster squadrons achieved an outstanding 32-to-1 victory/loss ratio. Even more astonishing is the fact that during the first six months of the

war, the Brewsters scored 135 combat victories without suffering a single loss in return. However, by mid-1943, and with the battle of the Gulf of Finland in full flow, the Buffalo was rapidly being out-paced and out-manoeuvred by

During the Winter War Risto Puhakka flew the D.XX and the G.50 with the first flight of LeLv 24. He used both aircraft types to destroy a total of six Soviet aircraft. By the beginning of the Continuation War, Puhakka had been posted to LeLv 26, which was also equipped with the G.50 'Freccia'. During the Continuation War he achieved a further 11 combat victories before the unit re-equipped with the Bf 109G-2/G-6, Puhakka scoring a further 25 victories over mostly fighters – including several lease-lend aircraft. His victory total during the two conflicts had reached 42 by July 1944. (via Finnish Defence Training Development Centre, photo no. 105103)

a new generation of Soviet fighters which included lend-lease aircraft like the Spitfire, Hurricane and P-40 Tomahawk.

Soviet pilots had also learned valuable combat lessons during the first year of the Continuation War, and those who survived were more experienced, confident, and skilled in aerial combat techniques. By contrast, the FAF continued to suffer from a lack of fighters, and their pilots would go to extreme lengths to bring their aircraft home, often at great personal risk. Trading with Germany continued apace, and arrangements were made for a new squadron to be formed in January 1943 equipped with German-constructed Bf 109G-2s.

LeLv 28 pilot Sgt Urho Lehtovaara achieved one combat victory during the Winter War flying MS 406 MS 327 – his usual mount of the conflict. He continued to fly the Moranes of LeLv 28 until he was posted to the new LeLv 34 in March 1943, whereupon he flew the Bf 109G-2/G-6 with outstanding success over the next 15 months. Lehtovaara claimed 28 personal and one shared Soviet aircraft with the German fighter, adding to his earlier total of 15 combat victories with the French-built MS 406. (via Finnish Defence Training Development Centre, photo no. 155483)

Sixteen FAF pilots and seven technicians were transferred to the new unit – LeLv 34 – and placed under the command of Maj Olavi Ehrnrooth. In February these men were transported by DC-2 from Helsinki-Malmi to Werneuchen, Berlin, to receive familiarization training on the Bf 109G-2. In preparation for the visit by the Finns, the Luftwaffe had prepared a detailed training programme in which each Finnish pilot was to receive elementary flying training with a Luftwaffe instructor, before gradually progressing onto other more advanced training aircraft as a lead up to flying the Bf 109. Maj Ehrnrooth protested strongly to the Luftwaffe training school commander, and as a result, the German CO allocated three Bf 109s immediately to the Finns with the terse comment that when the three aircraft had been destroyed, and three Finnish pilots killed, then perhaps the Finns would welcome the opportunity to enrol in the Luftwaffe's training programme which had

been so thoughtfully laid on for them.

In the event, each of the 16 pilots put the Bf 109s through a series of testing manoeuvres without any loss, winning the admiration of the German CO, who announced that there was nothing the Luftwaffe could teach them about flying ! Maj Ehrnrooth was later to lose his life in a Pyry training aircraft, and was replaced by Maj 'Eikka' Luukkanen, who was eventually to become the second-highest scoring Finnish pilot on Bf 109s.

Bf 109G-2s and -6s, like the Brewsters before them, achieved remarkable successes in the hands of the experienced Finnish fighter pilots, with men like 'Oippa' Tuominen (the first pilot to receive the Knight of the Mannerheim Cross), 'Eikka' Luukkanen, 'Hasse' Wind and 'Illu' Juutilainen building large scores with this aircraft. Some 15 of the 111 Bf 109G-6s originally supplied by the Luftwaffe had two 20 mm wing cannon fitted, but some (not all) FAF

cont. p.152

Aerial photos of Finnish fighters in flight are fairly uncommon. In this shot, the Buffalos of the 2nd flight of Lentolaivue 24 are captured by the camera on an operational sortie over Rukajarvi in September 1942. BW-354 is being flown on this mission by Sgt Heimo Lampi. The Brewster enjoyed considerable success in the hands of LeLv 24's pilots, with some 477 enemy aircraft being downed . (via The Finnish Air Force Museum, photo no. 179351)

TABLE 1 – Fighter Squadrons Of The Finnish Air Force – 1939-44

Lentolaivue 24 (LeLv 24) – renamed
Havittajalentolaivue 24 (HLeLv 24) on 14/2/44

	Aircraft
Winter War	D.XX
Continuation War	Buffalo (4/40)
	Bf 109G-2 (4/44)
	Bf 109G-6 (6/44)

Lentolaivue 26 (Lelv 26) – renamed
Havittajalentolaivue 26 (HLeLv 26) on 14/2/44

	Aircraft
Winter War	Bulldog
	Gladiator (1/40)
	G.50 (2/40)
Continuation War	G.50
	Buffalo (5/44)

Lentolaivue 28 (LeLv 28) – renamed
Havittajalentolaivue 23 (HLeLv 28 on 17/2/44.

	Aircraft
Winter War	MS 406
Continuation War	MS 406
	Bf 109G-2 (6/44)

Lentolaivue 30 (LeLv 30) – renamed
Havittajalentolaivue 30 HLeLv.30 on 14/2/44

	Aircraft
Winter War	– (founded 27/3/44)
Continuation War	Hurricane I (3/40)
	D.XX (3/40)
	I-153 (11/42)
	G.50 (2/44)
	Bf 109G-6 (5/44)

Lentolaivue 32 (LeLv 32) – renamed
Havittajalentolaivue 32 (HLeLv 32) on 14/2/44

	Aircraft
Winter War	– (founded 27/3/40)
Continuation War	D.XX
	Hurricane I (7/41)
	Curtiss Hawk 75A (7/41)

Lentolaivue 34 (LeLv 34) – renamed
Havittajalentolaivue 34 (HLeLv 34) on 17/2/44

	Aircraft
Winter War	– (founded 1/43)
Continuation War	Bf 109G-2 (3/43)
	Bf 109G-6 (4/44)

Ilmari Juutilainen's Model 239 (BW-364) of 3./LeLv 24 is caught by the camera on 25 June 1942 prior to taxiing. On this particular sortie 'Illu' Juutilainen claimed two lend-lease Hurricanes destroyed. In total he scored 36 combat victories with BW-364. (via The Finnish Air Force Museum, photo no. 17935)

Two photos of Hans Wind's Model 239 (BW-393) of 1./LeLv 24. Second only to Juutilainen as Fisland's highest scoring pilot, Wind achieved 26 aerial victories with this aircraft. BW-393 was credited with 41 aerial victories, including seven by Eino Luukkanen, during its operational career. (via The Finnish Air Force Museum, photo nos. 1069 – 32 and 18667)

Gladiator GL-276 of 2./LeLv 24 in the Spring of 1940. Lt Paavo 'Pate' Berg achieved real success with the agile biplane, destroying five Soviet aircraft during an 18-day period in February 1940. The Gladiator proved effective during the Winter War, but was rendered obsolete during the Continuation War, by which time the FAF had re-equipped with Italian, German, British and American-built aircraft. (via The Finnish Air Force Museum, photo no. 13861)

pilots had these removed to improve aircraft performance by reducing weight. Kyostia Karhila and Antii Tani were two who chose to keep the 20 mm cannon on their aircraft.

The victory/loss ratio of the Finnish Bf 109 was 25-to-1, a score which is even more impressive than the Brewster's ratio as by 1943/44 the tactically-sound Soviet pilots flew equipment at least equal to the Bf 109G. Even so, Finnish fighter pilots have continued to maintain that their Bf-109s were faster, and could climb and dive much better than most Russian fighters to the extent that no Soviet machine presented particular problems to the FAF.

Kyosti Karhila continued his record of success when he moved from the Curtiss Hawk to the Bf 109, going on to destroy a further 19 Russian aircraft. Here, he describes a single sortie with the Bf 109G on 4 May 1943:

I had only 3 hrs 45 mins flight time on the Bf 109 when I got an order to patrol with one other aircraft over the east coast past the Gulf of Finland. We found clear sky. I had yet to get used to flying the Bf 109, and found that the all-round visibility was not as good as the Curtiss Hawk, which I had been used to flying. But the instrument panel seemed reasonably assessable and the gun-sight excellent, and with every minute the Bf 109 began to feel to me more and more like home.

We patrolled for about 30 minutes, keeping a close look out for surprise attack from behind. I then spotted two aircraft below us, heading to the south east. I recognized them as Russian LaGG-3 fighters. I easily got behind the wingman, and my first shot went below the enemy aircraft (this was the first time that I had fired the guns of the Bf 109). I made a slight correction and the LaGG-3 exploded in a mass of flames. In a moment I was behind the other LaGG-3 and he tried to avoid my attack by turning left to right, diving hard towards the direction of his base at Kronstadt (near Leningrad). I found myself in a nice shooting position and again my bullets went below, which I quickly corrected – the Russian fighter exploded. These were my 14th and 15th combat victories, and my wingman saw the whole spectacle from the 'best seat in house'.

In June 1944 the great Soviet summer offensive commenced along a 435-mile front extending from the Gulf of Finland down to the Romanian border. The Soviet's massive aerial resources totalling some 13,400 aircraft, including 2,000 modern fighters, was opposed by the small FAF and a severely depleted Luftwaffe, chronically short of aviation fuel. Despite the valiant efforts of its fighter pilots, the Finns were compelled to accept the terms of the armistice on 4 September 1944. The Russo-Finnish war finally ended, and under the terms of the treaty, Finland was not permitted to provide any bases to Germany, who promptly moved their remaining presence to Lapland. Despite the enforced armistice, it was clear that Finland had managed to retain her independence.

Training

From 1929 the home of Finnish Air Force flying training was the flying school at Kauhava, in Western Finland. During the critical years of the Winter and Continuation Wars, the need for trained aircrew accelerated and, within 150 km of Kauhava, eight auxiliary airfields – Menkijarvi, Laajalahati, Karvia, Lappajarvi, Lestijarvi, Vaasa, Siikakangas and Ylivieska – were established to provide ab initio training. Further south, the two airfields at Parola and Vesivehmaa, were used for both basic and operational training.

Like the fighters employed by operational units, the training aircraft used were a very mixed bag. Between 1939 and 1944, a cadet pilot might well have received primary or elementary flying training on the Letov S 218A 'Smolik' (the main primary trainer), completing 58 flying hours on-type from 1941 onwards. Moving on to basic training, several different types of aircraft were used throughout the period. In the Winter War there was a shortage of training aircraft, which resulted in obsolete types such as the DH.60 Moth and VL Saaski II being pressed into service.

From 1941, the cadet pilot was given the opportunity to fly the first monoplane basic trainer employed by the FAF, the VL Pyry. Around this time obsolete fighters such as the Gamecock II, Bulldog IV, Gauntlet II, Jaktfalken II and I-15*bis* were also used for basic training. Basic training comprised some 82 flying hours, this figure including 13 hours of instrument training possibly on the VL Viima II or Fw 44J Stieglitz, 20 hours 'special training' (gunnery) probably on the VL Tuisku, 17 hours intermediate training with the VL Pyry and 32

Photographed during the summer of 1941, this G.50 (FA-26) was used by Oiva Tuominen of 1./LeLv 26 to score 13 aerial victories between 14 July and 3 September 1941. (via The Finnish Air Force Museum, photo no. 151111)

hours of combat training on the Pyry, Bulldog, Gamecock, Gauntlet and D.XXI.

Kyosti Karhila joined the FAF on 6 December 1939, and spent three-and-a-half months in flying training school completing 95 flying hours in total, prior to moving onto operational training. He describes the content of operational training for the FAF fighter pilot at that time in the following interview:

In our programme we completed take-offs and landings, a little aerobatics, low-level flights, instrument flying, dual, attacks on both ground and air targets, many check-flights, shooting at ground targets (my record was 96 per cent), air-to-air target work from different directions (my record was 60 per cent), and two aircraft patrol flights. My operational flight record shows 138 hours flying time, with 480 landings, taking a gross total of 16 months to complete under training in the FAF.

It was now time to report to a fighter squadron, which was equipped with D.XX1s made under licence in Finland. These aircraft were old, having been flown throughout the earlier Winter War, and were already too slow to fight Russian bombers and too clumsy for Russian fighters. On the squadron, we continued with take-offs and landings, turning, climbing, diving, aerobatics, low-level flights (very low!), patrol flights, tight formation flights, and gunnery-aiming practice towards ground and air targets.

Combat Tactics

Despite the paucity of fighter aircraft, pilots of the FAF had received an unusually intensive training in combat techniques – a practice which stretched back to 1935. By the mid-1930s the FAF had recognized that fighter pilots needed to develop high levels of tactical awareness, combined with exceptional aerial gunnery skills. Combat training seemed to be concentrated on three critical areas: loose, broad sections and finger-four formations, systematic gunnery training when pilots were trained to shoot at specific parts of an enemy aircraft, and the aggressive edict to be the first to attack, regardless of opposition numbers, so as to exploit the initiative. There was 'individual freedom of action' inside the fighter formation – the first to see the enemy was the first to shoot, regardless of their status in the squadron and position in the formation. This tactic minimized delay, and encouraged gunnery skills.

However, the Finnish fighter squadrons were not adverse to employing tactics which had been demonstrated to work successfully in other

Hawk CU-580 photographed over Syvari on 16 October 1943, piloted by Lt Jaakko Hillo of LeLv 32, who gained a half share of an Il-2 with this particular aircraft. Hillo scored eight victories throughout the Continuation War. (via The Finnish Air Force Museum)

FAF MS 406 of 2.LeLv 28 seen in the summer of 1941. (via BAK 591)

conflicts by other airforces. One of the more popular manoeuvres was the 'Furball', which was based on a Soviet fighter tactic from the Spanish Civil War known as the 'Spanish circle'.

The Finnish Air Force were fortunate to have a core of highly experienced and skilled fighter pilots by the start of the Winter War. Several of those to achieve ace status in the forthcoming wars had served as pilots in the air force for several years, their ranks including Ilmari Juutilainen, Eino Luukkanen, Risto Puhakka, Emil Vesa, Eero Kinnunen, Pekka Kokko, Per Erik Sovelius and Leo Ahokas. It was clear that basic training hours were comparable to those undertaken by RAF cadet pilots, but the emphasis placed on gunnery training was markedly different. Nevertheless, pilots straight out of basic training were propelled into flying squadrons with little operational training, being groomed by more experienced pilots once in the frontline.

The primary function of FAF fighters was to defend Finland from attack by Soviet bombers, and during the battle of the Gulf of Finland, the FAF tenaciously protected the air space over Kotka and Helsinki. By contrast, ground attack by Finnish fighters was deemed too risky a strategy in terms of the potential loss of irreplaceable aircraft to ground fire – such sorties had little or no effect on denting the vast numbers of aeroplanes produced by the Soviet Union. The FAF fighter squadrons, therefore, were instructed to concentrate on meeting Soviet aircraft in the air, and all combat training was used to ensure that FAF fighter pilots were physically and tactically equipped to perform well in this arena. Originally writing in 1956, Ilmari Juutilainen describes fighter tactics:

In combat formation the four fighters in the two leading sections flew in front and at a lower altitude. A little behind, and off to one side, flew the four fighters in the second high division. When engaged in aerial combat the forward division attacked and the second division only joined the combat if the situation called for it. The second division stayed high to provide cover and maintain control of the overall situation.

When large numbers of a/c were engaged in aerial combat the fighters usually spread out over a large area, and there was no way to maintain formation integrity. Individual sections of two fighters each tried to stay together to lend mutual support within the section or division.

Filing of Claims

On returning from an operational sortie, a Finnish fighter pilot was interviewed by the squadron intelligence officer, and required to make a written account of any claim made against an enemy aircraft. The FAF recognized

cont. p.157

Engine testing of G.50 FA-17 of 2./LeLv 2 during the summer of 1942 at Malmo. (via BAK 727)

FIGURE 1 – Example of Combat Claim Submission Form

Unit: 8523 Not to be completed in Squadron
(Series 11)

Flight 3	Gunner	Pilot Juutilainen
	Destroyed	3 x I-16
	(Definitely)	
	Damaged	–

Air Battle Report

1 Date: 18 August 1942 Time: 2000 hrs – 2120 hrs
2 Location of battle (area) and height: Kreivinlahti
   – Kronstadt 500 to 50 metres
3 Destroyed or damaged (type and number of
   aircraft): Destroyed 3 x I-16
4 Location where the destroyed aircraft fell, or
   clarification of what condition it was in and
   where the damaged aircraft was last seen: At the
   battle area, fell into the sea. The first was
   smoking, the pilot of the second was shot and
   the third fell into the sea burning.
5 A brief report of the battle events (please supply a
   drawing on the reverse, if necessary): We were
   notified of a battle to the East of Seiskari. The
   Flight set off with 4 aeroplanes heading for
   Kreivinlahti, where the enemy was met fighting
   the BWs. I shot one down straight away and it fell
   down, smoking, into the sea (I-16) next to some
   patrolling gun boats. The second was shot down
   straight into the sea in an enveloping attack to the
   south-west of Kronstadt. The third also fell into
   the sea, burning, approx. 500 metres to the south
   from the point where the previous plane was
   destroyed. I could not estimate the total number
   of enemy aircraft, but there were many of them.
6 Witnesses of the event (their own statements, if
   possible): I saw pilot Juutilainen shoot down one
   I-16. Capt (signature given).
   We saw pilot Juutilainen shoot a plane which
   dived into the sea burning. Sgt. (signature
   given), Second Lieut. (signature given).
7 Notes (tactical or other observation, damage to
   yourselves, etc.): The air attack was consistently
   heavy from the 14 patrolling gun boats below,
   from the Tolli Lighthouse, Kronstadt and from
   Oramisenbaum.

Your aeroplane (Type and num.): BW-364
(Signature given)
Title and name

the categories of destroyed, probable and damaged, but for score purposes no account was made of probable or damaged claims – destroyed claims only were considered to count towards the accumulation of a score. There are comparatively few aerial photographs of Finnish fighter aircraft, and perhaps unsurprisingly FAF fighters were not equipped with camera-guns, whose footage was therefore not a factor in the verification of combat claims.

Documentary evidence in support of the claim from the ground was often forthcoming as most aerial combats took place over Finnish territory. However, not all claims received verification from the ground, as battles were fought over the Gulf of Finland resulting in a number of Soviet aircraft crashing into the sea. Furthermore, Soviet aircraft often crashed in dense, inhospitable, forest areas.

Written claims were first referred to the unit flight staff, and then to the squadron staff. From there the claims were passed to the Wing and finally forwarded to the Air Force HQ. It appears that those who verified combat claims were unlikely to have been experienced combat pilots.

Psychological Stress
In the FAF we were not posted for a rest. We had no R&R centres, although we received one/two weeks 'holidays' to go home three or four times a year. For example, my operational service in the FAF lasted three years, four months and twenty-three days, and my only times away from the squadron and combat duties were on these 'holidays'.

Kyostia Karhila

Squadrons sought to combat the effects of stress by establishing in-house physical fitness regimes based upon sports, including blood sports, which were enjoyed regularly between operations and during quiet periods. Unlike RAF and USAAF pilots, Finnish fighter pilots did not serve on a squadron until an operational tour had been completed. Once on a squadron, the FAF fighter pilot could expect to remain there for the duration or was posted to another front-line squadron. These operational postings would be interspersed with short periods of rest and recuperation. Only very occasionally would a combat pilot be posted to training duties.

Awards and Decorations
The Knight of Mannerheim Cross Order was the highest military award proffered by Finland during the Continuation War. Whilst President Ryti was the political leader of Finland, the elderly Mannerheim held the title of Marshal of Finland, and the award was established some nine months after the end of the Winter War. It was presented to 19 pilots of the FAF during the two periods of conflict, with Oiva Tuominen being the first air force member to receive the

Maintenance on a Model 239 of 1./HLeLv 26 during the summer of 1944. (via BAK 391)

A rare photograph of a Hurricane of 2./LeLv 26, taken at Malmo, Helinski, on March 1943. (via The Finnish Air Force Museum)

award on 17 August 1941 – he was the sixth recipient of the award in the Finish armed forces. Two pilots – Juutilainen and Wind – were decorated twice with this award.

For fighter pilots of the FAF, the criteria for the award of the Mannerheim Cross was linked to the number of combat victories obtained. From the start of the Continuation War through to 1942, 20 combat victories were needed, this figure rising in 1943 to 30 and then 40 in the final years of the war.

Two other important medals for FAF personnel (there were no unit citations) were the Freedom Cross (*Vapauden Risti* – VR) for officers and NCOs and the Freedom Medal (*Vapauden Mitali* – VM) for NCOs – the former could be awarded as a 1st, 2nd, 3rd, and 4th class award, with Oakleaves to the 3rd and 4th class. NCOs were eligible to receive the VR 3 and 4 only if they had first been previously been awarded the VM 1 and 2. Most fighter pilots were awarded the VR 3 and 4, a few got the VR 2, but the VR 1 was awarded only once to Maj Gustav E. Magnusson.

Pilot Profiles
Gladiator Pilot – O. E. K. 'Oippa' Tuominen
Oiva Emil Kalervo 'Oippa' Tuominen was 31 years old at the start of the Winter War, and he had already been a member of LeLv 26 for almost two years. Air Master Sergeant Tuominen made his first claim in a D.XX on Christmas Day 1939, sharing in the destruction of a SB-2 over Kannas, close to the south-eastern Finnish-Russian border. A sole SB-2 kill was claimed a few weeks later, after which LeLv 26 re-equipped for a short period with Gladiators in place of its fleet of D.XXs and Bulldogs.

During the squadron's spell with Gladiators, Tuominen, and fellow LeLv 26 pilot Paavo D. 'Pate' Berg, achieved outstanding success with the agile biplane fighter. On 2 February 1940, Tuominen claimed two I-16s over southern Finland and Berg claimed a single I-153 over Lansi-Suomi. Eleven days later Tuominen downed four SB-2s and a single R-5 over Karjala, to the east of Finland. With six personal kills and one shared to his credit, 'Oippa' Tuominen became the highest-scoring Finnish Gladiator pilot – he was not to increase his gross score of seven and two shared until the start of the Continuation War.

Tuominen continued to fly with LeLv 26, which re-equipped with G.50s during the inter-war period, and he and gained a further 22 personal and two shared kills with the Fiat fighter. In January 1943 he was posted to the new

TABLE 2 – Leading Finnish Fighter Aces

Winter War

Name	Score	Aircraft	Units
J. K. Sarvanto	12 (2 sh)	D.XX	LeLv 24
O. E. K. Tuominen	8	D.XX	LeLv 26
		Gladiator	
V. Pyotsiä	7 (+1 sh)	D.XX	LeLv 24
R. O. P. Puhakka	6	D.XX	LeLv 24
		G.50	
K. J. T. Virta	6	D.XX	LeLv 24
T. M Huhantti	5 (3 sh)	D.XX	LeLv 24
P. T. Tilli	5 (1sh)	D.XX	LeLv 26
U. A. Nieminen	5	D.XX	LeLv 26
P. D. Berg	5	Gladiator	LeLv 26

Continuation War

Name	Score	Aircraft	Units
E. I. Juutilainen	93(+1 Sh)	Buffalo	LeLv 24
		Bf 109G-2 & G-6	
H. H. Wind	75	Buffalo	LeLv 24
		Bf 109G-2 & G-6	
E. A. Luukkanen	53 (+1sh)	Buffalo	LeLv 24
		Bf 109G-2 & G-6	LeLv 34
U. S. Lehtovaara	43.5	MS 406	LeLv 28
		Bf 109G-2 & G-6	LeLv 34
O. E. K. Tuominen	36	G.50	LeLv 26
		Bf 109G-2 & G-6	LeLv 34
R.O.P. Puhakka	36	G.50	LeLv 26
		Bf 109G-2 & G-6	Lelv 34

(Note – with the exception of H. H. Wind, all above pilots accrued scores in the Winter War, which are excluded in the figures for the Continuation War.)

LeLv 34, being one of 15 pilots transferred to Werneuchen, Berlin, to convert onto the Bf 109G-2. Flying the little Messerschmitt fighter brought him a further 13 victories, taking his total to 42 personal and three shared kills during 400 operational sorties.

Tuominen had a reputation for being 'laid-back' whilst on the ground, but in the air it was a different matter, and his final score demonstrates both his ability, and clinical approach, to combat in the air. Air Master Sergeant Tuominen was awarded the Mannerheim Cross on 2 August 1941, thus becoming the first of only nine FAF fighter pilots to receive this honour. Tuominen resigned from the air force on 6 January 1945 with a full pension and the rank of Warrant Officer. He later became a taxi driver, and subsequently died on 28 January 1976.

D.XX Pilot – J. K. Sarvanto
Lt Jorma Kalevi Sarvanto achieved high public acclaim when on 6 January 1940 he destroyed six DB-3 bombers in just four minutes in the skies over south-eastern Finland. As he closed in on the seventh, and final, DB-3 in the formation, the guns of his D.XX ran out of ammunition. However, the enemy bombers quickly fell victim to Sarvanto's LeLv 24 colleague, Lt 'Pelle' Sovelius. Unsurprisingly, Sarvanto not only became the highest scoring Fokker pilot of the Finnish Air Force during the Winter War, but he was also one of the leading aces of the conflict

The Finnish Air Force had very limited resources available to produce the large number of aircraft it required to wage war with the vast Russian air force. Home-designed aircraft were largely restricted to training aircraft such as the Tuisku and Viima biplanes, the Pyry advanced monoplane trainer and the Myrsky single-seat fighter monoplane, which was made in very limited numbers. Therefore, the FAF made considerable use of imported aircraft and, on occasions, captured machines. In these photographs, Soviet aircraft have fallen into Finnish hands and have been impressed into service with the FAF.

Above left *Polikarpov I-153 VH-12 of 3./LeLv on 6 May 1941.*

Below left *LaGG-3 LG-3 of LeLv 32, photographed in March 1943.*

Above and below *I-16 VH-201 is seen following restoration to airworthiness in April 1940, and then soon afterwards following a dead-stick landing on the ice.* (All photos via Russian Aviation Research Trust)

with 12 personal and two shared kills – all achieved with the D.XX.

Sarvanto continued to fly with LeLv 24 during the early months of the Continuation War, the unit now flying Brewster Model 239s. Indeed, it was Sarvanto who was entrusted with leading the first aerial combat of the Continuation War by long-standing LeLv 24 CO, Major Gustav E. Magnusson, who had also gained victories (four) with the Fokker during the Winter War.

Three days after the German invasion of Russia, some 150 Soviet bombers made a surprise attack on Finnish bases, whose aircraft had been mobilized and sent to southern Finland. Anticipating just such a pre-emptive strike, Maj Magnusson had despatched the second of his four flights to a another local base at Selänpää. Designated 2/LeLv 24, this flight was led into action by Lt Sarvanto at 0715 against the enemy formation, claiming some eight aircraft destroyed in two sorties before midday. A total of 26 unescorted Soviet bombers were destroyed by the FAF on this day, the Finnish government declaring war on the USSR in the aftermath of the action.

Despite this early success, Sarvanto's record with the Buffalo was less dramatic than that achieved with the D.XX, and he managed just four further victories – the last on 9 May 1943. In total, Sarvanto had scored 14 personal and 2 shared kills during his 251 operational sorties. By 1947 he had become CO of HLeLv 21, followed by a tour of duty as the military attaché in London 1954 between 1958. He then became the CO of the Karelian Wing, retiring from the FAF on 8 June 1960 with the rank of lieutenant colonel. Jorma Sarvanto died on 16 October 1963.

Buffalo pilot – H. H. Wind

At the tender age of 20, Hans Henrik 'Hasse' Wind's first operational posting to the Buffalo-equipped LeLv 24 came just six weeks after the start of the Continuation War. He was to remain with the squadron throughout the conflict, flying with the 4th, 1st and 3rd flights respectively. During this time, Wind enjoyed great combat success with both the Model 239 Buffalo and the Bf 109G – indeed, he became the highest scoring Buffalo pilot of the war with 36 personal and six shared victories. The first of the shared kills

came on 27 September 1941, and his credits went on to include claims against Russian-constructed aircraft and lease-lend fighters including the Spitfire and Hurricane. An example of the latter occurred on 14 August 1942 when Wind led five Brewsters of 1/LeLv 24 in a fight against thirteen Hurricanes – three of the latter crashed into the Gulf of Finland, some 13 miles west of Kronstadt. On 31 July 1943 Wind was awarded the Knight of Mannerheim Cross Order for the first time.

In May 1944, LeLv 24 re-equipped with the Bf 109G, and on 27 May Wind continued his high scoring by claiming two La-5s destroyed over Kannas. He subsequently achieved a further 34 victories with the Bf 109, producing a combined tally of 72 personal and six shared victories from just 302 operational sorties. This record made him the second-highest scoring FAF fighter pilot of the 1939-44 period. His scoring run came to a dramatic halt on 28 June 1944 when Wind was badly injured during a reconnaissance sortie, He managed to nurse his damaged Bf 109G-6 (MT-439) back to base at Lappeenranta, and he was subsequently hospitalized for the last few weeks of the war. So successful was Wind in coaxing his aircraft back to base, that the Bf 109 was repaired and flown the following day on operations by Lt Ahti, who was himself shot down flying MT-439 and taken prisoner! On the day that Wind made his last operational flight, he was awarded the Knight of Mannerheim Cross Order for the second time, a distinction shared with only Juutilainen.

Wind resigned from the FAF on 10 October 1945, having attained the rank of captain. He then went to university, graduating with a degree in economics. In a subsequent career in business, Wind also achieved high distinction. He died on 24 July 1995.

Bf 109 pilot – E. I. Juutilainen

Born on 21 February 1914 in Lieksa, Eino Ilmari Juutilainen graduated as a Finnish Air Force pilot with the rank of sergeant in 1935, and by the end of the Continuation War in 1944, he had become the highest-scoring Finnish fighter pilot of all time. 'Illu' Juutilainen scored a total of 93 (and one shared) confirmed victories, flying three aircraft types on 437 operational sorties. During the Winter War whilst part of 3/LeLv 24, he achieved two personal and one shared victory with the D.XX. With the commencement of the Continuation War, Juutilainen claimed a further 34 personal victories with the Buffalo before departing LeLv 24 to become a founder member of LeLv 34. As such he was sent to Werneuchen to convert onto the Bf 109G-2, and upon his return to Finland, Juutilainen continued to demonstrate his increasing prowess by destroying no less than 58 Soviet-built and American and British lend-lease aircraft.

Juutilainen received the Knight of Mannerheim Cross Order on two occasions, and with the award of his first became only the third FAF pilot to receive this distinction. Juutilainen remained with LeLv 34 until 16 May 1947, when he resigned from the air force and bought a light aeroplane. For the next ten years he performed as an airshow pilot, giving 'hospitality' flights. His autobiography, *Punalentajien kiusana*, was published in 1956, and has been recently reissued in a shortened form. Ilmari Juutilainen was still alive as this book went to press.

Chapter Six

The Luftwaffe

. . . we shot at each other several times in passing. It must be remembered that the P-38 Lightning, being a twin-engined aircraft, was a lot more powerful than my Me 109. We were doing head-on attacks and he managed to pull a curve earlier than me. On our third pass the situation became very critical as he managed to curve out much earlier, and so came into an ideal shooting position – we passed each other in an opposing curve. It was not, in this position, possible to recognize or see the hits, nor to feel the damage they cause because one had curved out before the shells strike home. In a head-on attack, the unwritten law amongst pilots was that each aircraft was to be pulled into a right-hand curve, so that the aircraft passed each other belly to belly, then around again for the next attack. With a combined approach speed of at least 1,000 kmh, we had to curve out at least 300 metres before the target, otherwise a crash would become imminent.

Emil Clade, Bf 109 pilot

This chapter seeks to provide an overview, rather than a detailed chronological account, of combat experienced by the Luftwaffe fighter pilot. The narrative provided by former leading Luftwaffe and Soviet fighter pilots is *the* focal point, whilst the reference to primary source material enables supportive archival data on combat training, the criteria and process of claim submission, and of awards and decorations to be provided. Firstly, it is important to set the scene by looking at the volume of Luftwaffe claims, the doubts expressed about their validity by the Allies, and the counter arguments which provide a rationale explaining how this overwhelming number were in fact scored.

Setting the Scene

The statistics derived from the sheer volume of Luftwaffe fighter claims during the Second World War are simply staggering. In total, across every theatre of operations, Luftwaffe day- and night-fighter pilots were credited with the destruction of some 70,000 enemy aircraft, including some 45,000 on the Eastern Front. The distribution of pilots claiming victories was typically skewed, for like the RAF, USAAF, Red Air Force and numerous other national air forces, a very small proportion of Luftwaffe pilots claimed a disproportionately large number of these combat victories – for example, 13,997 victories were credited to just 94 pilots.

There were 13 German *Experten* who shot down over 200 enemy aircraft, and two (Hartmann and Barkhorn) gained over 300 aerial victories. No less than 34 German fighter pilots scored 150 or more combat victories, shooting down 6,902 enemy aircraft between them. A

The following series of four photos of aerial combat depict the 57th individual victory by Adolf Galland in his career. It is not clear how, or who, took photos one, two and four in the sequence, but photo three appears to have been captured by Galland's own gun-camera. The trite German war time caption reads:

Oberstleutnant Galland gets his 57th kill. (1) The English fighters have been sighted and attempt to flee but the German fighters are faster and rapidly catch up with the English. The aircraft of the commander dives towards one of the English aircraft. (2) All attempts of the English aircraft to evade the German fighters fire are in vain. As can be seen by the cloud bank in this photo, Oberstleutnant Galland is flying a sharp curve and is sticking to the heels of the English aircraft. (3) The fire of his machine guns and cannon from his Messerschmitt aircraft are starting to tell. The enemy trailing smoke is about to crash. Again the enemy opponent is vanquished. (4) The end, trailing black smoke the aircraft is about to crash. (via BAK 961)

further 60 destroyed between 100-150 aircraft each, accounting for a total of 7,095 aeroplanes, whilst 103 pilots attained a score of a 100 or more victories. In contrast, no Allied fighter pilot came near to achieving 100 aircraft destroyed during the same period of time.

The disparity between the highest scoring fighter pilots of the Allied air forces and those of the Luftwaffe is often thought to be peculiar to the Eastern Front, where experienced Luftwaffe pilots enjoyed easy pickings against Soviet aircraft during the first 18 months following the instigation of Operation *Barbarossa*. However, the reality is that Luftwaffe pilots also claimed far higher numbers of victories than Allied pilots in other operational theatres too. For example, Heinz Bär achieved 124 victories in the ETO against the RAF and USAAF, whilst Hans-Joachim Marseille claimed 158 destroyed in the North African campaign.

During the Battle of Britain, leading RAF pilots Eric Lock (18 kills), Josef Frantisek (17), Bob Doe, Brian Carbury and Archie McKellar (all with 16) were easily outscored by their Luftwaffe counterparts Werner Mölders (he had 25 kills, even though he missed a whole month of the short conflict), Adolph Galland (37), Helmut Wick, Walter Oesau and Hans-Karl Mayer (all with over 30 victories).

Literature

In the years immediately following the end of the

war, doubts were expressed over the validity of Luftwaffe claims. It was clear, for a start, that overclaiming was widespread by fighter pilots of all air forces (a fact which had been recognized during the war itself), but the defeated Luftwaffe attracted special scrutiny. The vast quantity of claims made by their pilots was treated with scepticism and, in some circles, total disbelief. In his text on the German Air Force, W/C Asher Lee (1946) wrote:

. . . Mölders, Wick and Marseille were certainly first class pilots, equal in calibre to any of their opposite numbers in the Allied Air forces, but the mammoth claims of air combat victories, running sometimes over the 200-mark, were absurdly exaggerated.

In 1954, the USAF's Lt Gen E. R. Quesada wrote the following in an introduction to Luftwaffe fighter ace Heinz Knoke's autobiography, *I Flew for the Führer*:

I do not believe, as Knoke does, that any German ace shot down 150 Allied planes. Here and there his book contains other statements which I regard as obvious Nazi propaganda, swallowed whole by an eager youth.

In the 1960s W/C Roland Beamont wrote in a review of a book on fighter aces:

The lists of British, American and German leading scorers imply that the latter were some form of supermen. Where were these men who could shoot down six of our fighters in one sortie and more than a dozen in one day? . . . One remains unconvinced that differences in methods of recording victories have not given a completely misleading impression of the capabilities of the German leaders.

'Facts' were discovered through research to disprove the claims of some Luftwaffe pilots. Asher Lee described:

On one occasion a young German ace, who shall be nameless, returned from an engagement with Spitfires over the English Channel coast and claimed three of the Spitfires shot down. The ground staff noted that his guns had not fired and that all his ammunition was intact in the aircraft.

The story was circulated amongst the squadron and was transmitted to other flying units. The score of the ace pilot rose, but his stock fell, and he soon acquired a German staff appointment!

The RAF's official highest scoring ace, 'Johnnie' Johnson, wrote:

I have found it possible to make a detailed check of some of the claims of a well known German pilot who has been called the 'unrivalled virtuoso of the fighter pilots'. His greatest day in the Western Desert was on 1 September 1942 when he claimed 17 victories, eight of them in the space of 10 minutes. But our own records show that on this day we lost a total of only 11 aeroplanes, including two Hurricanes, a type which the German pilot did not claim. In fact, some of our losses occurred when he was on the ground.

It will be seen, however, that the process of combat claim submission was applied consistently by the Luftwaffe throughout the war, although there were subtle changes in interpretation over the same period. Therefore, taking into account that it was just as hard for a Luftwaffe pilot to have a claim confirmed by his superiors as it was for the RAF or USAAF pilot, what other reasons can be employed to explain the vast differences in scores?

Reasons for Differences – General Points

i) Continuous combat service not restricted by set tour lengths

Unlike their Allied equivalents, Luftwaffe fighter pilots did not fly a set tour of operations before being rested. Once with a fighter unit, the pilot flew on and on against the enemy until it was recognized – often by his CO – that he required a short period of rest and recuperation in the Luftwaffe-run facility at Bad Wiese, near the Alps. Only infrequently would fighter pilots be given a lengthy 'rest' spell as an instructor on a training unit, and only then after first volunteering for the position. As a result, some Luftwaffe fighter pilots flew well over 1,000 *feindflüge* (frontline) missions during the War.

ii) Frequency of sorties

Often, Luftwaffe fighter airfields were only a

Two dramatic photos from the Battle of Britain. The original German wartime caption claims that the Spitfire has been hit by the He 111's defensive fire, but it is more likely that the Spitfire has been damaged following attack by a Luftwaffe fighter. (via BAK R78)

Two Bf 109E-4 Trops of I./JG 27 flying over the desolate and parched landscape of North Africa in September 1941. 'White 8' is the aircraft of Lt Werner Schroer, who developed his combat skills in this theatre to become one of the Luftwaffe's greatest ever Experten. *He attained 61 victories in the North African campaign, and later kills against the USAAF and Soviet Air Force brought his tally up to 114 in only 197* feindflüge. *Schroer was awarded the Knight's Cross in October 1942 and Swords in April 1945. He died in Munich in 1985 aged 66.* (via BAK 435)

very short distance away from the combat area, thus allowing German pilots to fly several sorties in a day. During the latter years of the war, German fighter pilots were employed on defensive operations, meaning that they were often shot down over home territory. This usually meant that would survive to fight another day or, occasionally, even that same day. Gerhard Barkhorn, who scored a total of 301 combat victories in 1,107 frontline sorties, was shot down on numerous occasions over the Eastern Front.

iii) Operating from any airfield with any unit
The German practice of landing their fighters on any airfield available after they had exhausted their ammunition and fuel served to facilitate both a quick turn-round and swift return to action. All the fighters who had landed on a given airfield (no matter what squadron they hailed from) were grouped together and formed into combat units. These mixed units were then sent off again to engage the enemy. Order Number 321/43 HQ of 3 September 1943 read:

On landing on a foreign airfield, all fighters, no matter what their squadron, will be grouped together under a senior ranking officer and will be formed into a battle group to facilitate a speedy return to action.

The new take-off orders will be given by the fighter command of the relevant area, as they are aware of the operational strengths in their area.

If the unit leader is unable to communicate with fighter command he will order a start on his own initiative, relying on line of sight or other diverse reports of enemy activity. His call sign will be the name of the airfield he has taken-off from. Areas of enemy activity will be broadcast over the *Reichsjägerwelle* (Reich fighter radio station).

The sole function of this radio station was to broadcast a constant update of enemy aircraft activity over the Reich in unambiguous language. The radio station became operational under Order Number 23658/43 on 31 August 1943:

. . . the fighter pilots return to their home bases.

Auxiliary re-supply airfields dumps in the Reich will be marked on all pilots maps. These dumps will be so marked that they can be easily identified even from a great height.

iv) Durability of aircraft
It is also notable that every leading German ace flew the Bf 109 at some time in their operational career. Hans Joachim Marseille, for example, flew only the Bf 109, achieving 158 combat victories up to the time of his death. If nothing else, this says something about the longevity and operational durability of the Bf 109.

Pilots Recollections – Focus on the Eastern Front
The third-highest scoring Luftwaffe fighter pilot of the Second World War was Günther Rall, who here considers reasons for the large differences in claims between Luftwaffe and Soviet fighter pilots over the Eastern Front. Rall obtained 272 of his total number of 275 victories in this latter theatre – 241 of these were Soviet fighters:

When the war started against Russia we already had some combat experience. We met an opponent who was inferior to us in training, tactics, and equipment, which caused them tremendous losses in the first six months. Furthermore, we always found targets in the air, as many Russians flew a lot of missions without contact. In most cases we were outnumbered, but we felt superior. Anyway, I was shot down seven times, and on two occasions was seriously injured, but I returned to my squadron/group and flew again. I officially led and completed 800 operational sorties (*Feindflüge*), which means that I had contact with the enemy 800 times – all other sorties that we undertook were not counted. But Russian morale remained unbroken, and they recovered and came at us with better aircraft after the first year.

In contrast to Rall, Soviet pilot and HSU winner Scherbakov, who eventually became a test pilot after the war, describes his experiences with the 176th Proskurov FAR:

A Bf 109F is examined after taking a hit in the elevator from Allied flak in North Africa in late 1941. (via BAK 435)

A series of five photos showing Staffkapitän Emil Clade leading his Schwarm flying 'White 2', a Bf 109G of 7 Staffel III./JG 27. Clade explained:

We were on escort duty for Gen Oberst Fiebig, the Commander in Chief South East, and were flying over the Bay of Athens on our way to Crete – this was in November 1943. I was allocated 'White 2' at the beginning of the war, and although I was entitled to a 'White 1', I never changed my 'White 2' but kept it to the end.

The white fuselage recognition band was indicative of the North African and Mediterranean theatre of operations. All three aircraft are carrying drop tanks for the long flight. (for some reason Clade's aircraft does not sport the Baltenkreuz of III Group, nor the pierced apple as part of the William Tell emblem below the cockpit as seen on 'White 9 and 7'. This was the jealously-guarded logo of 7 Staffel). (via BAK 529)

Could German aces achieve better results than our pilots? Yes, I think so. There were some real reasons for this. Luftwaffe fighter pilots often operated under special conditions. They had permission to choose the time and place of attack, and avoid combat if the chances of being hit were too great. Our pilots often had no such opportunities. Free hunting for Soviet pilots became prevalent only after 1943, while there was no regiments of 'aces'. The protection of our troops on the ground and our assault and bombing aircraft was the greatest task for our fighters, and their successes in this sphere were more important than air victories.

When defending the assault aircraft, our fighters were not to engage in dogfighting. When defending crossing places and bridge-heads, our fighters were to avoid combat with the Germans even when faced by a stronger enemy. In 1942, and even into 1943, our fighters were detailed to patrol over a defensive position for as long as possible, and thus they had to fly at a low speed. The Germans knew the names and call-up signs of our 'aces', and made a warning when these pilots were flying. There was no similar practice in the Soviet Air Force, and our pilots did not know the names of enemy 'aces'.

Many Luftwaffe pilots built-up extremely high scores, and the leading ace of them all, Erich Hartmann, was seized by the Soviets at the end of the war and sentenced to 20 years in prison for 'the damage caused to the Soviet economy, as he destroyed 347 planes', as the Main military public prosecution department's case Number 463 read.

Hartmann's claims were not checked by the Soviets, and one of the court officials stated that the defendant had behaved with dignity. Hartmann conveyed that the Luftwaffe knew the names and call-up signs of the Soviet 'aces', and were warned when those men were flying. He is reported to have said that he highly appreciated Pokryskhin's skill, and stated that he had twice avoided an encounter with him.

It is clear that at least during the first 18 months of the Soviet campaign, logistical support and technical maintenance at the Luftwaffe units was superior to that practised by the Red Air Force. The smaller numbers of Luftwaffe fighter aircraft in-theatre were better prepared for battle, and professionally repaired if they returned from combat damaged. German pilots were also quickly returned to the frontline after bailing out of their aeroplanes – Hartmann

II./JG 52 Group Commander Gerhard Barkhorn is toasted on his 250th aerial victory at Kriwoi Rog, in Russia, in February 1944 whilst sat in his Bf 109G-6. With a final score of 301, he finished second only to Hartmann in terms of the total number of victories achieved. Barkhorn's Knight's Cross was awarded on 23 August 1942 and the Swords on 2 March 1944. He died in 1983, aged 64. (via BAK 483)

was shot down 14 times, Rall, Barkhorn and others on numerous occasions, whereas leading Russian fighter pilot Kozhedub was never shot down, neither was Skomorokhov, and Pokryshkin only twice, as were Savitsky and Popkov. A. Scherbakov explains why:

Of great importance was that the German pilots shot down managed to fly time and time again. The Bf 109 was able to take considerable punishment, being less vulnerable to fire than the Soviet-made fighters whose carburettor-fitted engines could easily be set on fire.

Training

i) Basic flying training

After a spell in the German Labour Service (the RAD – *Reichsarbeitdienst*), the aspiring Luftwaffe cadet pilot would undertake an induction course in military discipline at a *Fliegerersatzabteilung* (FEA). The function of the FEA was not dissimilar to the RAF's Initial Training Wing (ITW), and once students had completed the course, suitable candidates for flying duties were identified. At this point the similarity between the Luftwaffe system and RAF disappeared. By late 1941, the latter was sending successful cadets to an Elementary Flying Training School (EFTS) for 'Grading', whilst the Luftwaffe cadet could expect to be posted to a *Fluganwärterkompanie* for ground school tuition in the theory of aviation.

The Luftwaffe sought to identify officer material at an early stage, and suitable cadet pilots would then be posted to *Luftkriegschule* (LK) to receive flying training up to B Certificate level. The curriculum would include extra emphasis on aspects of air force law and regulations deemed as essential knowledge for officers. NCO cadet pilots would often remain at the FEA to receive their basic flying training.

The RAF, however, trained potential NCOs and officer cadets together, their rank status becoming known only at the point of graduation.

Luftwaffe flying training for pilots was divided into graded licences, and by 1942 the General Flying School Training Directive (Military) stipulated that the military pilots' licence be divided into four stages. This consisted of the A2 licence followed by B1, B2, and C2. The total training period time allotted was seven months, consisting of 174 flying training hours and 405 ground instruction hours. The A2 licence included 30 dual and 30 solo flights. Training for the B1 licence included conversion training, night flying (five hours dual and solo), aerobatics and formation flying.

For the B2 licence, a greater concentration was made on navigation and instrument flying. The C2 was essentially an instrument flying licence and pilots would often then move onto take a Blind-flying (IFR) certificate. Typical aircraft used by the Luftwaffe training schools were the Bücher Bü 181 Bestmann, Klemm Kl 35, Fw 44 Steiglitz, Fw 56 Stoeber, Fw 58 Weihe (with a covered cockpit for instrument flying), Italian Machetti, Gotha Go 145 (for aerobatics), Gotha Go 150, Siebel Si 202 Hummel, Seibel Si 204 and the Junkers W 34 (the final four aircraft were used primarily for a limited number of cross-country flights).

The *Jagdfliegervorschule* (JVS) was the next port of call for the pilot selected for fighters. Here, he would have the opportunity to fly obsolete single-engine types including the Ar 68 and He 51, both of which served in the Spanish Civil War, and early-mark Bf 109s. After successfully completing initial fighter training, the pilot would move to advanced fighter training at a *Jagdfliegerschule* (JFS).

ii) Operational training

'Raw' fighter pilots would be posted to a

FIGURE 1

25/4/44

OKL to General Flight Training:

As from now the following conditions apply for pilot training applicants. This order will apply until further notice. Minimum age 17, maximum age 26, minimum height 165 cm, maximum height 191 cm, volunteer, conscript, all to have had basic training.

France, August 1943, and Lt Josef Wurmheller of 9 Staffel III./JG 2 proudly poses by the rudder of 'White 2', a Fw 190A-5 which has been marked up with his 60 victories. The Ritterkreuz *with Oakleaves can be clearly seen around his neck. Wurmheller gained 93 aerial victories in the West from around 300 frontline sorties. He died on 22 June 1944 when he collided with his wingman during a dogfight. (via BAK 483)*

Ergänzungsgruppe (training group) attached to the combat squadron to which he had been posted. If fortunate, the new pilot could expect to be instructed in two operational techniques in particular upon his arrival in the training group – weapons training and low-level flying (the Luftwaffe referred to the latter as 'hedge-hopping'). For combat operations it was sometime necessary to fly very low, in and over the contours of the countryside. Increased urgency for combat ready fighter pilots as the war progressed meant that many inexperienced pilots were propelled into action without having sufficient operational training.

Towards the end of the war trainees would sometimes complete their training on Fw 190s and then get theoretical instruction on the new fighters of the time, the Me 262, Me 163 and He 162. However, many fully-trained Luftwaffe pilots from late 1944 to the end of the war never made it to operational units, finishing in the ranks of the Luftwaffe's infantry. By late 1944 flying training schools were being disbanded not necessarily through a lack of trainees or aircraft, but of aviation fuel, which had been an impediment since 1942.

In desperation, and facing defeat in the spring of 1945, a group of young cadet pilots flew their Bü 181 trainers to the operational airfield at Bad Aibling, near Munich, where JG 27 was based. The cadets had flown their aircraft from disbanded training schools and were worried that the war was going to finish without them. After fitting a *Panzerblitz* (infantry anti-tank weapon) under each wing of the little monoplanes, they took off to engage the advancing US Army in low level attacks. Very few returned.

Combat Tactics

i) Firepower

Galland had long and vigorously argued for an improvement in both the efficiency and potency of Luftwaffe fighter armament so as to improve the chances of bringing down USAAF multi-engined bombers conducting daylight raids over the Western Front. As the war progressed, the Luftwaffe began to increase the weight of fire-power and effectiveness of the armament used. This meant a decrease in the amount of machine gun firepower employed, but the ever-increasing use of cannon, and the bore size of the latter weapons.

By 1942, the Luftwaffe was well aware of the potential effectiveness of the armament used, calculating that it took between 20 to 25 20 mm cannon strikes to destroy a B-17. They also estimated that it would take only five strikes of 30 mm cannon to achieve the same effect.

FIGURE 2 – Battle Information for Fighter Units – circular to all squadrons, extracts

The Commander in Chief of the Luftwaffe
Berlin
10/11/1942

General for Fighter Command
Order Number 2522/42
JG 54

Battle information for fighter units
The Reichsmarschall (Göring) has, on 24/10/1942, given the following battle instructions:

Fighter pilots are to attack the enemy not just from a position of advantage, but also from every position which might not be to their advantage.

Through better flying and fighting abilities the disadvantage can be turned into an advantage.

When engaging enemy bomber formations it is essential to thrust through the fighter escort and to engage the bombers at close quarters in order to inflict losses which the enemy will find unacceptable.

The thrusting attack from superior height is not the only form of attack and must be supplemented with the attack from every possible position, as well as the tenacious curving attack. In order to negate the enemy's superior strength, his positional advantage, and the likely better turning circle of his aircraft, tenacious and ruthless combat, as well as

superior flying, is required. That is working with the throttle and using landing flaps and trimming.

Pulling the aircraft up after a thrusting attack can be achieved by throttling back and performing an acrobatic pull-up, or the aircraft can be let to slide off sideways, which can cause the enemy to miss his target. After this, the enemy is again to be rigorously attacked. The practice of breaking off the attack and seeking the horizon when the shout 'Spitfires behind us' is heard will cease forthwith.

When engaging the enemy, manoeuvrability whilst flying a curve is better in the horizontal, and constant positional change is strongly recommended, as is the engagement of the enemy at close quarters. Thrusting through escorting fighters to get at bombers has highest priority, and must be practised. Repeated attacks from all directions with several aircraft at the same time must be made. The time-consuming gaining of height for a positional attack only leads to a situation whereby the enemy fighters are able to push our fighters away from the bombers, thereby making them ineffective. Our objective is to disperse and destroy.

Finally note that in future awards will not be given for the number of kills, but for the completion of a successful mission.

Cannon produced a slower rate of fire than a machine gun, but the advantage for the Luftwaffe was increased potency and the ability to out-range the bombers' defensive fire, thus increasing the chances of scoring a kill.

The ultimate fighter of the Second World War in the shape of the turbo-jet powered Me 262 was extremely well-armed. Johannes Steinhoff, a Knight's Cross winner with 176 kills to his credit, including 6 with the Me 262, flew the jet in combat with JG 7 and then JV 44. In 1993, Steinhoff recalled the armament of the Me 262:

The armament of four 30 mm cannon, with 12 RTL (R4M) rockets underneath the wings, was impressive. When you placed the target in the reticule to the gun and released the rockets, the kill was guaranteed. However, the bullet velocity was so poor that in a turn you could see the bullets fly.

ii) Combat tactics determined by individual circumstances
On the Eastern Front there was little formal teaching of combat tactics for Luftwaffe pilots. Günther Rall recalled that 'there were no special instructions. The specific situation dictated case by case your action as an experienced fighter pilot'.

Emil Clade flew the Bf 109 with JG 27 in the Polish campaign, during the Battles of France and Britain, over the Eastern Front, North Africa and Mediterranean, the Balkans, Italy and finally in the defensive battles over Germany itself. He considered the proposition that individual Luftwaffe fighter pilots had favourite methods of attack:

It depended on who the opponent was. There were a number of attack possibilities, with the tactic for attacking a bomber being different from that used to attack a fighter. If it was a surprise attack – where the enemy was not aware of you – the usual method was from the rear. In North Africa, Hans-Joachim Marseille had an attack method which nobody was able to copy. His attacks were from every possible position. But for many of us the most common method was from the rear, with the hope that the opponent kept still long enough for the surprise attack to be effective. In an attack from the rear the speeds were much the same, and you could aim and fire much longer.

In North Africa we faced not only the British and, later, the Americans, but also colonial troops from India, South Africa and Palestine. These units had developed a method of aerial warfare as practised by the South Africans, which relied heavily on the so-called defensive circle – we could compare this circle with the infantry square of the Napoleonic era. This sort of defensive formation flying inhibited, of course, any sort of offensive flying as we knew it. The defensive circle usually had a diameter of about 300 metres. Now, if I wanted to attack this formation I immediately had an enemy fighter on my tail and it was quite deadly to intrude into this circle.

The idea of the South Africans to fly like this

was in itself not a bad one. But they did not reckon with the fact that some pilots were able to attack either from underneath or from straight down into the formation (a near vertical line of attack, up or down). Both methods were extremely difficult to put into practice, and this was a method of attack much favoured by Marseille – a pilot who could shoot and hit instinctively, and seemed not to have used his Revi gun-sight at all. It must be remembered that when approaching the target, the angles of attack are constantly changing, but Marseille seemed to us to have had a knack of hitting his target, and being able to break up such a defensive circle. Within five minutes he'd have taken out two or three aircraft.

Over the Western Front, as the large USAAF bomber formations made daylight sorties deep into the France and Germany, so Luftwaffe fighters made slashing attacks from high above, with the aim of shattering the defensive cordon of the American bombers.

iii) Head-on attacks
The Luftwaffe also made dangerous attacks from directly astern and head-on. The former had the

---

FIGURE 3 – Organizational Instructions, Circular to all Squadrons, Extracts.

The Reiches Minister for Aviation and Commander
   in Chief of the Luftwaffe
General Fighter Command
Order Number 745/42
Berlin
2/5/1942
JG 54

Ref: Increasing the battle capability of the fighters

The Reichsmarschall has ordered that the effectiveness of fighters be increased, in so much that the burden of aerial combat be more evenly divided amongst the pilots of the squadron. We need to increase the quality and effectiveness of all pilots so that the burden of the successful kill is not carried by a few highly-talented pilots, but by all.

In order to reach this objective, it is necessary to re-deploy the older fighter pilots who, after 200 and more missions, have achieved a pathetic three to five kills, although there has been plenty of

opportunity for further claims. These pilots can be transferred to bombers, battle squadrons, or to the reconnaissance units.

In short, it is strongly recommended that every pilot be given a chance – not just the successful ones. Successes, experience and casualties will therefore be spread over the whole unit. This will also give younger replacement pilots a better chance to integrate themselves.

It is recommended that when a pilot is to be given leave, it is left up to the discretion of the unit commander. However, a pilot is not to be kept in action at the front longer than six months. These periods of rest will also further his combat effectiveness.

It is recommended that squadron commanders do not fly every mission with their unit, but concentrate more on the leadership of their squadron.

                                        Signed for Galland

A scene that would be repeated in many air forces in Europe in the summer of 1941. The Bf 109F-4 has its starting handle in place, clearly suggesting that pilots lounging in their deck chairs are on standby, ready to scramble at a moment's notice. (via BAK 597)

advantage of reducing the deflection angles, but by dint of having to fly for longer periods directly at the enemy aircraft, left the attacking pilot vulnerable to defensive fire. The head-on attack took great nerve, as the aircraft would be closing at some 200 metres per second. Maj Werner Schroer, commander of III./JG 54 (who was also a *Ritterkreuz* holder with 114 kills, including 61 in North Africa), instructed his young pilots to attack the large B-17 formations by meeting the enemy head-on. He advised them to keep their eyes firmly closed so that they would not see the American tracer coming straight for them. Schroer's was a tactic not explicitly agreed with by General Fighter Command, yet it corresponded to Göring's directive in November 1942 that:

Fighter pilots are to attack the enemy not just from a position of advantage, but also from every position which might not be to their advantage . . . Through better flying and fighting abilities, disadvantage can be turned into an advantage.

Galland was forced to make something of this empty rhetoric, and in conveying the instructions of the Commander in Chief of the Luftwaffe, managed to describe attacking manoeuvres. Emil Clade remembered employing the head-on tactic on his return from a sortie over the Ardennes:

I was just on my way back to my base at Osnabrück (near Minden) from a sortie in the Ardennes. During this attack I was separated from my unit and was on my own flying back to my base, near Siegburg, when I encountered four P-38 Lightnings. I saw these aircraft from quite a way off, and as I came nearer three of the American fighters made off. I attacked the one remaining aircraft, which turned to meet me. We shot at each other several times in passing. It must be remembered that the P-38 Lightning, being a twin-engined aircraft, was a lot more powerful than my Me 109. We were doing head-on attacks and he managed to pull a curve earlier than me. On our third pass the situation became very critical as he managed to curve out much earlier, and so came into an ideal shooting position – we passed each other in an opposing curve. It was not, in this position, possible to recognize or see the hits, nor to feel the damage they cause because one had curved out before the shells strike home. In a head-on

A demonstration of jubilation as pilots and ground crew welcome this Bf 109G on its return from a successful mission in France in late 1943. Two 20 mm gun pods can be seen under the aircraft's wings. (via BAK 487)

attack, the unwritten law amongst pilots was that each aircraft was to be pulled into a right-hand curve, so that the aircraft passed each other belly to belly, then around again for the next attack. With a combined approach speed of at least 1,000 kmh, we had to curve out at least 300 metres before the target, otherwise a crash would become imminent. Almost inevitably I started to get hit. My fighter

FIGURE 4

The Commander in Chief Luftwaffe
H.Q.
3/9/1943
General Fighter Command
Order Number 321/43
JG 54

Combat instructions for fighter and destroyer formations in air defence. This order has priority over all previous orders.

Every fighter formation (Group/Flight) will engage only one and the same formation. If the attacked bomber formation should jettison its bombs, or become dispersed, it is to be left alone and the next bomber formation which can be seen will be attacked.

The aircraft of all flight leaders from Schwarm leader upwards will have white tail fins. Individual fighters or dispersed units will close up on these aircraft irrespective of the squadron. The leaders of these units will then again, without hesitation, engage the enemy formation.

The objective of the first attack is to disperse the enemy. The target is to be exactly divided and the best attack position sought. From this position the attack will be carried out so that each Schwarm is able to follow each other into the attack and maximize the opportunities to hit the same enemy formation. The distance between each Schwarm should be kept to a minimum. A quick assembly position for the fighters after the attack is essential, and this should be decided upon before the attack is carried out.

In further engagements with the enemy, it is to be noted that the attack should be carried by several aircraft at a time.

The attack from the front is from now on to be the exception to the rule. Only successful and experienced groups are to use this form of attack.

The standard attack method will be from the rear, with a shallow angle of attack.

The enemy is to be engaged at close quarters in order to get in the most effective fire. Flight leaders will observe and note their units' performance. Pilots who without good reason do not engage the enemy at the minimum ordered distance will be court marshalled for cowardice.

From now on, formations of bombers are only to be attacked irrespective of whether they are flying in, or flying out. Only after the whole formation has been dispersed, or if there is no further chance of engaging the formation, is it allowed to engage dispersed or single, damaged, aircraft to their final destruction.

After the Nebelwerfer aircraft have successfully fired off their grenades, permission is given to engage and destroy *Herausschüsse*. Industrial Rotten, nightfighter, and small units of the training formations can, if they are unable to close up with larger formations, engage *Herausschüsse* to their final destruction.

Unit leaders and fighter pilots who do not follow these orders are libel for prosecution, as they are endangering the security of the Reich and will be court marshalled.

Opening fire in a frontal attack is to be carried at a range of 800 metres (earliest). All other attacks will be carried out at a range of 400 metres. If the fire is opened at a longer range this will be considered as wasting ammunition, and is a sign of lack of courage.

All flight angles of attack in excess 30° are ineffective.

Shooting at tracer and smoke trails will not lead to a combat kill.

Combat will continue in and above areas of heavy flak, in flak zones and restricted areas.

The enemy bomber formations, if they have broken through to their targets, are, with all means available, to be prevented from achieving a targeted drop.

Any divergence of these orders is prohibited.

lost steerage and was losing oil at the same time, so that it became imperative to leave the aircraft and parachute out.

As I was hanging on my parachute I noticed a second parachute below me. Later, I was gathered up by a flak unit from Siegburg whose task it was to collect shot down Allied pilots. This unit thought at first that I was an American pilot because of the reports they'd received from the population about over-flying enemy aircraft. I accepted their offer of a lift so that I'd be able to get back to my base. As I got onto the lorry I noticed that there was already another pilot onboard. I struck up a conversation with him and it soon became evident that he was the American pilot I had shot down. It turned out that he had landed about 200 metres from me.

I had an opportunity to talk to my opponent on the lorry as we were transported away, I assumed he was an American although he said nothing. I asked him his name and where he came from, but all I got was that he was not allowed to say

anything, and I left it at that. During the journey back to Siegburg we had to abandon the truck three times because his comrades were shooting at the farmers in the fields. I said to him that I did not consider the enemy aircrafts' actions to be correct. He answered 'it was the Germans who had wanted the total war'. When we arrived at the flak unit's barracks at Siegburg, it was already past lunch time, so I organized some food for us which we had together. He was then transported off to the collection point for enemy pilots at Oberursal (on the Rhine).

Claim Process

i) Criteria

It is clear that the Luftwaffe's basic combat claim process remained constant throughout the duration of the war. What may have changed was the way in which claims were interpreted – occasionally, Galland was impelled to remind

---

FIGURE 5 – Combat Claim Directive. Circular to all Squadrons

The Commander in Chief of the Luftwaffe
Berlin
16/4/1942

General of Fighters
Order Number 582/42
Stamped: Staff JG 54, 7/5/1942 I.8./JG 54 9/5/1942

Ref: Combat claims
Because of the different ways combat claims are reported, it has again become necessary to clarify the report procedure.

1. The daily reports of combat claims are based on the report of the pilot. In his report the pilot must testify that he has plainly observed the destruction of the aircraft.

If the pilot can find no eyewitness for the destruction of the aircraft, his report will be marked as a probable and will be passed on for further review.

The flight commander and the group commander must check the correctness of the claim before passing it on, they will need to satisfy themselves that there are not two claims for the same destruction.

The squadron commander must also check the

correctness of a claim, and must compare subsequent claims with the first claim in order to avoid double claims for the same aircraft.

2. The pilot and witness must immediately write their claim and report on landing. These will be handed to the flight leader, who will pass them on to the group commander. This first written report will be seen as the basis for the final combat claim.

Claims for shot down aircraft without witnesses will only be passed on as probables if the pilot has achieved at least three previously reliable claims.

Where there are follow-on claims without witnesses, it is better to pass the report on, marked as a probable, than to waste time looking for witnesses whose testimonies will be, at the least, doubtful. On different fronts, and with the tactics used by ourselves and by the enemy, we will always get satisfactory claims with, or without, witnesses.

The personal ambition of the pilot to get enemy kills and decorations is all to the good – as is the competition between pilots, flights, groups and squadrons. This inter-unit and pilot competition furthers the achievements of fighter command.

Signed for Galland.

FIGURE 6 – Documentation Required for Consideration of a Combat Claim Issued 28/4/41

The application for the recognition of a shot down aircraft, or the destruction of one, is made up of the following parts:

a A completed report form (*L. V. Blatt – Luftwaffenverordnungsblatt*)
b The combat report (by flying units, the person who shot enemy down)
c The original witness report

d If destroyed on the ground (*L. V. Blatt*, paragraph B, 1, d) 276
e Opinion of the report by an intermediate commander (flight commander)

The intermediate commander must express his opinion of every combat claim or destruction report giving his reasons, and will verify and report any other units involved in a clear and precise way.

FIGURE 7 – Instructions to Luftwaffe Pilots Submitting Combat Claims

28/4/41
Combat report and eyewitness report

For every combat claim, a separate report is to be submitted. The reports must include the following details:

A Crew, aircraft type, registration number.

Combat report:
b Time (day hour minute)
c Type and number of own attacks, type and number of attacks of the enemy. Enemy a/c type and nationality
d How was it destroyed?
e Type of fire or smoke (for further details see *L. V. Blatt*)
f Type of crash, description of area and place

g If crash was not observed, why not?
h Fate of crew
i Other units involved

Part of c) Direction of (own individual attacks and that of the enemy), distance from which enemy was shot down, tactical position.

Type of ammunition used, how many rounds fired, type and number of weapons used in shooting down enemy aircraft?

Hits on own aircraft?

B Eyewitness: Eyewitness reports should include a description report of the combat, and if possible should correspond with the points made in the combat report.

FIGURE 8 – Definitions for the confirmation of a combat claim

28/4/41
Conditions: a flawless eyewitness report, if possible with photo.
Aircraft shot down this side of our own lines: look for and find aircraft wreckage.

Destruction means burnt out or destroyed so that the aircraft is of no further use to the enemy (destruction has been documented), or has been removed so that enemy can not repossess it.

Shot down means that the enemy aircraft has been hit by an attack in the air or from the ground and was damaged, destroyed or burned out on crashing.

If, after an emergency landing on the enemy side of the line, is the degree of damage on the aircraft visible? Or, if it is possible to destroy the aircraft through artillery fire or bombing before it is

removed by the enemy, then this will count as a claim.

Forced to land: If an aircraft is forced to land after taking hits either from the air or from the ground, the following will apply – if it landed on the enemy side of the front, this will not count as a claim; if it lands on our side of the front, then this will count as a claim.

Success on the ground: 1) Shot into flames on the ground; aircraft that are engulfed in fire or smoke, will count as burned out. 2) Diverse destruction on the ground: on aircraft where the under-carriage has collapsed, or showing other important parts as being damaged – for example, fuselage or wings – are considered to be destroyed

L. V. Blatt 1941, Number 18
28/4/1941

A relaxed session of tactical instructions is given to a group of pilots from II./JG 26 on a summer's day in France in mid-1942. The aircraft parked in the hangar is a Fw 190A-3. (via BAK 606)

fighter units of the process to be followed. Like most other air forces, the Luftwaffe used the criteria of 'destroyed' and 'probable' and, in addition, 'damaged' rather than 'possible'. With the advent of heavy bomber daylight raids a further category was introduced, for it was recognized that the defensive and protective cordon and durability of heavy bomber formations presented particular difficulties.

Combat victories by the Luftwaffe over multi-engined heavy bombers were far more difficult for pilots to achieve than destroying a single-engined fighter. As a result, the category of *Herausschiessen* (HSS – to shoot an aircraft out of a defensive formation) was introduced in order to give the pilot credit for such a feat, even though confirmation of its final destruction was not determined. The HSS held special significance in the new points system introduced in 1943 – the latter was an attempt by the Luftwaffe to equalize the criteria for the recommendation of awards and decorations for action over either front.

ii) Describing the process

Günther Rall details the process of claim submission:

For each claim we had to have an air or ground witness. Both you and he had to write a detailed report. Victories without witnesses were not recognized. The report was very detailed, and many questions were asked – 'how did I make the attack, the type and insignia of the enemy aircraft, its position, how much and which type of ammunition was used?' The witnesses also had to write a report independently. We got gun cameras very late, and only a few in Russia. The report was sent to Fighter Headquarters, and it took quite a long time to get confirmation."

Emil Clade achieved 26 victories with JG 27 and recalled:

After we had landed we had to go to operations for debriefing and make our report to the op's secretary, who wrote down the events of the mission. These reports were then passed on to division. Each group had an op's room, and every pilot had to report in after a mission. Normal office types took the report, and we were not asked about any specific incidents. All they did was write down what we told them. These documents were then passed on through channels up to Division. Most of the combat claims were confirmed by fellow pilots, which is understandable since we operated as a unit. In fact confirmation of a claim could be got even during the combat phase, or within a day or two, just by listening to the British radio traffic.

The British, in turn, used to listen to our radio traffic, as the general radio chatter of the pilots usually gave a good insight into the goings-on of a combat, so that we were able to reconstruct the events of a claim. I would say that half of the claims were confirmed over the radio. I have no personal knowledge of any pilot filing bogus claims, although anything is possible. The chances of being detected were very high – after all, we were seldom alone. Only rarely did it occur that

one could shoot down an enemy when flying alone, as happened to me when I met the P-38 over Siegburg, but that was an exception to the rule. When the American pilot and I were having lunch together at the camp in Siegburg, I asked him if he would confirm my claim for me, which he did. Even if he had not confirmed it for me I, still had the flak unit as a witness.

Clade recalled another interesting combat claim:

In North Africa I shot down Lt Gen Gott (W. H. B. Gott, who was on his way to assume command of the Eighth Army at Cairo). His aircraft (a Bristol Bombay transport) was attacked by my schwarm, and following his death as a result of this action, Lt Gen B. L. 'Monty' Montgomery was posted to command the Eighth Army as Gott's replacement. I waited until the latter's aircraft was over the desert and then dived down on him with four fighters. As I was the leader of this schwarm (four aircraft), I was able to fire on him first – he was flying at a height of

Instruction on methods of fighter attack on a B-24 Liberator. The B-24's defensive arcs of fire are represented by the wire caging on the model. (via BAK 565)

In 1942 the Focke-Wulf company released a series of photos depicting the Fw 190 in a variety of attacking roles. It is assumed that these were composite photos, and those shown here depict two very different roles for the Fw 190. The first, positioning for attack on a Spitfire on 16 September 1942, and the second, an attack on enemy shipping, dated 3 July 1942. (via BAK R93)

about 20-30 metres. They felt so secure that they
had not even occupied the rear gun pod. My fire was
effective on the engine, and the pilot immediately
reduced the power in order to land, which was no
problem in the desert. Meanwhile my remaining
three fighters came in after me also firing.

After the general's aircraft had landed, the crew
started to jump out of the aircraft, although it was
rolling along. Now, Gott did not die through my
gunfire, but by jumping out of the rolling aircraft
and breaking his neck. I still have one living eyewitness for this event, the other two having died in
the war. When the aircraft had come to a halt, I
instructed my Rotte leader to destroy it so he could
claim it as destroyed. The claim could only be
accredited if the aircraft was destroyed.

On another occasion I remember that I once shot
down a Spitfire, but the pilot managed to land the
aircraft. The causes for its landing were not really
clear, but I think I hit him in the engine because he
had a vapour trail behind him as he was going
down. Two days later we got a message from OKH
(Army High Command) that the aircraft had indeed
landed, but had not been destroyed, and therefore
could not be accredited as a kill. Two days later we
flew a special sortie just to shoot up this aircraft,
which stood there parked in a valley – these events
were then included in the combat claim. It was
confirmed as my Rotte leader's kill.

Psychological Impact of Combat
Emil Clade considered the question of the
psychological impact of combat, firstly in respect
to engaging the enemy:

I remember the first days in the Polish campaign –
at that time there was no opportunity, nor need, for
aerial combat. We were allocated for army co-
operation duties. After our first mission we came
back to our base and saw that our aircraft were shot
through with many bullet holes. We were instructed
to strafe the retreating Polish infantry and horse
drawn artillery, and I could see my flight leader's
hits taking their toll in all directions. In a situation
like this you are very much aware of the fact that
you are shooting at people. In return, the Polish
infantry shot at us with everything they had from
pistols to rifles, and some of our aircraft were like
sieves. I had six hits on my own aircraft – the holes
had ragged edges so one could tell that they were
from infantry weapons.

*A Fw 190 from JG 26 is parked in a field on a clear
summer's day, whilst above it vapour trails from a dogfight pattern the blue sky. (via BAK 604)*

On this first sortie I had not fired my guns in
anger, and this was noticed by my flight leader, a
Spanish Civil War veteran, who was flying ahead of
me (he could tell by lack of tracer bullets going past
him from my aircraft). In debriefing he asked me
why I had not fired? I said to him that I was unable
to shoot at people. My flight leader said, 'the next
time you shoot – IS THAT CLEAR?' So, as you
gained battle experience over a period of time, you
also developed a different attitude of mind to war.
With regard to aerial combat, what you see is the
aircraft and not the pilot. There was always some
armoured protection when sitting in your fighter, so

one was never quite certain when shooting at an enemy aircraft that you would also be hitting the pilot.

Later in the war, the emotional state you were in following a combat depended on the situation you were in. If it was a one-to-one dogfight and a turbulent aerial scrap, the radio airways filled with much shouting. When the radio traffic got too heavy the CO could be heard shouting at the top of his voice for everybody to shut their mouths.

When you fired at an enemy aircraft you were conscious of the fact that you were not just shooting at the aeroplane, but in all likelihood at the pilot as well. For example, if I fired on a bomber I would go for the engines to stop him flying on any further. Other pilots might do things differently. It was said that Marseille always went for the cockpit, which might be a bit unfair to him since the distance between engine and cockpit is quite small – still, it was strange that many of his opponents did not bale out. Over a period of time you develop an attitude of mind where you say to yourself 'it's him or me'.

In respect to rest and recuperation, Clade recounted:

On the Western Front in 1940 we had a high operational frequency, so that we flew four to five sorties a day, and this was considered to be quite high. But I would say that we flew an average during the war of around one to two sorties a day. Periods of rest were not automatic, and were left to the discretion of the commanding officer, who usually conveyed to the pilot concerned that in his opinion, he was *Abgeflogen* (suffering either physical or mental exhaustion), and that a holiday might be a good idea, or a short stay at the Luftwaffe fighter R&R centre at Bad Wiesee, near the Alps, where the *Abgeflogenen* pilots were made fit to fly again.

For Günther Rall, who spent three-and-a-half years in Russia, made the following comment about being rested from combat. 'I flew about 800 sorties with enemy engagement. My rest time was always spent in hospital – after having been injured.'

Many Luftwaffe fighter pilots were shot down on several occasions, and Emil Clade recalled:

I was shot down five times, including the once by my own flak, as I was on a front recon mission near Bonn. On my fourth bale out, I was hanging on my 'chute when I was attacked by American fighters – this happened over an airfield near Bremen. The

Russia 1942/43. Coming in to land on a bright winter's day is a Fw 190A of 3 Staffel I./JG 54 'Grünherz', the aircraft carrying the green heart squadron insignia and broad yellow recognition band for the Russian theatre of operations. The latter was also used by aircraft operating in the Scandinavian countries, the Channel area and in defence of the Reich. (via BAK 625)

Russia 1943, and well and truly bogged down. The atrocious weather conditions encountered in the east severely handicapped German fighter operations. This Bf 109G-6 of JG 3 is being battened down in the hostile climate. (via BAK 634)

airfield security flak, armed with 20 mm cannon, came to my rescue by taking the American P-51 Mustang fighters under fire and forcing them to turn off.

We noticed that American fighter pilots who had baled out and were hanging on their parachute used to stretch out their arms in the sign of a 'T', which signified to their fellow pilots that they too were American. We soon caught on to this sign language, and used it to our own advantage when we were hanging on the 'chute.

Awards and Decorations

During the Great War, the *Pour le Merite* had been the most prestigious of all awards available to members of the German armed forces. The populace thrived on accounts of individual heroism in popular magazines including *Signal*, which gave fulsome coverage of the careers and exploits of personnel awarded the *Pour le Merite*. For fighter pilots, the *Pour le Merite* was usually awarded after achieving 20 kills. This medal

could be granted only to officers, and following the end of the First World War was never again awarded.

The need for a replacement for the medal was caused by the commencement of German aggression in Europe in the latter half of the 1930s. Awarded for special acts of valour, this new decoration was to have two significant differences from the *Pour le Merite*. Firstly, all ranks would be eligible to receive it, and secondly, that it could be awarded only with Hitler's permission. The name of the new decoration was the Knight's Cross (*Ritterkreuz*) of the Iron Cross and, for the Luftwaffe pilot, it was to become the most coveted award.

The Knight's Cross was in fact an extension of the original Iron Cross, which had been first commissioned in 1813 during the reign of Friedrich Wilhelm III, King of Prussia. The Iron Cross had achieved considerable respect in its own right with the German fighting man

The cramped cockpit confines of a Bf 109G. (via BAK 680)

throughout the various campaigns of the 19th and 20th centuries, and it was awarded to personnel regardless of rank. Divided into two classes, Second and First Class, the latter could not be presented until the former had been issued. The Iron Cross could only be awarded for valour in the field of battle when engaged with the enemy, or for exceptional deeds. A third Iron Cross award was also detailed – namely the Great Cross. Unlike the first two classes of the Iron Cross, the Great Cross of the Iron Cross was awarded to field commanders only, and it was not necessary to have previously received the Iron Cross First and Second Class in order to qualify.

The Iron Cross was first awarded to allied foreign powers on 16 March 1915, and during the Second World War both the Iron Cross, Second and First Class, and the more prestigious Knight's Cross were given to fighter pilots of Germany's allies.

The latter award was used throughout the duration of the Second World War. By 3 June 1940, the Oak Leaves to the Knight's Cross had been introduced so as to give those who had already achieved the highest award that Germany could proffer another target to aim for. It was simply not enough to alter the criteria by which the decoration would be recommended, so the Knight's Cross hierarchy developed further in direct response to the achievements of Germany's top scoring U-boat captains, tank commanders and fighter pilots. On 28 September

---

FIGURE 9 – Citations for the Award of the Oak Leaves to the Knight's Cross of the Iron Cross

General Command XII Air Corps
Corps Operations
27/2/1943
II Br, B, Number 3006/43
Corps orders of the day Number 94
Bearer of the Knight's Cross Oberleutnant Gilder
Flight captain of 1./*Nachtjagdgeschwader* 1, died
in action on the night 24–25/2/1943.

In recognition of his excellent service and heroic valour, the Führer, Commander in Chief of the Wehrmacht, has awarded the Oakleaves to the Knight's Cross of the Iron Cross.
With the loss of Oberleutnant Gilder, our

nightfighters have lost one of their best, and most experienced, pilots. Oberleutnant Glider was one of the first in the newly-formed units of nightfighter command.
With a total of 2 day and 42 night combat claims.
He has earned unforgettable glory in the defence of the his homeland.
The Fatherland will not forget this hero.
He will be remembered for his sense of duty and victorious deeds for the Führer and Reich.

Signed
Lieutenant General

FIGURE 10 – Citations for the Award of the Oak Leaves to the Knight's Cross of the Iron Cross

General Command XII Air Corps
Corps Operations
28/2/1943
II Br, B, Number 3201/43
Corps orders of the day Number 96

In recognition, the Führer, Commander In Chief of the Wehrmacht, has for Major Streib, Commander of I./N.J.G.1, awarded the Oakleaves to the Knight's Cross of the Iron Cross, and with the following telex citation:

For Herrn Major Streib. I./N.J.G.1
In recognition of your excellent deeds for the freedom of our nation. I award you, as the 197th soldier of the German Wehrmacht, the Oak Leaves to the Knight's Cross of the Iron Cross.

Adolf Hitler

Congratulations also from XII Air Corps for Major Streib on receiving this high award.

1940, the Oak Leaves with Swords, and the Oak Leaves with Swords and Diamonds, were commissioned. Just two days before the end of 1944, Hitler commissioned the order of the Golden Oak Leaves, but gave the instruction that this would be awarded on only 12 occasions. Indeed, the sole recipient of this award was the Ju 87 Stuka pilot Hans Ulrich Rudel.

For the fighter pilot, the Knight's Cross was a visible recognition of his high flying skill and personal courage, but there were no hard and fast guidelines regarding the distribution of these awards. Until 1943, the *Ritterkreuz* was awarded for a specific number of combat victories. However, from then on a points system was introduced to try to restore a balance between the high number of claims made over the Eastern Front and the far lower scores being achieved against the heavy day and night bomber formations, and their deadly escorting fighters, in the western theatre of operations. It would seem that the following sequence applied:

September 1939 – June 1941 – 20 kills appeared to be the average number of combat victories achieved enabling a recommendation for the Knight's Cross to be made. Introduced in June and September 1940 respectively, the Knight's Cross with Oakleaves required 40 kills, and Oakleaves with Swords 70.

July-August 1941 – rapidly increasing scores over the Eastern Front led to the *Ritterkreuz* being recommended after 25, and then by September, 30 kills.

November 1941 – 40 kills were required.

May 1942 – 50 combat victories required. For the award of the Knight's Cross with Oak

Adolf Galland is seen seated in his Bf 109E in France in late 1940. (via BAK 345)

Adolf Galland's Bf 109E-4 Wk-Nr. 5819 shortly after he had scored his 50th victory on 1 November 1940. All his kill markings have been applied to the starboard side of the rudder. Yet . . .

. . . this photo was taken on the same day showing the port side of Wk-Nr. 5819's rudder, which has Galland's victory tally totalling 44 kills! Clearly, the artist had yet to bring the port rudder up to date by the time this photo was taken. (both via Rick Chapman)

Leaves, fighter pilots progressively needed 60, 80, 100, 125, and then 150 victories over the Eastern Front, whilst on the Western Front, 60-70 kills were required. For the Oak Leaves with Swords, 100 kills were required over the Western Front.

Spring 1943 – the rapidly increasing effectiveness of Soviet air power had significantly impeded fighter pilots' opportunities to gain the necessary high number of combat victories, and the score needed is duly reduced to 75 kills on the Eastern Front. The Oak Leaves with Swords in the same theatre required 200. In September 1943, the figure for award of the Knight's Cross rose to 100 kills along the Eastern Front, but by December 1943 had been reduced to 75 in view of the small number of awards being given. The Oakleaves with Swords at the turn of the year needed 200-225 victories, whereas on the Western Front 100 kills were required.

End of 1943 – a points system was introduced to run in parallel with combat reports in an attempt to recognize the higher strategic value in shooting down a heavy bomber making an attack on Germany: 0.5 point for the destruction of an already damaged twin-engined aircraft; 1.0 point for the destruction of a straggler (a heavy bomber having already been damaged and shot out of formation) or the destruction of a single-engined aircraft or damaging a twin-engined machine; 2 points to shoot an enemy heavy engined bomber out of formation (*Herausschiesse*), even without confirmation of its final destruction, or the downing of a twin-engined aircraft; 3 points for the destruction of a heavy bomber.

1944 – the number of combat kills remained set at 75, having been carried over from the end of the previous year. However, for those returning from the Eastern Front to the defence of the homeland and then going on to score additional kills over RAF or USAAF aircraft, their combined tally from both fronts was converted into points. It quickly became apparent, however, that the points system and the combat claim did not run in tandem. By 1945, Germany was in a desperate situation and many, of the highest scoring fighter pilots who had survived so far, were killed in the last months of the war. Increasingly, fighter pilots were instructed to undertake ground attack missions, and combat victories were credited for the destruction of tanks.

APPENDICES
A. Example of Confirmed Combat Claim and supporting documentation – Heinz Bär

II./*Jagdgeschwader* 1
Operations, 23 April 1944

Shot down one Liberator on 22/4/44 at 20:08 hours, grid ref JQ 8-9 north of Ahlen. By Major Bär, Heinz – Staff II./J.G.1

179th confirmed claim (200th claim) of pilot, to be confirmed. 122nd claim of Staff, 687th claim of II./JG 1 in for confirmation.

Contents
1 Combat claim
2 Combat report of pilot
3 Combat witness report: Air
4 Combat witness report: Ground
5 Statement made by intermediate assessment office

Signed Bär
Major
Unit. II./Jagdgeschwader 1
Place. Operations
Date. 23/4/44

Abschussmeldung

1 Time (Date, Hour, Minute) and Location of Crash – 22/4/44, 20:08 hours, Grid ref JQ 8-9 north of Ahlen, height 6000 m
2 Name of Crew making Claim – Major Bär, Heinz, Staff II./JG 1
3 Type of Aircraft Destroyed – Liberator
4 Enemy Nationality – America

Serial Number or Markings – National emblem

5 Nature of Destruction – Hit on fuselage and wings, vertical crash dive
   a) Flames and black smoke, flames and white smoke
   b) Did aircraft shed pieces (name them)? – burst apart
   c) Was it forced to land (Our side or their side of front, normal or crash landing)?
   d) Was it shot into flames while on the ground on their side?
6 Nature of Crash (only if this could be observed)

a) Our side or their side of the front?

b) Vertical, flat angle, fire on crashing, in cloud of dust?

c) If not observed, why not?

7   Fate of enemy Aircrew (killed, four men baled out, not observed)

8   Combat report of Pilot is attached

9   Witnesses

a) Air – Ofw Schuhmacher

b) Ground – Ground crew from II./JG 1

10 Number of Attacks on enemy Aircraft – 1 attack from behind

11 Direction from which each Attack was carried out – below and behind

12 Range from which effective Fire was directed – 400-100 m

13 Tactical position of Attack – not known

14 Were any Enemy Gunners neutralized?

15 Type of Ammunition used – Brdgr.M-patr 151/20 Pzbrdgr. Pzgr.151/20 and 131 Brdsprg

16 Consumption of Ammunition – MG 151/20 400 rounds, MG 131 160 rounds

17 Type and number of Guns used in shooting Enemy down – 2 MG 151/20. 2 MG 131

18 Type of own Aircraft – Fw 190A-7 ('Red 23')

19 Anything else of tactical Interest – no

20 Hits on own Aircraft – none

21 Other Units involved (incl. Flak)

Signed Bär
Major

Nos 5–7 Relevant Question To be underlined
Bär, Major
Operations, 23 April 1944
II./*Jagdgeschwader* 1
Staff

Combat report

Shot down one Liberator on 22/4/44
20:08 hours
Grid Ref. JQ 8–9
Major Bär, Staff II./JG 1
Fw 190 – 'red 23'.

On the 22/4/44 at 19:53 hrs I started with Ofw. Schuhmacher to intercept a lone flying Liberator NW of our airfield. The aircraft was dropping smoke canisters as aiming points. I assumed that the aircraft was a pathfinder. The four engines of the Liberator were running smoothly as I started my attack from behind and at a range of 400-100

metres. The Liberator immediately jettisoned its bombs, soon after four men of the crew baled out. Light coloured flames were shooting out of the fuselage. The Liberator started to go down in a left-hand curve and broke apart in to air. The wreckage falling to the ground north of Ahlen.

Date and time of claim: 22/4/44 – 20:08 hours
Area of claim: JQ 8-9 – north of Ahlen
Height: 6,000 m
Witnesses: Air: Ofw Schuhmacher
Ground: Ground crew of II./JG 1
Bär

Schuhmacher, Ofw
Operations, 23rd April 1944
II./*Jagdgeschwader* 1
Air combat witness report

On 22/4/44 at 19:53 hours I took-off in a Rotte led by the commander to intercept a lone flying Liberator NW of our airfield. On attaining altitude we noticed that the aircraft was dropping smoke canisters as aiming points. The four engines of the Liberator were running smoothly. Major Bär started his attack from behind and at a range of 400-100 metres. The Liberator immediately jettisoned its bombs, soon after I saw four men of the crew bale out. The Liberator, its fuselage burning, started to go down in a left-hand curve and broke apart in the air. I observed the wreckage falling to the ground north of Ahlen.

Date and time of claim: 22/4/44. – 20:08 hours
Area of claim: JQ 8-9 – north of Ahlen
Height: 6,000 m
Schuhmacher

II./*Jagdgeschwader* 1
Operations, 23/4/1944
Ground combat witness report

On the 22/4/44 we observed a lone flying Liberator NW of the airfield. The aircraft was dropping smoke canisters as aiming points. After the sighting had been reported, the commander took-off along with Ofw Schuhmacher as his wingman. On attaining altitude, we could observe from the airfield Major Bär attack the Liberator from behind. Soon after we saw explosions in the distance, we assumed these were from the bomb drop of the aircraft. The Liberator was burning brightly as it went into a crash dive, soon after it broke apart in the air. We could not see where the wreckage came down, the distance being too great.

Witnesses: Voigt Oblt, Bückhof, Seebach Staff Dr, Kahl, Huffer Ofw and six more witnesses.

Authors' Notes

It can been seen that this is Bär's 179th combat victory, although he had already put in over 200 claims for evaluation.

With regard to the combat claim form used, there are some changes in the wording from earlier examples. Question 5b) has the addition category 'burst apart', and this seems to have appeared quite often in claims in 1944. Note the high number of 20 mm shells used by the two 20 mm MG (incendiary, explosive, armour piercing). The expenditure of ammunition in this case is unusually high, with most other claims from this period against other bombers being much lower.

Note that the claim form is now headed *Abschussmeldung* only (used on the Western Front, for bombers and fighters – on the Eastern Front the original combat claim is still in use), the wording destruction having been deleted. This is very much in line with the directives given out by OKL Order Numbers 2522/42 and 321/43, stating that the primary function of the fighter was the dispersal of the enemy bomber formation and to prevent the bombers from achieving an aimed bomb drop over their targets.

As can be seen, Bär made no attempt to follow the enemy aircraft down to its final destruction but relies on the 11 eyewitnesses to support his claim. The practice of verifying the destruction of an enemy aircraft was, of course, no longer feasible when engaging large enemy bomber formations. Clearly, not every engaged aircraft in the initial attack was shot down, but instead began to lag behind the formation, becoming prey to the marauding operational combat training school (*Ergänzungsgruppe*), ISS (industrial protection) and any other fighters which were in reach and active behind the main centre of action. See OKL Order Number 321/43 for further details.

B. Example of Order of Day Report

File RL 8 90
General Command XII Air Corps
Corps Operations
28/2/1943

II Br, B, Number 3101/43

Corps orders of the day Number 95

The following aerial victories where achieved for the night 25–26/2./943

Leutnant Marxen – 12./JG 1
Shot down one Boeing

Leutnant Knoke – 2./JG 1
Shot down one Liberator
In co-operation with 5./Ln.-Regiment 202

Leutnant Frey – 2./JG 1
Shot down one Liberator
In co-operation with 5./Ln.-Regiment 202

Leutnant Demetz – 3./JG 1
Shot down one Liberator

Comment
Note that some of the claims are divided between the fighters and the Luftwaffe flak regiment. Note that the claim is divided between the flak regiment and the fighter pilot.

C. Example of Operational Reports

Br Telex: 04.45 hours   2/12/1942
End of Day Report from F.d.L. Tunis from 1/12/1942

1 Operations: 25 Ju 87 of II./StG 3 on 3 missions 32 Me 109 of II./JG 53. Of these, 2 missions with 4 Me 109s for harbour protection, 3 missions with 26 Me 109s for escort duty and low level attacks, 1 mission with 2 Me 109s for reconnaissance (missions from JG 53 will be reported later), 8 reconnaissance aircraft (Me109) from 2./(H)14 on 4 missions for battle reconnaissance and low level attacks on reported paratroops.
2 Losses: None
3 Successes: II./St 3 1 tank destroyed by a direct hit, the destruction of further tanks and an artillery position can be reckoned with.
   II./JG 53 5 Spitfires shot down.
   2./(H)14 Results of Low level attacks on paratroops were not observed.
4 Note:
   5./S G.2 No missions.
5 Enemy activity:
   In bomb attacks at 10:00 and 11:15 hours; 8 dead, 16 wounded, 5 vehicles and 1 motor-bike.

F.d.R. Signed

Bibliography

Abbott, P. E., and Tamplin, J. M. A., *British Gallantry Awards* (Nimrod Dix & Co, 1981).

Anon, *The Army Almanac: A Book of Facts Concerning the United States Army* (The Military Service Publishing Company, 1957).

Anon, *Itrebitel'naya aviasionnaya diviziya (The Fighter Division)* (Voenizdat, 1982).

Anon, *Aviatsionny polk (The Air Regiment)* (Voenizdat, 1985).

Anon, *Eskadril'ya – Ekipazh (The Squadron and Individual Aircrew)* (Voenizdat, 1985).

Anon, *Wolfgang Späte – 70 years of age* (Luftfahrt International, September 1981).

Arnold, H. H., *Global Mission* (Hutchinson & Co Ltd, 1951).

Baker, D., *Flight and Flying: A Chronology* (Facts on File, Inc, 1994).

Bekker, C., *The Luftwaffe War Diaries* (Macdonald, 1967).

Bowyer, C., *For Valour: The Air VCs* (Grub Street, 1992).

Boyd, A., *The Soviet Air Force since 1918* (Macdonald and Jane's, 1977).

Boyd, A., *Vstrecha s prolavennym letchikom trizhdy Geroem Sovetskovo Soyuza marshalom aviatsii A.I.Pokryshkin. A complete translation from O. Frantsev* (Voennoistoricheski zhurnal No 3, 1983).

Butler, P., *War Prizes* (Midland Counties Publications, 1994).

Caidin, M., *Me 109. Purnell's History of the Second World War, Weapons Book, No 4* (Macdonald & Co Ltd, 1968).

Caidin, M., *Zero fighter. Purnell's History of the Second World War, Weapons Book, No 4* (Macdonald & Co Ltd, 1969).

Cottam, J. K., *Soviet Airwomen in Combat in World War II* (Sunflower University Press, 1983).

Craven, W. F., *The Army Air Forces in World War II, VI: Men and Planes* (Office of Air Force History, University of Chicago Press, 1983).

Department of the Air Force, *USAF Historical Study No. 81. USAF Credits For The Destruction Of Enemy Aircraft, Korean War* (Office of Air Force History Headquarters USAF. Albert F. Simpson Historical Research Center Air University 1975).

Department of the Air Force, *USAF Historical Study No. 85. USAF Credits For The Destruction Of Enemy Aircraft, World War II* (Office of Air Force History Headquarters USAF. Albert F. Simpson Historical Research Center Air University, 1978).

Dougherty, J. E., *Flying Fatigue: the Effects of Four Months Combat Flying in a Tropical Combat Zone on Fighter Pilots* (Josiah Macy

Jnr Foundation, 1942).

Fowler, S., Elliot, P., Conyers Nesbit, R., and Goulter, C., *RAF Records in the PRO* (PRO Publications, 1994).

Galland, A., *The First and the Last* (Methuen, 1956).

Gilbert, A. & The Imperial War Museum, *The Imperial War Museum Book of the Desert War* (Book Club Associates, 1992).

Golley, J., *Aircrew Unlimited: The Commonwealth Air Training Plan during WW 2* (Patrick Stephens Ltd, 1993).

Grinker, R. R. and Spiegel, J. P., *War Neuroses in North Africa: The Tunisian Campaign, January to May 1943* (Josiah Macy, Jnr, Foundation, 1943).

Guest, C. F., Keskinen, K., and Stenman, K., *Red Stars: Soviet Air Force in World War Two* (Ar-Kustannus Oy, 1993).

Guest, C. F., *Under the Red Star, Luftwaffe Aircraft in the Soviet Air Force* (Airlife, 1993).

Hastings, D.W., *Psychiatric Experiences of the Eighth Air Force: First Year of Combat 4 July 1942 – 4 July 1943* (Josiah Macy, Jnr, Foundation, 1943).

Hardesty, V., *Red Phoenix: The Rise of Soviet Air Power, 1941-45* (Arms and Armour Press, 1982).

Hata, I. and Izawa, Y., *Japanese Naval Aces and Fighter Units in World War II. Translated by D. C. Gorham* (United States Naval Institute, 1989).

Historical Research Division, *USAF Historical Study No. 133: USAF Air Service Victory Credits, World War 1* (Aerospace Studies Institute, Air University, 1969).

Holmes, H., *Allied Air Aces of World War Two. Victory Through Air Power* (Flypast Special, 1995).

James, T. C. G., *Notes on Claims and Casulties during the Battle of Britain. AHB/II/117/(2B), App 36* (Air Historical Branch Narratives, 1945).

Johnson, J. E., *Wing Leader* (Ballantine Books, 1957).

Johnson, J. E., *Full Circle: The Story of Air Fighting* (Pan Books Ltd, 1968).

Juutilainen, E. I., *Double Fighter Knight* (Apali Oy, 1996).

Ketley, B. & Rolfe, M., *Lutfwaffe Fledglings 1935-45: Luftwaffe Training Units and their Aircraft* (Hikoki Publications, 1996).

Knoke, H., *I Flew for the Führer* (Reinhardt & Winston, 1954).

Krosnick, G., *Anxiety Reactions in Fighter Pilots: Italy 1942* (Josiah Macy, Jnr, Foundation, 1942).

Lee, A., *The German Air Force* (Harper and Row, 1946).

Lerche, H-W., *Luftwaffe Test Pilot* (Jane's, 1980).

Maelor, C., *Witches of the Eastern Front* (*Daily Telegraph*, April 1994).

Mau, H. J. and Stapfer H. H., *Lend-Lease Flugzeug fur die Sowjetunion* (Transpress, 1991).

Michulec, R., *Stalinowskie Sokoly (Stalin's Falcons)* (A. J. Press, 1995).

Miller, R., *Die Sowjetunion Im Luftkrieg. Eltville am Rhein. Bechtermünz* (Verlag/Time Life Books, 1993).

Mikesh, R. C., *Broken Wings of the Samurai* (Airlife, 1993).

Morgan, H., *By the Seat of Your Pants: Basic Training of RAF pilots in Rhodesia, Canada, South Africa & USA during WW2* (Newton, 1990).

Morgan, H., *The RFC in Texas, 1917-18* (Aeroplane Monthly, 1992).

Morgan, E. B. & Shacklady, E., *Spitfire: The History* (Guild Publishing, 1988).

Myles, B., *Night Witches: The Untold Story of Soviet Women in Combat* (Mainstream Publishing, 1981).

Nesbit, R. C., *An Illustrated History of the RAF* (Colour Library Books, 1990).

Noggle, A., *A Dance with Death: Soviet Airwomen in World War II* (A&M University Press, 1994).

Obermaier, E., *Die Ritterkreuzträger der Luftwaffe* (Verlag Dieter Hoffmann, 1966).

Okumiya, M., Horikoshi, J., with Caidin, M., *The Zero Fighter* (Cassell, 1958).

Olynyk, F., *Stars and Bars* (Grub Street, 1995)

Pokryshkin, A. I., *Nebo voiny (War Sky). Translated and edited as Sky War Over Russia: The wartime memoirs of Alexandr Pokryshkin. R. Wagner and L. Fetzer, editor and translator* (Unpublished manuscript, Russian Aviation Research Trust, 1966).

Price, A., *Battle of Britain: The Hardest Day, 18 August, 1940* (Arms and Armour Press, 1988).

Royal Air Force, *RAF Heaton Park, Manchester. A Guide for Newly Arrived Cadets* (Royal Air

Force Publication, 1942).

Ramsey, W. G. (Ed.), *The Battle of Britain Then and Now – Mk V* (After the Battle Magazine, 1980).

Russian Aviation Research Trust, *An unpublished collection of pilots recollections of the Great Patriotic War* (RART, 1995).

Scherbakov, A., *No Confidence, No Explanation* (Aviatsiya/Kosmonavtika, Vol 11, 1995).

Scutts, J., *Bf 109 Aces of North Africa and the Mediterranean: Osprey Aircraft of the Aces 2* (Osprey Aerospace, 1994).

Seago, E., *High Endeavour* (Collins, 1944).

Shores, C. and Williams, C., *Aces High* (Grub Street, 1994).

Shores, C., Franks, N., and Guest, R., *Above the Trenches* (Grub Street, 1990).

Shuckman, H., *General Dmitri Volkogonov* (*The Independent*, 7 December, 1995).

Skulski, P., *Asy Przestworzy 1939–1945* (ACE Publication, 1995).

Stenman, K., *38 To 1: The Brewster 239 in Finnish service* (Air Enthusiast Vol 46, 1992).

Steinhoff, J., *The Last Chance: The Pilots' Plot Against Göring* (Hutchinson, 1977).

Stokes, D., *Paddy Finucane: Fighter Ace* (William Kimber, 1983).

Sultanov, I., *Vozdushnye asy – kto oni? (The Air aces – Who Are They?)* (Krylya Rodiny, 1992).

Symonds, C. P., Bradford Hill, A., Reid, D. D., & Williams, D. J., *Psychological Disorders In Flying Personnel Of The Royal Air Force Investigated During The War 1939–45* (Air Ministry Air Publication – 3139, HMSO, 1947).

Tavender, I. T., *The Distinguished Flying Medal: A Record of Courage 1918–1982* (J. B. Hayward., 1982).

Technical Air Intelligence Center, *Japanese Aircraft: Performance and Characteristics, TAIC Manual No 1* (NAS Anacostia, D.C., 1945).

Terraine, J., *The Right of the Line* (Hodder and Stoughton, 1985).

Tolubko, V. F., & Kovalenko, A. P. (Eds.), *Na Grani Vozmozhnogo (On the Brink of what*

Tolubko, V. F., & Kovalenko, A. P. (Eds.), *Na Grani Vozmozhnogo (On the Brink of what one may)* (Moscow, 1990).

Townshend Bickers, R., *The Battle of Britain* (Salamander Books Ltd, 1990).

USAF, *Air Force ACES: Background Information* (Secretary of the Air Force, Office of Information Internal Information Division, 1970).

US Army Air Forces, *Headquarters Eighth Air Force, Office of the Commanding General: Awards and Decorations, 29 November 1942* (1942).

US Army Air Forces, *German Fighter Tactics Against Flying Fortresses. Special Intelligence Report No. 43–17. 31 December, 1943* (IWM, 1943).

US Army Air Forces, *Memorandum for Assistant Chief of Air Staff, Personnel: Automatic AAF Awards, 24 June, 1944* (1944).

Watkins, D., *Fear Nothing: The History of No 501 (County of Gloucester) Fighter Squadron, Royal Air Force* (Newton,1990).

Watry, C., *Washout! The Aviation Cadet Story* (Caifornia Aero Press, 1983).

Wells, M. A., *Courage and Air Warfare* (Frank Cass, 1995).

Williamson, G., *Aces of the Reich* (Arms and Armour, 1989).

Zaitsev, A. D., *Khronika vozdushnykh taranov (Chronicle of Air Rams)* (Voenno-Istorichesky Zhurnal (Journal of Military History), 1989).

Archive Sources

US AFHRA 16 mm microfilm Roll Nos A1208, K1009, K1016, 31374, 35196, 23509.

Bundesarchive Freiburg File nos, RL 4 236. RL 7 31. RL 7 119. RL 8 90. RL 10. 433 p18. RL 10. 375 p70. RL 10. 375 p69. RL 10 580 Claim Helm. RL 10 580 p162. RL 10 580 p186. RL 10 580 p187 to 188. RL 90.

Public Records Office Files, Air 49/376. Air 2/207. Air 2/4900. Air 41/9. Air 40/1691. Air 16/954. Air 41/15. Air 41/16. Air 41/17. Air 41/18. Air 41/24. Air 41/55. Air 49/145. Air 50/166. Air 50/350. Air 50/406.

Index

Aeronautica Nazionale
  Repubblicana (ANR) (Italy)
  35, 107–139
Ahokas, Leo 155
Aircraft types
  A-20 Havoc 85
  Ar 68 173
  Arado 51
  A. S. 1 Breda 25 112
  AT-6 Texan 22, 41, 76
  AVIA Fl. 3 112
  B-17 Flying Fortress
    130–132, 174, 177
  B-24 Liberator 131, 183,
    191, 193
  Ba. 24 Breda 111
  Ba. 25 113
  Ba. 65 126
  Battle 49
  'Betty' bomber 85
  Bf 109 27, 29, 31, 35, 49,
    51, 56, 68–71, 73, 81, 82,
    109–110, 113–114, 129,
    143, 164, 173, 175, 177,
    193
  Bf 109E 46
  Bf 109E-4 168, 189–190
  Bf 109F 55, 169
  Bf 109F-4 TROP 106
  Bf 109G 46, 97–98, 105,
    108, 122, 152, 162, 170,
    172, 177, 188
  Bf 109G-2 148–150, 159, 163
  Bf 109G-2/G-6 142,
    144–145, 147–148
  Bf 109G-4 123
  Bf 109G-6 124, 146,
    149–150, 159, 187

Bf 109G-10 126, 128
Bf 109G-10/AS 129
Bf 110 30, 43, 105, 108
Blenheim I 140
Blenheims 49, 128
Boeing 193
Bombay 183
Boston 143
Breda 128
Bücker Bü 181 113, 173–174
Buffalo, Brewster Model 239
  141–147, 149–151, 157,
  159, 162, 163
Bulldog IV 153
Bulldog 140, 145, 150, 154,
  158
C. 200 Saetta, Macchi 107,
  112–113, 119, 128–129
C. 202 Folgore, Macchi 107,
  111, 116, 121, 126,
  128–129, 130–132
C. 205 Veltros 108, 118, 122,
  124–126, 128, 130
Ca. 164 Caproni 112
Ca. 309 126
CANSA C. 5 112
Cessna 172 73
CR. 30 Fiat 112–113
CR. 32 112–113, 129
CR. 42 110, 112–113, 117,
  120
CR. 100 112
C. VE Fokker 140
C. X Fokker 140, 146
DB-3 141, 143, 159
DH. 60 Moth 153
'Dinah' reconnaissance
  86–87

D. XX Fokker 140, 143,
  145–147, 150, 158–159,
  162–163
D. XXI Fokker 103, 146,
  154
F-80 97
F-86 48, 75, 97
FN. 305 Nardi 112
FN. 315 Nardi 112
Fury 46
Fw 44 Steiglitz 153, 173
Fw 56 Stoeber 173
Fw 58 Weihe 173
Fw 190 31, 33–34, 46,
  48–49, 56, 64, 73, 84,
  174, 184–185
Fw 190A 186
Fw 190A-3 182
Fw 190A-5 174
Fw 200 Condor 73
G. 10 124
G. 50 Fiat 108–109, 112,
  114, 118, 144–147, 150,
  153, 156, 158, 159
G. 55 Fiat 108
Gamecock 140, 153–154
Gauntlet II 153–154
Gladiator GL-276 152
Gladiator 43, 144–145, 150,
  158–159
Gotha Go 145 173
Gotha Go 150 173
Hart 43, 144
Hawk 75A Curtiss 104, 146,
  150, 152, 154
He 51 51, 173
He 111 60, 167
He 111P 29, 49

He 162 174
Heinkel 30
Hs 129 73
Hurricane 22, 26, 29, 35, 67,
  144, 146, 148, 150, 158,
  162, 166
Hurricane I 43, 49
Hurricane IIC 49
I-15 (Polikarpov) 51–54
I-15bis 52–53, 144, 153
I-153 52, 54, 143–145, 150,
  158, 161
I-16 51, 54–56, 58, 60, 71,
  140, 143–145, 156, 158,
  161
I-16bis 146–147
Il-2 65, 73, 154
Jaktfalken II 153
Ju 52 55
Ju 87 57, 64, 73, 189, 193
Ju 88 57
Ju 88A-5 29
Junkers K 43 140
Junkers W 34 173
K. 14 126
Ki-27, Nakajima 52
Kittyhawk 33
Klemm Kl 35 173
LaGG 56
LaGG-3 63, 65, 71, 152, 161
La-5 63–65, 73, 162
La-5FN 72
La-7 Lavochkin 65, 72, 101
'Lily' 78–79, 80
Machetti 173
Magister 20
Master I 22
Master II 22

MC. 202 97
Me 109 (see Bf 109)
Me 163 109, 174
Me 262 109–110, 174–175
MiG-3 59, 66
MS 406 Morane 144, 146, 148, 150, 155, 159
Mustang III 88
Myrsky 160
'Oscar' 96, 97
P-36A Hawk 96
P-38 Lightning 75, 91, 164, 183
P-38G 96
P-38H 96
P-38H-1 87, 89, 97, 177
P-38J 92
P-39 Airacobra 78–80, 97, 143
P-39N 50–51, 73
P-40 69, 76, 91, 97–98, 128, 130, 148
P-40F 97
P-40L 97
P-47 Thunderbolt 74, 79, 85–86, 90, 96–98, 128, 133
P-47D 93, 96, 98
P-47D-5 102
P-51 Mustang 84, 88, 96, 98, 187
P-51D 96–97
P-63 Kingcobra 68
Pe-2 dive-bomber 69
Po-2 54, 70
PT-17 Stearman 22, 76
Pyry 149, 153, 154, 160
Queen Bee 46
R-5 158
Re. 2000 120
Rippon, 140
Ro. 41 IMAM 111, 113
S. 79s 118
S. 218A 'Smolik', Letov 153
SAIMAN 200 112
SAIMAN 202 112
SB-2 52, 144, 158
Siebel Si 202 Hummel 173
Siebel Si 204 173
Spitfire 20, 33, 43–44, 72, 128, 130, 148, 162, 167, 184–185, 193
Spitfire I 23, 27, 29–30, 33
Spitfire II 46
Spitfire IX 71
Spitfire IXb 48
Spitfire VB 34, 46, 48, 76, 99
Su-2 70, 73
Sunderland Flying Boat 129
TB-3 52
Tempest 28, 30–31
Tempest V 49
Tempest VI 49, 100

Tiger Moth DH. 82A 20
Tomahawk 33, 148
Tomahawk Mk IIB 69
Tuisku 160
Typhoon 22, 30
Typhoon IA 46
Typhoon IB 46
UT-1 54
UT-2 54
UTI-4 54
'Val' dive-bomber 96
Valiant Vultee BT-13 22
Valiant Vultee BT-13A 76
Victor 23
Viima 160
VL Saaski II 152
VL Tuisku 153
VL Viima II 153
Yak-1 57, 60, 61, 70–72
Yak-3 62, 72
Yak 7B 71
Yak-9 64, 71
Zeke 52, 96, 97
Zero type A6M2 52, 76, 81, 85, 97
Alessandrini, T. Col Aldo 133
Ancillotti, Allievo Pil. Rolando 113
Alexander, Cadet Pilot 4 BFTS 41
Arnold, Gen H. H. 'Hap', Chief USAAF 84, 94

Baldwin, Johnny 46
Balgoveshchenski, Gen A. S. 63
Ball, Albert 22, 34
Bär, Maj Heinz 165, 191–193
Barbaglio, M. llo Aldo 113, 121
Barkhorn, Gerhard 68, 164, 168, 172
Battle of Britain 22, 32, 165, 167, 175
Battle of France 175
Beamont, Roland, W/C 19, 25, 27, 30, 42, 166
Bellagambi 113, 126, 139
Bellagambi, Maggiore Mario 126, 139
Benz, Capt Walter T. 86
Berg, Lt Paavo D. 'Pate' 152, 158–159
Biron, Gen Giuseppe 107, 112, 116, 124
Boelke, Oswald 35
Bong, Richard 'Dick' 75, 95, 97–98
Bonet, Capt Giovanni 126, 135
Bordoni-Bisleri 111
Broadhurst, Harry 40
Brooker, W/C 28
Brown, Harry W. 96
Brown, Capt Roy 31
Budanova, Lieut. Ekaterina 57, 69–70

Carbury, Brian 165
Carlo, Cap Miani 133
Cavatore, Ten Mario 130
Chase, Levi R Jr 97
Churchill, Winston 35
Clade, Emil 164, 170, 175, 177, 182–183, 185–186
Claims filing 24–34, 60–65, 79–84, 117–124, 155–157, 180–185, 191–193
Continuation War Finland/Soviet Union 140–142, 144, 146–147, 149, 152, 154, 157–158, 162
Corner, G/C Hugh 33–34
Cronk, Lt Charles Jr 86

Daymond, G. A. 'Gus' 76
Decorations 42–43, 70, 94–96, 124–126, 157–158, 187–191
Deere, S/L Al 23, 40, 44
Demetz, Lt 193
Doe, Bob 165
Donaldson, W/C Teddy 41
Dougherty, Lt Col John E. 90
Dowding, ACM 24
Drago, Capt Ugo 113, 128, 132–133, 136
Duncan, Col Glenn E. 93
Dundas, John 22

Eddy, Lt Charles C. 128
Edge, 'Gerry' 22
Egyptian Air Force 48
Ehrnrooth, Maj Olavi 149
Emory, Capt Frank N. 81, 84, 98

FAF (see Finnish Air Force)
Fairbanks, David C. 'Foob' 48
Farnes, Paul C. P. 49
Farquhar, S/L A. D. 29
Fiebig, Gen Oberst 170
Fiedler, William F. Jr 97
Filippi, Fausto 126
Finnish Air Force bases
Helsinki-Malmo 147, 149, 156, 158
Hollola 147
Immola 143–144
Joutseno 144
Karvia 153
Kauhava 153
Laajalahati 153
Lappajarvi 153
Lappeenranta 162
Lemi 144
Lestijarvi 153
Menkijarvi 153
Parola 153
Ristiina 144
Ruokolahti 145
Selanpää 162
Siikakangas 153
Vaava 153

Veisvehmaa 153
Ylivieska 153
Finnish Air Force (FAF) 140–163
Finnish Air Force units
1. /HLeLv 26 157
1/LeLv 24 162
1. /LeLv 26 153
2. /LeLv 2 156
2. /LeLv 24 152, 162
2. LeLv 28 155
3. /LeLv 161
3/LeLv 24 143, 162
2 Wing 146
3 Wing 146
Fighter Squadrons, table 150
HLeLv 21 162
Karelian Wing 162
LeLv 22 147
LeLv 24 140–141, 143–147, 149–152, 159, 162
LeLv 26 140, 144–147, 159
LeLv 28 140, 146, 148, 159
LeLv 30 140, 146
LeLv 32 146, 154, 161
LeLv 34 148–149, 159, 162
Lentorykmenti 140
Finucane, Brendan E. F. Paddy 23, 33, 43–46
Flieger, General der 133
Fornaci, Serg Magg pil Fausto 131–132
Franchini, Capt 116
Frantisek, Josef 165
Frey, Lt 193

Gabreski, Francis S. 'Gabby' 75, 90, 98
Gaffney, Brig Gen Dale V. 68
Galland, Oberlt Adolf 110, 165, 174, 176–177, 180, 189–190
Gentile, D. S. 'Don' 48, 75–76, 78
Gilger, Oberlt 188
Giudice, Cap pil Eber 131–132
Godfrey, John T. 48, 78
Göring, Reichmarshall, Hermann 110, 177
Gott, Lt Gen 183, 185
Great Patriotic War 48–71
Green, Sgt Paul 34
Greim, Generaloberst von 110
Grinker, Lt Col Roy 91, 93
Gun cameras 28–31, 65, 84–86
Guynemer, Georges 35

Habermann, Uffz Robert 29
Hartmann, Erich 67, 73, 164, 172
Hastings, Maj Donald 89
Haw, F/Sgt Charlton 'Wag' 35, 67
Heinilä, Capt Erkki 147
Hillo, Lt Jaakko 154
Hitler, Adolf 189
Hogan, H. A. V. 'Harry' 40–41

Holloway, Lt Col B. K. 75
Holmes, F/O Ray 35
Huhantti, T. M. 159

Italian Air Force bases
    Bresso Airport, Milan 108
    Campoformido (Udine) 108,
        130
    Ciampino 110
    El Daba 130
    Florence 108
    Lagnasco (Cuneo) 108, 126
    Martuba 130
    Mirafiori 108
    Pantelleria Island 114
    Reggio Calabria 131–132
    Sardinia 116
    Sciacca 123
    Sicily 120, 123
    Tunisia 128
Italian Air Forces (see Regia
    Aeronautica and Aeronatica
    Nazionale Repubblicana . . .)
Italian Air Force units
    I° Gruppo 109, 111
    I° Gruppo Caccia 108, 113,
        122, 124, 125, 126
    I° Periodo (training schools)
        111, 113
    1ª Squadron, 1° Gruppo
        Caccia 128
    1st Squadron 'Gigi
        Caneppele' 133
    II° Gruppo Caccia 108, 113,
        114, 136
    II° Gruppo Caccia 1a
        Squadron 114
    II° Gruppo Caccia 2a
        Squadron 114
    3° Gruppo Autonomo 108
    III° Gruppo Caccia 113
    10° Gruppo, 4° Stormo CT
        130
    12 Stormo 'Sorci Verdi' 118
    19ª Squadriglia 'Asso di
        Bastoni' 10° Gruppo, 4°
        Stormo CT 22° Group
        107, 116
    23ª Squadron OA/2 Gr
        Colonial Aviation 126
    51 Stormo 118
    76ª Squadron, 16° Group,
        54° Stormo 128
    84° Squadriglia 130
    101° Gruppo Autonomo
        Caccia Terrestre 108
    150° Gruppo Autonomo 108
    159ª Squadron, 12° Group,
        50° Stormo 126
    300 Squadriglia 110
    Scuole di 2° Periodo 112
    Settore Aeronautico Est 113
    Squadriglia Complementare
        'Montefusco' 108, 126,
        135

Ivanov, Lt I. I. 60

Japanese Air bases
    Lae, New Guinea 85–86
Japanese Army Air Force
    (JAAF) 52, 59, 63
Johnson, Amy 68
Johnson, G/C (later AVM)
    'Johnnie', 23, 48, 166
Johnson, Robert S. 75, 98
Juutilainen, Eino Ilmari 'Illu'
    143, 145, 149–150,
    155–156, 158–159, 162

Kahl, Ofw Huffer 193
Kain, F/O Edgar 'Cobber' 38
Kamikaze pilots 59
Karhila, Kyöstia K. E. 140,
    146, 152, 154, 157
Kearby, Neel 90, 95
Keillor, Col Russell 68
Kent, Johnny 40
Khalkin, Gol 52
Khlobystov 60
Kingaby, Donald Ernest 43
Kinnunen, Eero 155
Kirvan, Sgt/Pilot 29
Kisilev, Col Peter S. 68
Kleshchev, Ivan 72
Knoke, Lt Heinz 166, 193
Kobzan, Lt Boris 60
Kokko, Pekka 155
Koldunov, Aleksandr I. 72–73
Kopets, Ivan I 65
Kozhedub, Ivan Nikolaevich
    50, 68, 70
Krosnick, Maj Gerald 92–93
Kuter, Maj Gen 95
Kuznetsov, Maj. Gen. A. A. 29
Kuznetsova, Mariya 57
Kuznetsove, Vera 57

Lacey, J. H. 'Ginger' 32
Lampi, Sgt Heimo 149
Lee, W/C Asher 166
Lefebre, Col Fred H. 82, 88, 98
Lehtovaara, Sgt Urho S. 148,
    159
Litvyak, Lily 57, 69–70
Lock, Eric 165
Loud, Bill 44
Lucchini, Franco 129–130
Luftwaffe 22, 50, 51, 56, 58,
    67, 90, 92, 107, 109–111,
    113, 116, 121, 123, 128,
    149, 164–193
Luftwaffe Air bases
    Bad Aibling 174
    Bremen 186
    Furth 113
    Holzkirchen 113
    Kriwoi Rog, Russia 172
    Liegnitz 109, 113
    Oberursal 180
    Osnabrück 177

Reichersberg 84
    Werneuchen, Berlin 149,
        159, 163
Luftwaffe units
    I. /Nachjagdgeschwader 1
        188
    I. /N. J. G. 1 189
    1. /KG30 29
    1. /JG27 168
    1. /JG77 29
    II. /Jagdgeschwader 1 191
    II. /JG1 192
    II. /JG26 182
    II. /JG52 172
    II. /JG53 193
    II. /JG77 126
    II. /St 3 193
    II. /StG 3 193
    II. /ZG26 43
    2. /(H)14 193
    2. /JG1 193
    2. /SG 2 193
    III. /JG54 177
    3. /JG 1 193
    3 Staffel I. /JG54 186
    6. /JG27 46
    7 Staffel III. /JG27 170
    9 Staffel III. /JG2 174
    12. /JG 1 193
    JG3 187
    JG7 175
    JG26 185
    JG 27 174, 175
    JG53 193
    JG 54 55
    JG 77 108, 122
    JV 44 110, 175
    ZG 26 108
    Jagdfliegerführer Oberitalien
        109–110
    Luftwaffe Fighter Command
        in Italy 139
Lundquistat, Lt Gen J. F. 142,
    144
Lutzow, Oberst Günther
    'Frankel' 110
Luukkanen, Maj 'Eikka' 143,
    149, 151, 155, 159
Lynch, Maj Thomas J. 87

McCormack, J. M. 28
McGregor, F/O A. J. 29
McGuire, Thomas B. Jr 75, 95,
    97
McKellar, Archie 165
McKennon, Pierce 48
Magnusson, Maj Gustav E.
    158, 162
Malan, Adolf 'Sailor', S/L
    22–23, 25, 40
Maltzahn, Oberst Baron
    Günther von 109–110
Marseille, Hans-Joachim 126,
    165–166, 169, 176, 186
Marxen, Lt 193

Mayer, Hans-Karl 165
Meagher, S/L 23
Meyer, J. C. 75
Miller, S/L 35
Miller, P/O Norman 46
Mölders, Werner 165–166
Montgomery, Gen B. L.
    'Monty' 183
Moore, Capt John T. 86
Mottet, Serg Giuseppe 135
Muirhead, P/O Ian J. 26

Naidenko, Capt 69
Neumann, Oberst 'Edu' 110,
    139
Nicolson, James Brindley
    'Nick' 42
Nieminen, U. A. 159
Noggle, Anna 69

Oesau, Walter 165
Operation Barbarossa 50, 54,
    66, 68, 165
Operation Phoenix 109–110
Orekhov, Vladimir A. 54,
    63–64, 71–72

Pacini, Serg Magg pil Giuseppe
    131–132
Park, AVM Keith 24
Pattle, Marmaduke T. St J.
    'Pat' 43
Peterson, Chesley 48, 78
Peterson, R. A. 75
Petsamo 29
Pierce, Sir Richard 24
Pokryshkin, Alexandr
    Ivanovich 51, 54–57, 68, 70,
    172
Polunina, Yekaterina 69
Portal, CAS Charles 35
Powers, J. H. 75
Preddy, George Earl Jr 75, 98
Proudman, P/O 29
Puhakka, Risto 147, 155, 159
Pyles, M/Sgt Max 92
Pyotsiä, Victor 'Vikki' 142, 159

Quesada, Lt Gen E. R. 166

Raffaelli, Generale 113
Rall, Günther 68, 169, 175,
    182, 186
Ramsbottom-Isherwood, W/C
    35
Raskova, Marina 68–69
Rechkalov, Grigori A. 50, 56,
    73
Regia Aeronautica (RA) (Italy)
    35, 107–139
Richthofen, Count Manfred
    von 31, 35
Rickenbacker, Eddie 75, 98
Risk, Lt Edward J. 84
Roller, Gen 110

Rook, S/L 'Mickey' 35
Rosen, Count Erik von 140
Royal Air Force 19–47, 109,
    111
Royal Air Force bases
    Bentley Priory 46
    Biggin Hill 25
    Boscombe Down 48
    Cottesmore 23
    Farnborough, RAE 33
    Filton 49
    Gravesend 49
    Hawarden 46
    Henlow 46
    Heston 25
    Kenley 33, 49
    Lympne 34
    Manston 46, 48
    Middle Wallop 49
    Montrose 43
    Shellingford 46
    Sywell 43
    West Malling 49
Royal Air Force units
    2 BFTS 46
    2nd TAF 25, 48, 49
    3 Squadron 49
    4 BFTS 39
    6 EFTS 43
    7 OTU 46
    8 SFTS 43
    11 Group 24
    33 Squadron 43
    59 OTU 46
    61 OTU 25
    65 Squadron 46
    71 Eagle Squadron 76
    73 Squadron 38
    74 Squadron 23
    80 Squadron 43
    81 Squadron 29, 35, 67
    92 Squadron 43
    103 Squadron 47
    123 Wing 48
    133 Eagle Squadron 76
    134 Squadron 29, 35, 67
    146 Wing 48
    145 Squadron 76
    151 Wing 29, 35, 67
    198 Squadron 46
    209 Squadron 31
    229 Squadron 49
    249 Squadron 48
    274 Squadron 49
    303 Squadron 76
    452 Squadron 46
    486 Squadron 28
    501 Squadron 40, 48, 49
    602 Squadron 23, 29, 44, 46
    605 Squadron 26
    609 Squadron 'West Riding'
        46
Rudel, Hans Ulrich 189

Safonov, Boris 35, 67

Sanderson, 'Jock' 44
Sarvanto, Lt Jorma Kalevi 141,
    159–162
Savitsky Ye Ye 68
Scherbakov, A. 65, 169
Schilling, David C. 75, 98
Schmidt, Lt Herbert 46
Schroer, Lt Werner (later Maj)
    168, 177
Schuhmacher, Air Ofw 192
Scott, Col R. L. Jr 75
Sellege, Uffz Walter 29
Serves, Lt Hermann 29
Shaffer, Lt Joseph 75
Shahan, Lt Elza 75
Sinclair, Sir Archibald 24
Smushkevich, Yakov V. 66
Sovelius, Per Erik 'Pelle' 155,
    159
Soviet air bases
    Chungking 52
    Hankow 52
    Lanchow 52
    Nanking 52
    Paldiski, Estonia 142
Soviet Air Force (Voyenno-
    vozdushnyye sily – VVS)
    50–73
Soviet Air Force units
    1st Czechoslovak Fighter Air
        Regiment 63
    III Fighter Corps 59
    4th Air Army 59
    15th Air Army 59
    17th Air Army 72
    16th Guards Fighter Air
        Regiment 73
    22nd Fighter Air Regiment
        52
    32nd GIAP (Guards Fighter
        Air Regiment) 65, 71, 72
    72nd Regiment of the
        Russian Naval Air Fleet
        67
    73rd Fighter Air Regiment 69
    122nd Composite Air Group
        68
    176th Proskurov FAR 65,
        169
    177th Fighter Air Regiment
        PVO 60
    178th Guards Fighter
        Regiment 73
    184th Fighter Air Regiment
        60
    240th Fighter Air Regiment
        73
    286th Fighter Division 59
    434 Fighter Air Regiment 71
    586th Fighter Air Regiment
        69
    587th Dive-Bomber Air
        Regiment 69
    866th Fighter Air Regiment
        73

Air Force of the Western
    Military District 66
Spiegel, Capt John P. 91, 93
Stanford-Tuck, W/C R. R. 34,
    40
Steinhoff, Oberst Johannes
    110, 175
Strait, Maj Gen Don J. 96
Strobell, Bob 74, 79, 82, 85, 88
Suprun, Stepan 52
Sylvester, P/O E. J. H. 49

Tactics, FAF 154–155
    Italian 114–116
    Luftwaffe 174–180
    RAF 22–24
    Soviet air forces 55–61
Talalikhan, Victor 60
Tani, Antii 152
Thorne, Len 23, 27, 30, 32–33,
    44–46, 88
Tilli, P. T. 159
Training, FAF 153–154
    Italian pilots 111–116
    Luftwaffe 173–174
    RAF 19–22
    Soviet air forces 54–55
    USAAF 77–81
Tumlin, Rupert M. 98
Tunis, F de L 193
Tuominen, Oiva Emil Kalervo
    'Oippa' 144, 149, 153,
    157–162

Urbanowicz, Witold 76
USAAF 19, 40, 74–96, 111
USAAF units
    VIII Fighter Command 82
    5th Fighter Command 87
    5th AAF 91
    8th AAF 75, 81, 82, 89, 96
    9th AAF 83
    2nd Air Commando Group
        97
    14th Air Force 75, 76
    15th Air Force 108, 124
    2nd Bombardment Division
        83
    49th FG 98
    56th FG 98
    348th FG 86
    51st FIW 48
    9th FS/49th FG 96
    27th FS/1st FG 75
    33rd FS 75
    39th FS 87
    40th FS 80
    41st FS 80
    60th FS 'Fighting
        Crows'/33rd FG 97
    61st FS 98
    68th FS 97
    70th FS/347th FG 97
    75th FS 76
    79th FS/20th FG 92

    308th FS/31st FG 75
    328th FS 98
    334th FS 76
    336th FS 76
    341st FS 86
    342nd FS 86
    346th FS/350th FG 128
    351st FS 82, 84
    351st FS/353 FG 79, 98
    352nd FS/353rd FG 93
    361st FS/356th FG 96
    431st FS/475th FG 96
    487th FS/352nd FG 98
    23rd Fighter Group 75
    16th Fighter Interceptor
        Squadron 48
    1st Provisional Fighter
        Group 97
    47th Pursuit Squadron/ 15th
        Pursuit Group 96
    American Volunteer Group
        75
    Flying Tigers (see American
        Volunteer Group)
US Air bases
    Bodney 98
    Broadwell (Bradwell Grove)
        Oxfordshire 90
    Clark Field, Phillipines 97
    Fort Dix, New Jersey 97
    Guadalcanal 97
    McGuire AFB (see Fort
        Dix)
    Martlesham Heath 96
    Metfield, Suffolk 79
    New Caledonia 97
    Pensacola 75

Valenzano, Raffaele 133
Vesa, Emil 155
Virta, K. J. T. 159
Visconti, Adriano 111,
    126–129, 138
Voight, Oblt 193
Voll, Capt John 75
VVS (see Soviet Air Force)

Wade, Lance 40, 76
Wagner, Lt Boyd 'Buzz' 74–75
Walker, P/O James 35
Ward, Kenneth 67
Wick, Helmut 165, 166
Wiese, Johannes 73
Wilson, W/C H. J. 43
Wind, Capt Hans 'Hasse' 142,
    146, 149, 151, 158–159,
    162
Winter War 52, 53, 56, 66,
    140–145, 148–149, 152,
    154–155, 157–158
Wurmheller, Lt Josef 174

Yevstigeyev, Kirill A. 73

Zemke, Col Hubert 75, 98